www.wadsworth.com

www.wadsworth.com is the World Wide Web site for Wadsworth Cengage Learning and is your direct source to dozens of online resources.

At *www.wadsworth.com* you can find out about supplements, demonstration software, and student resources. You can also send email to many of our authors and preview new publications and exciting new technologies.

www.wadsworth.com
Changing the way the world learns®

Guide to Criminal Procedure
for California

JEFFREY B. SNIPES
San Francisco State University

WADSWORTH
CENGAGE Learning

Australia • Brazil • Japan • Korea • Mexico • Singapore • Spain • United Kingdom • United States

Guide to Criminal Procedure for California

Jeffrey B. Snipes

Executive Editor: Sabra Home

Development Editor: Julie Sakaue

Assistant Editor: Jana Davis

Editorial Assistant: Elise Smith

Marketing Manager: Terra Schultz

Marketing Assistant: Annabelle Yang

Project Manager, Editorial Production: Jennifer Klos

Print Buyer: Emma Claydon

Permissions Editor: Chelsea Junget

Cover Designer: Yvo Riezebos

Cover Image: Donovan Reese/Getty Images

© 2005 Wadsworth Cengage Learning

For product information and technology assistance, contact us at
Cengage Learning Customer & Sales Support, 1-800-354-9706

For permission to use material from this text or product, submit all requests online at **cengage.com/permissions**
Further permissions questions can be emailed to
permissionrequest@cengage.com

Library of Congress Control Number: 2004109559

ISBN-13: 978-0-534-64344-7

ISBN-10: 0-534-64344-2

Wadsworth
10 Davis Drive
Belmont, CA 94002-3098
USA

Cengage Learning is a leading provider of customized learning solutions with office locations around the globe, including Singapore, the United Kingdom, Australia, Mexico, Brazil, and Japan. Locate your local office at:
international.cengage.com/region

Cengage Learning products are represented in Canada by Nelson Education, Ltd.

For your course and learning solutions, visit **academic.cengage.com**

Purchase any of our products at your local college store or at our preferred online store **www.ichapters.com**

Printed in the United States of America
4 5 6 7 11 10 09 08

For my loving parents, Roberta and Wally, and siblings, Greg and Jan

Table of Contents

CHAPTER ONE

Introduction to Guide to Criminal Procedure for California

This is a casebook designed at introducing the reader to the law of criminal procedure in California. In this chapter we'll provide an overview of the material to come and discuss how this casebook can be used in conjunction with the study of criminal procedure in the United States. Additionally, we'll discuss the general structure of the California court system, relating it to the appellate process for criminal procedure cases.

Section One: Overview of Text

The structure of this book is generally parallel with Joel Samaha's *Criminal Procedure* (Belmont, CA: Wadsworth, 8th ed., 2004). Beginning with Chapter Two, the chapter topics will run parallel with Samaha's text, which focuses on criminal procedure in the U.S. generally, but will focus on how each topic has been handled within the California court system.

Each chapter is divided into sections. These sections predominantly correspond to the subtopics in Samaha's text, with a few exceptions. Subtopics of minor importance which are handled in a matter of paragraphs in the main text are eliminated in this book—any necessary information from these areas will be addressed in the chapter's introduction. Additionally, in a couple of instances, small sections from the main text are grouped into one major section in this book. At times a section will be added that is relevant to California law but not to federal, such as the Three Strikes section in Chapter Fourteen. The reader will discover, though, that this book will read complementarily and at the same pace with the federal approach offered in Samaha's edition.

Each chapter will begin with an introduction that summarizes the federal approach to the chapter content, and follows with discussion of the fit between the federal and California approaches. Next, each section is introduced in series, beginning with an overview of the section material, and followed by any relevant statutes, and finally, any cases that have been chosen to highlight key issues from that section. Statutes will invariably come from the California Penal Code, but the reader will spot other relevant codes throughout the text as well, such as Evidence Code, Government Code, Rules of Civil Procedure, Rules of Court, and Rules of Professional Conduct (for lawyers). In some chapters, such as sentencing, statutes will abound; in others, such as the question of when a police action constitutes a search, the law is entirely driven by federal and state cases. The California Constitution may be relevant at times, and the reader will be referred to the pertinent section of the Constitution, which is included in this text's Appendix.

Cases will be introduced by a brief discussion of the significance the case offers to the study of criminal procedure in California. Next an edited version of the case will be presented, divided into two sections: background (facts behind the case), and discussion (the court's analysis of the major issues posed by the appeal). For the sake of readability and overall length, cases are trimmed of many citations and quotes from citations (unless crucial to the understanding of the case). That said, most cases are not significantly pared down in terms of overall content. When part of the court's analysis is simply not relevant to that section's content, it may be eliminated—if necessary for comprehension, a summary of the court's analysis in that deleted portion will be summarized in brackets. In some instances a dissenting opinion may follow the majority's opinion. Following each case a short conclusion will summarize the holding and its significance. Finally, we provide several review questions for the reader, aimed both at reinforcing the reader's comprehension of the court's analysis, and at times, putting the case in a larger context.

Now, let's review the sequence of topics to be covered in this text.

Chapter Two will discuss constitutional issues of criminal procedure. The most important task in this chapter will be to relate criminal procedure in California to the federal approach. We'll find out that after Proposition 8 was passed by voters in California, in 1982, the California approach merged with the federal approach, such that for most of the topics in this book there are not any dramatic differences between the approaches. However, we'll also see that California courts are allowed to interpret federal case law—this has import because there are many gaps in Supreme Court case law when it comes to procedures governing police investigations, and ensuing court proceedings; thus, California courts have considerable discretion in shaping the law.

Chapter Three introduces the three-step process that is applied when analyzing questions of whether certain evidence against criminal suspects will ultimately be admissible against them in court. It then discusses the first step of this approach, which is determining when a seizure occurs and when a search occurs, such that the Fourth Amendment is implicated.

Chapter Four discusses an important aspect of police work: stops based on reasonable detention. These are based on less evidence than arrests, but are important to patrol officers who have the difficult job of preventing crimes from occurring and have a great deal of sensory stimuli to contend with while on patrol. Potential targets of these stops also have an interest in not being subjected to police encounters when they are in fact not doing anything wrong.

Chapter Five moves on to arrests, which are based on a higher objective standard of proof—probable cause. Arrest is defined, and the difference between arrests with and without warrants is discussed.

Chapter Six handles one of the most important areas of the law of criminal procedure: searches. Some searches require warrants; others do not, when an exception to the general warrant requirement exists. Since the fruit of searches is often the core of a prosecutor's case-in-chief, it is important that police follow proper procedures and adhere to current law when carrying out these searches. This chapter deals with the second step of the three-step process introduced in Chapter Three: determining whether a search was reasonable under the Fourth Amendment.

Chapter Seven briefly considers administrative or "special-needs" searches, which are not necessarily conducted for the purpose of criminal investigation, but more often for public safety—whatever their purpose may be, however, criminal cases are often the outcome of these searches. We'll see that the standards are relaxed for these searches, since there are societal interests that are implicated in addition to the usual interest of crime control.

Chapter Eight covers police interrogations and confessions. Like physical evidence found during searches, confessions and information resulting from interrogations are often key to a prosecutor's case. When a confession is thrown out for violating a procedural right (such as the right to be informed of *Miranda* rights, an entire case may be damaged. In addition, faulty interrogations may provide information that leads the police to evidence that then must be squashed as "fruit of the poisonous tree."

Chapter Nine covers yet another part of prosecutorial cases: identification of suspects through either eyewitnesses or DNA analysis. In this substantive area, the law is stacked in the prosecutor's favor, as we'll see it is very difficult for defense attorneys to have these identifications stricken, and even more difficult for it to negatively impact the outcome of the case.

Chapter Ten arrives at the third step in the process of determining when evidence is admissible, by asking whether illegal obtained evidence is inadmissible under the exclusionary rule, or when it may still be admissible due to some exception to the exclusionary rule.

Chapter Eleven traverses an important avenue available to victims of government conduct that is separate from exclusion of evidence: the right to sue the police for violations of their rights. We'll mostly focus on state actions that are independent from opportunities for lawsuits supplied by federal statutes.

Chapter Twelve discusses the procedures necessary when a case is turned over from the police to the prosecutor, including the decision to charge, a probable cause declaration (or first appearance), bail, and appointment of counsel.

Chapter Thirteen broadly surveys procedures from the preliminary hearing or grand jury indictment all the way though the trial to the verdict. Especially important in this chapter are motions made prior to trial, such as to suppress evidence or to change venue.

Chapter Fourteen addresses sentencing following conviction. We'll review California's sentencing philosophy, specific sentencing procedures, and will discuss at some length the state's well-known Three Strikes law.

Chapter Fifteen examines the reaction the state has taken to the federal Patriot Act, which has diluted individual liberties for the purpose of protecting the country from post-9/11 terrorist activities. We'll see that many California communities are resolving not to cooperate with the federal government's approach, and we'll see how complex things can become when states governments clash with the federal government.

The Appendix provides key selected provisions of the California Constitution that relate to issues of criminal procedure.

Section Two: California Court Structure

With few exceptions, every case you read in this text will be from a California appellate court. For it is in these courts that most issues of criminal procedure are decided in the state. For federal offenses, which are far rarer than violations of state crimes, criminal procedure issues will be heard out in federal district and appellate courts. Even though criminal procedure necessarily implicates federal law (especially in California, after Proposition 8—see Chapter Two), you can imagine how stressed the federal court system would be if every federal issue in every state criminal case had to be heard by federal judges. Instead, state courts interpret criminal procedure issues, regardless of whether they are governed by federal or state law, or both.

California courts consist of trial courts and appellate courts. Each of the state's 58 counties has a trial court. Prior to mid-1998, trial courts were comprised of superior and municipal courts, each with separate jurisdiction. Subsequent to that, superior courts have jurisdiction over all felony cases; municipal courts can handle misdemeanors. The 58 trial courts have approximately 400 court locations across the state, with about 1,500 judges.

Each trial court is located in one of six appellate districts: First (San Francisco); Second (Los Angeles and Ventura); Third (Sacramento); Fourth (San Diego, Riverside, Santa Ana); Fifth (Fresno); and Sixth (San Jose). These six districts have 19 divisions and over 100 justices (appellate judges, unlike trial judges, are called justices).

A criminal defendant starts out in a trial court—either a municipal or superior court. Following a conviction (or in some cases a guilty plea), an appeal may occur, which will be made to the appellate district within which the trial court resides. This court may in its discretion agree to hear the appeal, and will render its decision. If it affirms the trial court, the defendant may appeal to the California Supreme Court (which has a chief justice and six associate justices). If it decides to take the case, it will render the final decision in the state. If a defendant is still out of luck, the U.S. Supreme Court is their last resort, and it reviews only a minute percentage of cases coming its way.

The state can also appeal cases through this process. It cannot appeal an acquittal, due to the rule against double jeopardy, but it can appeal rulings on such matters as motions to suppress evidence. (These may be handled in an expedited fashion, so the ruling is administered before the case goes to trial.) Most importantly, it can appeal a reversal of conviction made at the appellate district level, since a reversal of this reversal does not violate double jeopardy.

In this book, each case will contain a citation following the case name. Any citation that has "App." in the middle is an appellate case (e.g., "Cal.App.4th"). If the citation is missing this phrase (such as "Cal.3d") the case was heard at the California Supreme Court.

CHAPTER TWO

The Constitution and Criminal Procedure

In this chapter we'll discuss how the federal and state constitutions relate to each other in governing the law of criminal procedure. The primary sources of law for criminal procedure within the state of California are: U.S. Constitution and interpretative federal and state case law, California Constitution and interpretive state law, California Penal Code provisions and state case law, and other miscellaneous state codes and rules and interpretive case law, such as the Evidence Code, Government Code, Rules of the Court, Rules of Professional Conduct, and so forth.

We'll first review the major provisions of the U.S. Constitution that relate to criminal procedure; next we'll discuss similar provisions in the California Constitution. Finally, and crucially, we'll examine the significance Proposition 8 has had in California, in terms of the relationship between federal and state laws governing criminal procedure.

Section One: Federal Constitution

OVERVIEW

Within the main body of the U.S. Constitution, two important provisions reside pertaining to criminal procedure: habeas corpus (right to challenge illegal detentions) and right to a jury trial by the community in which the crime occurred. All other rights reside in the amendments. These include:

Fourth Amendment: Guarantee against unreasonable searches and seizures

Fifth Amendment: Guarantee of grand jury indictment
Guarantee against double jeopardy
Guarantee of due process of law
Protection against self-incrimination

Sixth Amendment: Right to public, speedy trial
Right to impartial jury
Right to notice of the nature and cause of the accusation
Right to confront opposing witnesses
Right to compulsory process
Right to assistance of counsel

Eighth Amendment: Prohibition against excessive bail
Prohibition against excessive fines
Prohibition against cruel and unusual punishment

Section Two: California Constitution

You have probably learned that the federal constitution sets minimum standards for protecting individual rights, and that states, usually through their largely parallel state constitutions, can afford individuals greater protection. In California, section 24 of Article I of the state constitution says that criminals are not to be afforded greater rights by the state than the federal constitution. Section 28, codifying Proposition 8, also makes it clear that federal law is the guide for state law. However, for some issues of criminal procedure that do not relate to the introduction of evidence against criminal suspects, the various provisions of the California constitution are still important, and may at times provide individuals with greater rights than does the federal constitution. Additionally, governing state statutes (usually in the Penal Code) at times afford greater protection to individuals in the state. For example, in California's penal code, all indigent misdemeanants have the right to counsel, whereas the minimum standard set by the U.S. Supreme Court is cases where an actual prison sentence will be imposed upon a conviction. And the California Constitution's bail clause is more generous than that of the U.S. Constitution, because it goes beyond the prohibition against "excessive bail." It's probably clear to the reader by now, that the relationship between the U.S. and California Constitutions can at times be complex.

The following are the key provisions of the state constitution affecting criminal procedure. To see these in much more detail, see the Appendix. All of the following sections come from Article I of the California Constitution, which is the Declaration of Rights.

Section Four:	Religion cannot make one incompetent to be witness or juror
Section Nine:	Prohibition of ex post facto laws
Section Ten:	Witnesses cannot be unreasonably detained
Section Twelve:	Right to bail with some exceptions Prohibition against excessive bail Release on own recognizance in court's discretion
Section Thirteen:	Guarantee against unreasonable searches and seizures
Section Fourteen:	Requirement of indictment or information for felony prosecutions Procedures for first appearance Waiver of preliminary hearing if indictment has occurred
Section Fifteen:	Right to speedy, public trial Right to compulsion of witnesses Right to counsel, and to be present with counsel Right to confront witnesses Guarantee against double jeopardy

Section Sixteen:	Right to trial by jury, by 12 persons
	Waiver of right by consent
Section Seventeen:	Prohibition against cruel and unusual punishment
	Prohibition against excessive fines
Section Twenty-three:	Requirement that each county have a grand jury
Section Twenty-four:	Independence of state constitution from U.S. Constitution
	Criminal defendants' rights under state constitution to be construed consistently with the rights in the U.S. Constitution
Section Twenty-seven:	Authorization of death penalty
Section Twenty-eight:	Victim's Bill of Rights (Proposition 8)
Section Twenty-nine:	People's (as opposed to defendant's) right to speedy, public trial
Section Thirty:	Authorization of joining of criminal cases
	Admissibility of hearsay evidence in preliminary hearings
	Reciprocal discovery in criminal cases

Section Three: Proposition 8

In California, many laws are passed by voters, through state and local initiatives. The Three Strikes law (see Chapter Fourteen) is one example. Another example is Proposition 8, or the Victim's Bill of Rights, which went into effect in 1982, and resulted in section 28 of Article I of the California Constitution, which is presented in its entirety in the Appendix.

The most important part of this bill, for the purposes of criminal procedure, is 28(d)'s right to truth-in-evidence: "Except as provided by statute . . . relevant evidence shall not be excluded in criminal proceeding . . . ." What this means is that admission of evidence in California is generally limited only by federal law. Thus, for all matters of criminal procedure that relate to admission of evidence, such as search and seizure law, state courts are constrained to limit their analysis to the U.S. Constitution and interpretations of that constitution. Federal case law reigns; but amidst any ambiguity in federal case law, state courts are allowed to interpret the federal constitution as may be necessary. Additionally, although state courts are bound by Supreme Court precedent, they may be able to rely on their own precedent over that of the lower federal courts (see case below).

In *California v. Greenwood*, 486 U.S. 35, the major Supreme Court case involving the question of whether police need a warrant to search curbside trash, the defendant challenged the validity of Article I, section 28(d), arguing that it violated the Due Process Clause. The Supreme Court found no basis for this argument whatsoever, declaring that states can choose to abandon the practice of affording individuals greater rights for the practice of affording individuals only those rights guaranteed in the federal constitution. California made this choice when its voters passed Proposition 8.

CASES-

I. People v. Camacho, 23 Cal.4th 824 (2000)
Article I, section 28, California Constitution

Does Proposition 8 mean that California judges have no autonomy, no leeway whatsoever when deciding questions of criminal procedure? Absolutely not. This first case deals with the question of when California courts can still rely on California precedent on matters pertaining to exclusion of evidence—specifically, on precedent that predates Proposition 8.

*****

Werdegar, J.

BACKGROUND

On June 26, 1997, police received an anonymous complaint of a "loud party disturbance" at defendant Cayetano Calderon Camacho's house. Officers Wood and Mora, responding to the complaint, arrived at defendant's home around 11:00 p.m. Officer Wood testified that, on arrival, he heard no noise upon exiting his patrol car. Approaching defendant's home, the officers heard no excessive noise. Officer Wood testified, rather, that he heard merely an unidentifiable "audible noise," one that was neither loud, disturbing nor violative of the city's noise ordinance.

The officers did not knock on the front door. Instead, while Officer Wood remained on the front lawn, Officer Mora walked into the side yard of the single-story house. The officers did not have a warrant. The side yard was an open area covered in grass. No fence, gate or shrubbery suggested entrance was forbidden. Neither, however, did anything indicate the public was invited to enter; there was neither a path nor a walkway, nor was there an entrance to the home accessible from the side yard. An opaque brick wall, about six feet nine inches high, blocked entrance into the backyard. A cement block wall of similar height marked the property line between defendant's side yard and the home of his immediate neighbor.

Defendant's home was set back about 20 feet from the public sidewalk. About 20 feet from the front of the house and 40 feet from the sidewalk, Officer Mora came upon a large side window. The window is visible from the public street or sidewalk, but the inside of the room is not. The neighbor on that side of the house would have difficulty seeing into the window because of the high cement block wall separating the two homes. The yard had no exterior lighting.

The window, which was open a few inches, had no blinds, curtains or other covering. Officer Mora, standing in the darkened side yard outside the window, heard music coming from the stereo inside the room, although the music was not loud. A red light bulb dimly lit the room. Returning to the front of the house, Mora reported to Officer Wood that he had seen a man in a room but was unsure whether the man was committing a crime. The two officers proceeded together back through the side yard to the window. There, Officer Wood saw defendant, sitting with his back to the window, manipulating some clear plastic baggies. Wood saw several baggies with a white powdery substance on the bed and dresser in the room, as well as a cellular phone and a pager. The officers retreated to the front of the house, called for backup, returned to the side yard and entered the house through the window, whereupon they arrested defendant.

Defendant was charged with possession of a controlled substance (cocaine) for sale. He moved to suppress the evidence, relying on *Lorenzana v. Superior Court* (*Lorenzana*). The trial court denied the motion to suppress, observing: "Well, I think the key to the analysis, the important key, and that's using *Lorenzana*, is the expectation of privacy. [¶] And I don't think there can be an expectation of privacy on the initial threshold because, in looking at this window, even with the lights on, to me, an expectation of privacy is what the defendant in *Lorenzana* had because he had his window really covered and the officer had to get within five to six inches and look through a little, tiny slot. In other words, the window was opaque.

"Here, the window was closed, pretty much. There is nothing covering up the defendant's activity, which is clearly drug-type activity. And the only other question is the intrusion issue. And I don't know whether it's close or not, but the officer was on a legitimate call for a legitimate reason.

"And I think you can probably argue, explicitly, they had a right to try to look to find the music. So I think the key to the defendant's expectation of privacy-I think he gave it away by at least not having the blinds closed. [¶] If, in fact, the blinds were closed-I would look at it differently-and the officer had to go up to the window and peer down and look through a one-inch opening. Just walking by this window you can see fairly well ...."

After his suppression motion was denied, defendant pleaded guilty and appealed. The Court of Appeal reversed.

DISCUSSION

The Fourth Amendment provides "[t]he right of the people to be secure in their persons, houses, papers and effects, against unreasonable searches and seizures, shall not be violated ...." This guarantee has been incorporated into the Fourteenth Amendment to the federal Constitution and is applicable to the states. A similar guarantee against unreasonable government searches is set forth in the state Constitution but, since voter approval of Proposition 8 in June 1982, state and federal claims relating to exclusion of evidence on grounds of unreasonable search and seizure are measured by the same standard.

Footnote: Contrary to the suggestion in the dissent, for this court to look to our own precedent (i.e., *Lorenzana*, for guidance in Fourth Amendment jurisprudence is not inappropriate, notwithstanding Proposition 8. We are not bound by lower federal court decisions in this area. Although *Lorenzana* was decided before passage of Proposition 8, it was based expressly on both the federal and state constitutional guarantees against unreasonable searches and seizures, and thus constitutes a decision by this court on the federal constitutional issue we face in this case. Nothing in [the case] cited by the dissent, suggests we should devalue decisions of this court construing the Fourth Amendment in favor of the views of lower federal courts from around the country merely because our decision was rendered before June 8, 1982, the effective date of Proposition 8.

In reviewing the action of the lower courts, we will uphold those factual findings of the trial court that are supported by substantial evidence. The question of whether a search was unreasonable, however, is a question of law. On that issue, we exercise "independent judgment." Because the officers lacked a warrant, the People bore the burden of establishing either that no search occurred, or that the search undertaken by the officers was justified by some exception to the warrant requirement.

The "ultimate standard set forth in the Fourth Amendment is reasonableness" and, after *Katz v. United States*, we ask two threshold questions. First, did the defendant exhibit a subjective expectation of privacy? Second, is such an expectation objectively reasonable, that is, is the expectation that one society is willing to recognize as reasonable? Although the trial court's finding on the first point is obscure, we conclude defendant exhibited a subjective expectation of privacy, in that he did not expect people to be intruding onto his private property at 11:00 p.m. and looking into his windows.

"At the risk of belaboring the obvious, private residences are places in which the individual normally expects privacy free of governmental intrusion not authorized by a warrant, and that expectation is plainly one that society is prepared to recognize as justifiable." Indeed, "the 'physical entry of the home is the chief evil against which the wording of the Fourth Amendment is directed.' " A central principle of the Fourth Amendment is that a person may "retreat into his own home and there be free from unreasonable governmental intrusion."

Balanced against this solicitude for privacy in the home is the need for effective law enforcement. Thus, "[t]he Fourth Amendment protection of the home has never been extended to require law enforcement officers to shield their eyes when passing by a home on public thoroughfares. Nor does the mere fact that an individual has taken measures to restrict some views of his activities preclude an officer's observations from a public vantage point where he has a right to be and which renders the activities clearly visible. [Citation.] 'What a person knowingly exposes to the public, even in his own home ..., is not a subject of Fourth Amendment protection.' "

Officers Wood and Mora were not, of course, standing on a public thoroughfare when they observed defendant packaging cocaine; they were in his yard. Nevertheless, their observations would not constitute a search and thus not violate the Fourth Amendment if they were standing in a place where they otherwise had a right to be. This case thus turns on whether Officers Wood and Mora were legally entitled, under all the circumstances, to be in defendant's side yard.

We addressed this precise point in *Lorenzana*. In that case, the police, responding to an anonymous tip about drug dealing at the defendant's home, went into the side yard of his house. As here, the side yard was an otherwise barren, grass-covered patch of land bearing neither a fence, gate, landscaping nor a path to indicate that the public was expressly or impliedly invited in. Unlike in this case, when the investigating police officer in *Lorenzana* entered the side yard, he found the window largely obscured by drawn curtains. Undeterred, he crouched down and looked through a two-inch gap between the curtains and the windowsill, but could not see into the room until his face was five or six inches from the window. The officer watched and listened for 15 minutes; in this manner, he acquired evidence of drug dealing and made the arrest.

In issuing a writ to reverse the denial of a suppression motion, Justice Tobriner, writing for the court, relied principally on the fact the officer had trespassed on the defendant's property and thus, when he observed the evidence of criminality, he was not standing on property that had been expressly or impliedly opened to the public. "[Past cases] clearly demonstrate the salutary rule of law that observations of things in plain sight made from a place where a police officer has a right to be do not amount to a search in the constitutional sense. On the other hand, when observations are made from a position to which the officer has not been expressly or implicitly invited, the intrusion is unlawful unless executed pursuant to a warrant or one of the established exceptions to the warrant requirement."

"[A] resident of a house [may] rely justifiably upon the privacy of the surrounding areas as a protection from the peering of the officer unless such residence is 'exposed' to that intrusion by the existence of public pathways or other invitations to the public to enter upon the property. This justifiable reliance on the privacy of the non-common portions of the property surrounding one's residence thus leads to the particular rule that searches conducted without a warrant from such parts of the property always are unconstitutional unless an exception to the warrant requirement applies."

Defendant argues *Lorenzana* controls this case, while respondent and the dissent contend *Lorenzana* is distinguishable on its facts. Although we find slight factual differences between *Lorenzana* and the instant case, none implicate the core holding of *Lorenzana*, to wit, that observations by law enforcement officers intrude on a person's reasonable expectation of privacy if made from private property onto which neither the public nor the police has been invited, and in circumstances wherein police lack a legal justification for being on the property.

Respondent and the dissent emphasize that, unlike in *Lorenzana*, Officers Wood and Mora did not peer into a small opening or aperture in the curtains to intrude on defendant's privacy. Instead, defendant's rather large (four-by eight-foot) window was completely uncovered, so that any person in the side yard could easily have viewed his unlawful activity. From this circumstance, respondent and the dissent would have us conclude defendant failed to exhibit an expectation of privacy that was reasonable.

Although it is true the officer in *Lorenzana* was forced to peer through a small opening between the drawn curtains and the windowsill to observe the defendant's illegal activity, our decision in that case did not turn on the surreptitious nature of the officer's observation. Instead, *Lorenzana* identified a broader proposition: a warrantless search cannot be justified by police observations "made from a position to which the officer has not been expressly or implicitly invited."

None of the cases cited by respondent support a contrary conclusion. All either involve the police making observations from a public vantage or are silent as to whether the police were standing in a place open to the public.

Thus, while it is certainly true that " 'in striking a balance between the rights of the individual and the needs of law enforcement, the Fourth Amendment itself [does not] draw[] the blinds the occupant could have drawn but did not' " Accordingly, [no cases] create an "unshuttered window" exception to the Fourth Amendment's warrant requirement that supersedes *Lorenzana*'s reliance on the fact that police were not entitled to be in the defendant's side yard.

Nor is it significant, as respondent argues, that Officers Wood and Mora observed defendant for only a short time (perhaps only a minute), whereas the officer in *Lorenzana* watched and listened for 15 full minutes. It is the nature, not the duration, of the intrusion that controls this case. Had Wood and Mora been standing on a public sidewalk, they could have observed defendant for as long as they wished. Conversely, had the officer in *Lorenzana* peered through the small opening in the window for only 60 seconds, he would still have conducted an illegal warrantless search because he was standing on private property onto which he had not been invited.

Respondent and the dissent also argue *Lorenzana* is distinguishable because the officers in that case were directed to the house by a tip of drug dealing, and thus were investigating the very crime they ultimately discovered. By contrast, Officers Wood and Mora were investigating a noise complaint, had not targeted defendant's house for surveillance, and only by accident-characterized by the dissent in the Court of Appeal as a "luck out arrest"-discovered defendant packaging cocaine.

That police had not targeted defendant's house for an investigation into drug dealing, and only inadvertently discovered him engaging in that crime, does not change the fact that police acquired the evidence of his crime by watching him through a window from a vantage point to which neither they nor the public had been invited. The relevance of police motive was raised in where the defendant suggested the fact police were in a public airspace when they viewed the marijuana plants in his yard was insufficient to compromise his expectation of privacy when "the viewing is motivated by a law enforcement purpose, and not the result of a casual, accidental observation."

The high court accorded no weight to the police officer's motive, relying solely on the fact the officer's vantage point was open to the public. "That the observation from aircraft was directed at identifying the plants and the officers were trained to recognize marijuana is irrelevant.... Any member of the public flying in this airspace who glanced down could have seen everything that these officers observed. On this record, we readily conclude that respondent's expectation that his garden was protected from such observation is unreasonable and is not an expectation that society is prepared to honor." Similarly, we fail to see why the fact that Officers Wood and Mora entered defendant's side yard for reasons unrelated to seeking evidence of drug sales should be relevant to determining the reasonableness of defendant's expectation of privacy.

Respondent contends that Officers Wood and Mora's observations were constitutionally permissible because "nothing prohibited access to and from [the] side yard from the street along the side of the house." We might add that, from the photographs of the scene included in the record, one might expect that at some point, a neighbor's child, should the need arise, might retrieve an errant ball or loose pet from the side yard of defendant's home. Similarly, an employee of the local utility company might at some point enter the yard to read the meter, were one located there. Admittedly there was no fence, no sign proclaiming "No trespassing," no impediment to entry.

Nevertheless, we cannot accept the proposition that defendant forfeited the expectation his property would remain private simply because he did not erect an impregnable barrier to access. Recalling that the lodestar of our inquiry is the reasonableness of defendant's expectation of privacy, we assume for the sake of argument the meter reader or the child chasing a ball or pet may have implied consent to enter the yard for that narrow reason, for a limited time, and during a reasonable hour. Certainly the same cannot be said for the unconsented-to intrusion by police at 11:00 o'clock at night.

That is not to say we find Officers Wood and Mora's search unlawful merely because they were trespassing on defendant's private property. ["Since *Katz*, we have consistently held that the presence or absence of physical trespass by police is constitutionally irrelevant to the question whether society is prepared to recognize an asserted privacy interest as reasonable."] For example, *Katz*, a seminal case in Fourth Amendment jurisprudence, involved wiretapping, an intrusion into privacy not easily amenable to a trespassing analysis. The high court found police invaded that defendant's reasonable expectation of privacy even though they did not trespass on his property.

Moreover, even without a warrant, police officers may intrude onto private property if the surrounding facts provide cause to believe an emergency situation exists. Thus, had Wood and Mora been dispatched to defendant's house in response to a report of gunshots being fired, of screams being heard, or of a riot, a stabbing or some other serious crime, we cannot say their entry into the side yard would have been unlawful. Indeed, had the officers on their arrival at defendant's house heard a raucous party, confirming the anonymous complaint that brought them there in the first place, and had they then banged on the front door to no avail, their entry into the side yard in an attempt to seek the source of the noise would likely have been justified.

12

The facts here paint quite a different picture: Called to investigate a complaint of excessive noise, an infraction under the city's municipal ordinances, the officers arrived at defendant's home late in the evening and heard no such noise. Without bothering to knock on defendant's front door, they proceeded directly into his darkened side yard. Most persons, we believe, would be surprised, indeed startled, to look out their bedroom window at such an hour to find police officers standing in their yard looking back at them.

In short, we find this case is governed by *Lorenzana*. Although *Lorenzana* was decided prior to the enactment of Proposition 8 in 1982, no post-*Lorenzana* decision by the United States Supreme Court casts any doubt on its primary reliance on the public or private nature of the police officer's vantage point as a controlling factor in determining the lawfulness of the officer's warrantless observations of citizens' conduct inside the privacy of their homes. [Prop. 8 constrains this court to follow Supreme Court decisions; those of lower federal courts are persuasive but not controlling]. Significantly, respondent does not cite any Supreme Court authority requiring we uphold the trial court's denial of defendant's suppression motion.

Nor are we persuaded by the lower federal court decisions cited by the dissent in support. First, none is as close to the facts of this case as *Lorenzana*. Second, of those that indicate the site of the observation, most pose distinguishable facts, in that the observations were made from arguably public areas. In short, none of the cited lower federal court cases convince us to abandon our decision in *Lorenzana*.

The decision of the Court of Appeal is affirmed.

*****

CONCLUSION

The California Supreme Court was asked by the state in this case to disregard California precedent because the governing case predated the passing of Proposition 8, and asked instead to rely on precedent from lower federal courts (from a variety of federal circuits). The court refused to comply, stating that the fact that precedent predates Proposition 8 does not mean it is no longer relevant. Additionally, it reinforced the rule that even after Proposition 8, California courts must abide by Supreme Court precedent but do not necessarily have to favor decisions by lower federal courts over state case law that interprets the federal and state constitutions.

REVIEW

1. What were the facts and holding in *Lorenzana*?

2. Why did the trial court make its decision to deny the motion to suppress?

3. What are the reasons the court in this case affirms the reversal of the trial court?

4. What are the arguments put forth by the state (prosecutors) in this case?

5. Do you think that the California Supreme Court is "defending its turf" with this decision? How so?

CHAPTER THREE

Searches and Seizures

California follows the three-step process that is in accordance with federal law, in handling the legality of searches and seizures. First, it must be determined whether the government action qualifies as a search or a seizure (the purpose of this chapter). Second, if it is a search or seizure, is it reasonable under the Fourth Amendment? And finally, if it is unreasonable, must the evidentiary results be excluded? We deal with two questions in this chapter: when does a search occur; and when does a seizure occur? These are important preliminary questions, because if the government action isn't considered a search or a seizure, then the Fourth Amendment is not even implicated, and the remaining questions need not be addressed.

Section 1. Searches

OVERVIEW

A search occurs only if the government violates an individual's "reasonable expectation of privacy." The Supreme Court has adopted a two-prong test, where an individual must have a subjective (personal) expectation of privacy, and this must be objectively reasonable by societal standards. States are free to assess reasonable expectation of privacy as they wish, as long as they stay within these bounds. We'll see below how California courts have proceeded. The Fourth Amendment is also not implicated if government actors discover evidence in plain view or in "open fields." We will discuss a Supreme Court case that originated in California that eliminated the "inadvertency requirement" for plain view searches. We'll look at a California case that extended plain view to "plain smell."

CASES-

I. People v. Shepherd, 23 Cal.App.4th 825 (1994)

As mentioned, whether a person has a reasonable expectation of privacy in something (that will be claimed as evidence by the prosecution) depends on their personal subjective expectation as well as on what society would reasonably presume to be private. Courts can provide further guidelines as well, however. When you read this case pay attention to several characteristics the court uses in its analysis of the "privacy doctrine."

*****

Sims, J.

BACKGROUND

The following facts are adduced from the transcript of the preliminary examination. In the late evening hours of November 27, 1992, El Dorado County Sheriff's Deputy Murphy observed defendant and codefendant Harris standing in front of a Cameron Park liquor store. Harris was arrested on two outstanding traffic warrants. Murphy let defendant go when a warrant check on a false name she provided revealed no warrants.

In the early morning hours of November 28, 1992, El Dorado County Sheriff's Deputy Kenneth Danielson observed a truck parked around the corner from the Cameron Park liquor store. He noticed the license plate on the front of the truck differed from the back plate. Danielson learned the truck apparently had been stolen in Sacramento the day before.

Sheriff's deputies searched the truck. The truck's doors were unlocked, and the ignition had been punched out. A purse containing documents bearing defendant's name lay on the driver's side floorboard. The deputies also found duffel bags in the bed of the truck, which contained papers bearing defendant's and Harris's names.

From a photograph found in the purse, Deputy Murphy identified defendant as the individual he had released earlier. He later arrested defendant. Defendant told Murphy someone had given the truck to Harris. She also stated she did not know the truck was stolen, but should have presumed it had been stolen because the ignition was punched.

The trial court denied the suppression motion, ruling neither defendant nor codefendant Harris had "standing" to challenge the search of the truck.

DISCUSSION

Defendant contends "she had a reasonable expectation of privacy in the contents of her purse, and her Fourth Amendment right to privacy was violated when Deputy Sheriff Danielson searched her purse and seized the contents; therefore, the trial court erred in finding that [defendant] lacked standing to challenge the search of her purse."

"Before reaching the question whether the officer's [action] was a ' search' ..., we must determine whether the challenged action by the officer ' has infringed an interest of the defendant which the Fourth Amendment was designed to protect.' An illegal search or seizure violates the federal constitutional rights only of those who have a legitimate expectation of privacy in the invaded place or seized thing. [Citation.] The legitimate expectation of privacy must exist in the particular area searched or thing seized in order to bring a Fourth Amendment challenge. [Citations.] A defendant bears the burden to show he had such an expectation. [Citations.] Factors to consider in the determination include ' "whether the defendant has a [property or] possessory interest in the thing seized or the place searched; whether he has the right to exclude others from that place; whether he has exhibited a subjective expectation that it would remain free from governmental invasion, whether he took normal precautions to maintain his privacy and whether he was legitimately on the premises." ' [Citations.]"

Here, defendant had no legitimate expectation of privacy in the stolen truck. She contends she retained a privacy interest in her purse, left in the truck. We cannot agree. [A]n important consideration in evaluating a privacy interest is whether a person has taken normal precautions to maintain his or her privacy. Whether a woman has a legitimate privacy interest in the contents of her purse depends in part on where the purse is located. Thus, a woman who forgetfully leaves her purse on a chair at the dress shop may reasonably expect someone to look inside it to ascertain the rightful owner. Similarly, one who leaves her purse in a stolen vehicle may reasonably expect someone to look in the purse to ascertain the identity of the victim or the thief. In short, by leaving her purse in a stolen vehicle, defendant failed to take normal precautions to maintain her privacy interest in the purse.

The trial court correctly denied the motion to suppress evidence.

The judgment (order granting probation) is affirmed.

*****

CONCLUSION

The court focused its analysis in this case on whether the defendant took "normal precautions" to protect her property from the eye of the public, and since she didn't, by leaving her purse in a stolen car, she lost her privacy interest in the purse.

REVIEW

1. What are the guidelines the court provides for evaluating reasonable expectation of privacy?

2. Would it have made a difference to the analysis if the defendant hadn't known the truck was stolen and shouldn't have reasonably known it was stolen?

II. Horton v. California, 496 U.S. 128 (1990)

The next case is a Supreme Court Case originating in California, involving the plain view doctrine. This rule previously had three prerequisites for its use by governmental actors: that they are legally present when they view the evidence, that they do not use high-tech enhancements of normal senses, and that they inadvertently (rather than strategically) come across the evidence. This last requirement is of interest in *Horton*.

*****

Stevens, J.

BACKGROUND

Petitioner was convicted of the armed robbery of Erwin Wallaker, the treasurer of the San Jose Coin Club. When Wallaker returned to his home after the Club's annual show, he entered his garage and was accosted by two masked men, one armed with a machine gun and the other with an electrical shocking device, sometimes referred to as a "stun gun." The two men shocked Wallaker, bound and handcuffed him, and robbed him of jewelry and cash. During the encounter sufficient conversation took place to enable Wallaker subsequently to identify petitioner's distinctive voice. His identification was partially corroborated by a witness who saw the robbers leaving the scene and by evidence that petitioner had attended the coin show.

Sergeant LaRault, an experienced police officer, investigated the crime and determined that there was probable cause to search petitioner's home for the proceeds of the robbery and for the weapons used by the robbers. His affidavit for a search warrant referred to police reports that described the weapons as well as the proceeds, but the warrant issued by the Magistrate only authorized a search for the proceeds, including three specifically described rings.

16

Pursuant to the warrant, LaRault searched petitioner's residence, but he did not find the stolen property. During the course of the search, however, he discovered the weapons in plain view and seized them. Specifically, he seized an Uzi machine gun, a .38-caliber revolver, two stun guns, a handcuff key, a San Jose Coin Club advertising brochure, and a few items of clothing identified by the victim. LaRault testified that while he was searching for the rings, he also was interested in finding other evidence connecting petitioner to the robbery. Thus, the seized evidence was not discovered "inadvertently."

DISCUSSION

The criteria that generally guide "plain-view" seizures were set forth in *Coolidge v. New Hampshire*. The scope of that doctrine as it had developed in earlier cases was fairly summarized in these three paragraphs from Justice Stewart's opinion:

> It is well established that under certain circumstances the police may seize evidence in plain view without a warrant. But it is important to keep in mind that, in the vast majority of cases, *any* evidence seized by the police will be in plain view, at least at the moment of seizure. The problem with the 'plain view' doctrine has been to identify the circumstances in which plain view has legal significance rather than being simply the normal concomitant of any search, legal or illegal.

> An example of the applicability of the 'plain view' doctrine is the situation in which the police have a warrant to search a given area for specified objects, and in the course of the search come across some other article of incriminating character. Where the initial intrusion that brings the police within plain view of such an article is supported, not by a warrant, but by one of the recognized exceptions to the warrant requirement, the seizure is also legitimate. Thus the police may inadvertently come across evidence while in 'hot pursuit' of a fleeing suspect. And an object that comes into view during a search incident to arrest that is appropriately limited in scope under existing law may be seized without a warrant. Finally, the 'plain view' doctrine has been applied where a police officer is not searching for evidence against the accused, but nonetheless inadvertently comes across an incriminating object.

> What the 'plain view' cases have in common is that the police officer in each of them had a prior justification for an intrusion in the course of which he came inadvertently across a piece of evidence incriminating the accused. The doctrine serves to supplement the prior justification-- whether it be a warrant for another object, hot pursuit, search incident to lawful arrest, or some other legitimate reason for being present unconnected with a search directed against the accused--and permits the warrantless seizure. Of course, the extension of the original justification is legitimate only where it is immediately apparent to the police that they have evidence before them; the 'plain view' doctrine may not be used to extend a general exploratory search from one object to another until something incriminating at last emerges.

Justice Stewart then described the two limitations on the doctrine that he found implicit in its rationale: First, that "plain view *alone* is never enough to justify the warrantless seizure of evidence,"; and second, that "the discovery of evidence in plain view must be inadvertent."

Justice Stewart's analysis of the "plain-view" doctrine did not command a majority, and a plurality of the Court has since made clear that the discussion is "not a binding precedent."

Justice Stewart concluded that the inadvertence requirement was necessary to avoid a violation of the express constitutional requirement that a valid warrant must particularly describe the things to be seized. He explained:

> The rationale of the exception to the warrant requirement, as just stated, is that a plain-view seizure will not turn an initially valid (and therefore limited) search into a 'general' one, while the inconvenience of procuring a warrant to cover an inadvertent discovery is great. But where the discovery is anticipated, where the police know in advance the location of the evidence and intend to seize it, the situation is altogether different. The requirement of a warrant to seize imposes no inconvenience whatever, or at least none which is constitutionally cognizable in a legal system that regards warrantless searches as '*per se* unreasonable' in the absence of 'exigent circumstances.' "If the initial intrusion is bottomed upon a warrant that fails to mention a particular object, though the police know its location and intend to seize it, then there is a violation of the express constitutional requirement of 'Warrants ... particularly describing ... [the] things to be seized.'

We find two flaws in this reasoning. First, evenhanded law enforcement is best achieved by the application of objective standards of conduct, rather than standards that depend upon the subjective state of mind of the officer. The fact that an officer is interested in an item of evidence and fully expects to find it in the course of a search should not invalidate its seizure if the search is confined in area and duration by the terms of a warrant or a valid exception to the warrant requirement. If the officer has knowledge approaching certainty that the item will be found, we see no reason why he or she would deliberately omit a particular description of the item to be seized from the application for a search warrant. Specification of the additional item could only permit the officer to expand the scope of the search. On the other hand, if he or she has a valid warrant to search for one item and merely a suspicion concerning the second, whether or not it amounts to probable cause, we fail to see why that suspicion should immunize the second item from seizure if it is found during a lawful search for the first.

Second, the suggestion that the inadvertence requirement is necessary to prevent the police from conducting general searches, or from converting specific warrants into general warrants, is not persuasive because that interest is already served by the requirements that no warrant issue unless it "particularly describ[es] the place to be searched and the persons or things to be seized," and that a warrantless search be circumscribed by the exigencies which justify its initiation. Scrupulous adherence to these requirements serves the interests in limiting the area and duration of the search that the inadvertence requirement inadequately protects

18

In this case the items seized from petitioner's home were discovered during a lawful search authorized by a valid warrant. When they were discovered, it was immediately apparent to the officer that they constituted incriminating evidence. He had probable cause, not only to obtain a warrant to search for the stolen property, but also to believe that the weapons and handguns had been used in the crime he was investigating. The search was authorized by the warrant; the seizure was authorized by the "plain-view" doctrine.

The judgment is affirmed.

Brennan, J. (Dissenting)

Although joined by only three other Members of the Court, Justice Stewart's discussion of the inadvertent discovery requirement has become widely accepted. It has been accepted generally for over a decade"). Forty-six States and the District of Columbia and 12 United States Courts of Appeals now require plain-view seizures to be inadvertent. There has been no outcry from law enforcement officials that the inadvertent discovery requirement unduly burdens their efforts. Given that the requirement is inescapably rooted in the plain language of the Fourth Amendment, I cannot fathom the Court's enthusiasm for discarding this element of the plain-view doctrine.

The Court posits two "flaws" in Justice Stewart's reasoning that it believes demonstrate the inappropriateness of the inadvertent discovery requirement. But these flaws are illusory. First, the majority explains that it can see no reason why an officer who "has knowledge approaching certainty" that an item will be found in a particular location "would deliberately omit a particular description of the item to be seized from the application for a search warrant." But to the individual whose possessory interest has been invaded, it matters not *why* the police officer decided to omit a particular item from his application for a search warrant. When an officer with probable cause to seize an item fails to mention that item in his application for a search warrant--for whatever reason--and then seizes the item anyway, his conduct is *per se* unreasonable. Suppression of the evidence so seized will encourage officers to be more precise and complete in future warrant applications.

Furthermore, there are a number of instances in which a law enforcement officer might deliberately choose to omit certain items from a warrant application even though he has probable cause to seize them, knows they are on the premises, and intends to seize them when they are discovered in plain view. For example, the warrant application process can often be time consuming, especially when the police attempt to seize a large number of items. An officer interested in conducting a search as soon as possible might decide to save time by listing only one or two hard-to-find items, such as the stolen rings in this case, confident that he will find in plain view all of the other evidence he is looking for before he discovers the listed items. Because rings could be located almost anywhere inside or outside a house, it is unlikely that a warrant to search for and seize the rings would restrict the scope of the search. An officer might rationally find the risk of immediately discovering the items listed in the warrant--thereby forcing him to conclude the search immediately--outweighed by the time saved in the application process.

The majority also contends that, once an officer is lawfully in a house and the scope of his search is adequately circumscribed by a warrant, "no additional Fourth Amendment interest is furthered by requiring that the discovery of evidence be inadvertent." Put another way, " 'the inadvertence rule will in no way reduce the number of places into which [law enforcement officers] may lawfully look.' ". The majority is correct, but it has asked the wrong question. It is true that the inadvertent discovery requirement furthers no privacy interests. The requirement in no way reduces the scope of a search or the number of places into which officers may look. But it does protect possessory interests. The inadvertent discovery requirement is essential if we are to take seriously the Fourth Amendment's protection of possessory interests as well as privacy interests. The Court today eliminates a rule designed to further

19

possessory interests on the ground that it fails to further privacy interests. I cannot countenance such constitutional legerdemain.

*****

CONCLUSION

After the Supreme Court's 7-2 opinion in Horton, the inadvertency requirement was eliminated from the plain-view doctrine, leaving only the prerequisites that officers must be legally in place when they view the evidence and they may not use advanced technology to enhance their senses (such as thermal heat imaging devices).

REVIEW

1. What does it mean that Justice Stewart's analysis in *Coolidge v. New Hampshire* is "not binding"?

2. What was Stewart's reasoning behind the inadvertency requirement?

3. What "flaws" did the Court find in Stewart's reasoning?

4. How did Brennan, in his dissent, pick apart the majority's argument? Which position do you find more convincing?

III. Guidi v. Superior Court, 10 Cal.3d 1 (1973)

The "plain view" doctrine is not limited to vision: it can extend to touch, smell, and hearing as well. A leading California Supreme Court Case sets the parameters for its "plain smell" corollary.

*****

Wright, C.J.

BACKGROUND

For some months prior to his election to cooperate with Orange County authorities as an undercover operative seeking to deal in narcotics, Joe Del Sesto had frequented various commercial establishments patronized by narcotics traffickers. Acting in his undercover capacity he entered into preliminary negotiations with petitioners Guidi, Lefort and Neilson and thereafter went to an apartment in Long Beach in order to inspect hashish proffered by such petitioners in exchange for an agreed purchase price of $7,500.

The door of the apartment opened into a living room which was partially separated from the adjacent kitchen by a counter or bar six to eight feet long and three and a half feet high. A hall led to two bedrooms and a bathroom at the rear of the apartment. Upon his entrance Del Sesto went through the hall to the bathroom but was unable to observe the occupants of either bedroom as the doors to those rooms were closed. Having returned to the living room Del Sesto observed petitioner O'Connor withdraw 20

20

bricks of hashish, wrapped in pairs in separate plastic "baggies," from a brown grocery bag.

Del Sesto left the apartment to get the purchase money. Petitioners Lefort and Neilson, who had left with Del Sesto, were arrested on the street as they returned with Del Sesto to the apartment. Del Sesto told the officers that two other suspects were in the apartment and that the hashish was in a shopping bag on the floor of the living room. Del Sesto also said he had not been able to see if other occupants of the apartment were within the bedrooms.

Petitioner O'Connor responded to a police officer's knock and was arrested at the door of the apartment. Moving inside with weapon drawn and accompanied by two fellow officers, Officer Holt arrested petitioner Guidi in the living room. Both O'Connor and Guidi were handcuffed immediately. During this time Holt heard sounds coming from the rear of the apartment. He crossed the room to the kitchen. Behind the counter Holt saw a shopping bag with the opening squared shut. For the first time the officer became aware that the distinctive odor of hashish permeated the room and seemed to come directly from the vicinity of the bag. Seizing the bag he found the 10 "baggies" of hashish within. Holt then searched the bedrooms of the apartment, first for occupants and then more thoroughly to the point of rifling through drawers and opening shoeboxes. A small child was found in one bedroom and the tenant of the apartment in the other. The officers possessed neither search nor arrest warrants.

DISCUSSION

Petitioners contend that the search of the bag of hashish in the kitchen falls within [no exception to the presumptive invalidity of a warrantless search]. The People argue that the odor emanating from the bag put the contraband inside it within the "plain smell" of Officer Holt, and urge that we treat "plain smell" as the legal equivalent of "plain view," thus invoking or creating, with respect to items possessing unique or distinctive odors, a rule similar to the long-standing concept that contraband seen in plain view may be seized without a warrant.

[Next, the court addressed the question of whether the officers were legally where the bag was, since this a requirement for the plain view exception. It concluded they were, since upon making an arrest, the offices could search for additional suspects (for their own safety), and a suspect could have been hiding behind the kitchen counter.]

We now address ourselves to the central issue: the question of the inadmissibility of the hashish on the ground that although the view of the brown paper bag was constitutionally obtained, the viewing of the interior of the bag resulting in the disclosure of the hashish was constitutionally impermissible.

In the instant case, the officers entering the apartment were possessed of substantially contemporaneous information describing the container of contraband as a paper shopping bag. In the course of a lawful inspection of the premises he had entered, Officer Holt saw in plain sight a bag conforming to that described as bearing the hashish previously offered for sale to Del Sesto.

These factors alone would not suffice as reasonable justification for the seizure, but Officer Holt also detected an odor of hashish which was strongest near the bag. The reasonableness of the seizure must be judged with due consideration to the total circumstances.

Two additional elements must be weighed in the balance in the determination of the reasonableness of the seizure by Officer Holt. First, the bag was highly portable and second, as described to Holt, the contents of the bag consisted solely of the proffered hashish and nothing else. [T]he power to seize carries with it the power to "search" the seized item. Where contraband is believed to be hidden among several items within a container, such as a suitcase or a dresser drawer, seizure of the container may well be more difficult to justify. The type of container which may reasonably be seized as evidence of a transaction involving narcotics is a container which reasonably appears to hold contraband and little else. Moreover, the less portable a container, the less subject it should be to warrantless seizure as evidence merely by virtue of its role as a container of contraband.

The above standards render clearly justifiable some types of plain view seizures of evidence - such as the seizure of a marijuana "joint" even though the cigarette paper completely obscures the contraband itself from view. It is equally clear that the seizure of other literal containers of contraband would be insupportable - such as the "seizure" of a suspect's entire house. We deem under the totality of circumstances heretofore described that Officer Holt could reasonably conclude that the bag matched the description and location of the bag containing the hashish baggies, gave the appearance of utilization for such storage, emanated a strong smell of hashish and was removable, and that its invasion constituted a minimum infringement of privacy. The seizure was thus constitutionally reasonable.

The petition is . . . denied.

*****

CONCLUSION

The court upheld the use of smell in order to seize the bag of hashish, but cautioned that more factors than smell alone were necessary to justify the seizure.

REVIEW

1. Is smell as powerful a sense as sight, in terms of justifying a seizure of evidence? Will smell almost always lead an officer to contraband?

2. The court takes a "totality of the circumstances" approach to analyzing the warrantless seizure. What circumstances supported the government's position? Did anything support a view for the defense?

3. What is necessary, besides smell alone, to justify the taking of the evidence?

Section 2: Seizures

OVERVIEW

Before *California v. Hodari* was decided by the U.S. Supreme Court, it was unclear amongst states as to when a seizure occurred. The view California courts had taken was that a seizure occurred once an officer displayed authority and the suspect would not reasonably feel free to leave. Physical restraint was not necessary, nor was compliance with a show of authority. In *Hodari,* the government argued successfully that the seizure should not occur until a suspect complies or is forced to comply with the show of authority (through police restraint). Thus, when someone runs from the police they are not "seized" until the police catch them. Any evidence discarded during the run is not the product of the detention (which becomes important if the detention is unlawful). The decision has cleared up most confusion in this area of law. The following case demonstrates an application of *Hodari*.

CASES-

I. Lara v. County of San Mateo, 163 F.Supp.2d 1107

This case is not criminal; rather, it is a civil action brought by a plaintiff, alleging that her constitutional rights have been violated by a sheriff's deputy. We'll discuss this in more detail in Chapter 11. Criminal procedure is implicated, because the plaintiff must first show that the defendant violated the Fourth Amendment, before she can receive a positive verdict. This is a preliminary for the federal court, since the defendant is asking that the case be dismissed prior to trial.

*****

Spero, Magistrate Judge

BACKGROUND

This action is based on an incident that occurred on September 18, 2000, at Sequoia Hospital in Redwood City, California, where Plaintiff was employed as a kitchen helper. Plaintiff alleges that she was transporting a metal cart full of dishes via the elevator, as part of her normal duties. The elevator stopped at the second floor and two uniformed officers of the San Mateo Sheriff's Office, Dep. Kazeszki and Sgt. Flahavan, entered the elevator. After the doors to the elevator closed, Dep. Kazeszki, "without uttering a word to Plaintiff proceeded to handcuff Plaintiff's wrist, and then immediately handcuffed the other end of the handcuffs to a bar" of the metal cart. When the elevator reached the first floor, the officers exited and Plaintiff followed them, still handcuffed to the cart. At this point, Deputy Kazeszki made a "joke" about not having the key to the handcuffs, and then released Plaintiff. The next day, another officer from the San Mateo Sheriff's Department came to Plaintiff's workplace and told her that she had been handcuffed as a "joke" and that she had not really been arrested.

DISCUSSION

The Supreme Court has explained that not every encounter with a police officer rises to the level of a seizure. Rather, an encounter only triggers Fourth Amendment scrutiny when it "loses its consensual nature." "Only when the officer, by means of physical force or show of authority, has in some way restrained the liberty of a citizen may we conclude that a 'seizure' has occurred." Thus, the appropriate test to determine whether a police officer's conduct constitutes a seizure is whether, "taking into account all of the circumstances surrounding the encounter, the police conduct would have communicated to a reasonable person that he was not at liberty to ignore the police presence and go about his business."

Here, Plaintiff alleges that she was handcuffed to a cart by an officer of the Sheriff's Department. As a pleading matter, this adequately alleges a seizure. Nor do Defendants present any authority in support of the proposition that a reasonable person, having been handcuffed to a cart, would nonetheless believe as a matter of law that she was free to go about her business because the officers had not pointed a gun at her or told her she was under arrest.

Defendants suggest, however, that Plaintiff was not seized because "a seizure does not occur if an officer applies physical force in an attempt to detain a suspect but such force is ineffective." Defendants' reliance on *California v. Hodari* is misplaced. There, the defendant began to run when he saw a police car approaching One officer became suspicious and pursued the defendant. Before the officer had caught up with him, the defendant tossed away a small rock that turned out to be crack cocaine. The officer then tackled the defendant, handcuffed him and radioed for back-up. In considering whether the discarded drugs constituted the fruit of an illegal seizure, the California Court of Appeal held that the defendant was seized when he saw the officer following him because the pursuit itself was a show of authority sufficient to constitute a seizure. The California Supreme Court affirmed. The United States Supreme Court reversed, explaining as follows:

> The word seizure readily bears the meaning of a laying on of hands or application of physical force to restrain movement, even when it is ultimately unsuccessful... It does not remotely apply, however, to the prospect of a policeman yelling "Stop, in the name of the law!" at a fleeing form that continues to flee. That is no seizure.... An arrest requires *either* physical force ... *or,* where that is absent, *submission* to the assertion of authority.

Here, [p]laintiff's claim is based on the allegation that she was restrained by *physical* means rather than by a show of authority. Therefore, the rule articulated in *California v. Hodari* has no relevance to the facts alleged here.

The Court also rejects Defendants' argument that Plaintiff was not seized-- even though Defendants had handcuffed her to a cart--because she would not have been free to leave the moving elevator in any event. The fact that an individual's freedom of movement is restricted by a factor independent of police conduct *is* relevant in determining whether an individual who has not been physically restrained has nevertheless been restrained by a *show of authority.* In *Florida v. Bostick* the Court explained that where an individual was being questioned by police on a bus, the mere fact that the individual did not feel free to leave did not give rise to a seizure in light of the fact that a passenger on a bus that is about to depart generally does not feel free to leave.

Here, as discussed above, Plaintiff alleges that she was *physically* restrained by Defendants. Therefore, the reasoning of *Florida v. Bostick* does not apply. In particular, Plaintiff could reasonably have believed on the facts alleged that she was not free to go about her business because an officer of the Sheriff's Department had handcuffed her to a cart. Thus, the possible existence of an independent factor which might have made Plaintiff feel that she was not free to leave is not relevant to the question of whether Plaintiff was seized.

[T]he Court finds that Plaintiff has alleged sufficient facts to state a claim under [Section 1983].

*****

CONCLUSION

Notice how the court differentiated between seizures involving shows of authority and those involving physical restraint. The court refused to apply *Hodari* as they defendants wanted it to, because *Hodari* involved an initial show of authority rather than physical restraint.

REVIEW

1.   At what point did the seizure occur, according to the plaintiff? According to the defendants?

2.   What were the two arguments put forth by the defendant? How did the court dispel each of these?

CHAPTER FOUR

Stop and Frisk

Recall that pursuant to *Terry v. Ohio*, 392 U.S. 1 (1968) police officers are entitled to stop and detain an individual for investigation, when they have reasonable suspicion to believe that criminal activity may be afoot and the individual may be connected to such activity. The burden of proof required to justify such a stop is less than probable cause, but such a stop may still constitute a seizure, compared to an encounter in which officers merely pose voluntary questions to person. These investigative stops are supposed to be limited in scope, meaning that they should be relatively short, noninvasive, and place-specific. Reasonable suspicion is often based on an officer's observation of behavior, sometimes coupled with knowledge of the context of that behavior. But it can also be based on things such as anonymous tips, which must reach a certain level of substantiation before they qualify as reasonable suspicion.

There are several exceptions to the normal framework of reasonable suspicion. These include ordering passengers of a car after stopping the driver, detaining drivers at DWI checkpoints regardless of having any individualized suspicion they are breaking the law, and expanding the normal time scope of detentions at international borders. These exceptions have all been justified by the Supreme Court on the basis of special governmental needs (safety of officers during traffic stops, protection of public from drunk drivers, protection of country's borders from narcotics and illegal aliens).

Once an officer validly stops someone for an investigative detention, this does not automatically enable the officer to "frisk" or pat down the individual. The officer must have an articulable basis for thinking the person may be armed and dangerous. Upon having this basis, an officer may engage in a limited search of outer clothing for weapon, and upon discovering the feeling of what may be a weapon, the officer can remove the object to affirm that it is a weapon. If it turns out to be contraband, this may still be admissible evidence.

California must follow these general federal rules. However, there is still some room for variation. For example, we'll discover in this chapter that California had laid out a framework for investigative detentions similar to that in *Terry*, but several years prior to *Terry*. We'll examine how a California court has applied federal law in determining when anonymous tips may or may not justify a stop. Next, we'll see how California has dealt with the Supreme Court's unwillingness to provide an exact time length for a stop reasonable in scope. A comparison of two cases in which a suspect was frisked—one declaring the frisk to be legal, the other voiding the frisk—will allow us to see how California courts have applied the law of patdowns. And finally, we will see how California has dealt with the confusion left in the wake of the Supreme Court case that allows passengers to be ordered out of cars.

Section 1. Stops, Frisks, and the Fourth Amendment

OVERVIEW

The Supreme Court of California first declared the legitimacy of an investigative stop based on proof shy of probable cause in its 1963 decision *People v. Mickelson*, five years before the Supreme Court's *Terry* decision. Generally speaking, California follows an approach similar to the federal framework. However, it defines reasonable in a manner that focuses more on the objective basis for the stop, and less on the officer's prior training and experience. See *People v. Conway*, 25 Cal.App.4th 385 (1994). Unlike violations of criminal law, where statutes are very important in laying out the parameters of violations of state law, penal statutes are not very relevant to search and seizure law in the state—rather, federal and state case law are almost entirely determinative. Still, occasionally a statute will exist on the books, but usually will not be relevant simply because it is redundant to case law. A prime example is Penal Code Section 833.5.

> **Penal Code Section 833.5. Detention to determine whether crime relating to firearms or deadly weapons has been committed; reasonable cause; search incident to detention; disposal of seized firearm or weapon**
>
> (a) In addition to any other detention permitted by law, if a peace officer has reasonable cause to believe that a person has a firearm or other deadly weapon with him or her in violation of any provision of law relating to firearms or deadly weapons the peace officer may detain that person to determine whether a crime relating to firearms or deadly weapons has been committed.
>
> For purposes of this section "reasonable cause to detain" requires that the circumstances known or apparent to the officer must include specific and articulable facts causing him or her to suspect that some offense relating to firearms or deadly weapons has taken place or is occurring or is about to occur and that the person he or she intends to detain is involved in that offense. The circumstances must be such as would cause any reasonable peace officer in like position, drawing when appropriate on his or her training and experience, to suspect the same offense and the same involvement by the person in question.
>
> (b) Incident to any detention permitted pursuant to subdivision (a), a peace officer may conduct a limited search of the person for firearms or weapons if the peace officer reasonably concludes that the person detained may be armed and presently dangerous to the peace officer or others. Any firearm or weapon seized pursuant to a valid detention or search pursuant to this section shall be admissible in evidence in any proceeding for any purpose permitted by law.

Note that this penal code section allows officers with "reasonable cause" to believe a person may have a firearm to detain the individual as well as engage in a limited search of the person. This is a subset of case law allowing officers to detain people for a broader range of reasons and allowing them to frisk people upon suspicion that they are armed and dangerous in any way. Because case law is determinative, one is not likely to see this statute appear in court decisions.

CASES-

I. People v. Mickelson, 59 Cal.2d 448, 380 P.2d 658 (1963)

At the time of this case, *Terry v. Ohio* had not been decided. Therefore, the California Supeme Court was forging new ground in laying out a rule similar to that in *Terry*. Pay special attention to the reasoning the state supreme court uses in justifying this rule as not conflicting with the U.S. Constitution's Fourth Amendment, which prohibits unreasonable searches and seizures.

*****

TRAYNOR, J.

BACKGROUND

Defendant was charged in two counts of an information with committing burglaries of telephone booths. His motion to set aside the information was granted, and the People appeal. The Attorney General concedes that there was no evidence at the preliminary hearing to support count I and seeks a reversal only as to count II.

A Burbank police officer discovered the physical evidence supporting count II in the course of searching an overnight bag found under the front seat of an automobile in which defendant had been riding and which Don Zauzig had been driving. The bag contained $85.90 in nickels, dimes, and quarters. At defendant's preliminary hearing, the bag and its contents were introduced in evidence, and Zauzig testified to his and defendant's commission of the burglary. Zausig's arrest and his availability as a witness were direct results of the search that disclosed the physical evidence of the burglary. If that search was illegal, neither the physical evidence nor Zauzig's testimony is competent to support the information.

The Attorney General contends, however, that the arresting officer had reasonable cause to arrest Zauzig for a recent robbery in the neighborhood and that the search of the car was therefore justified as incidental to the arrest. Before the decision of the United States Supreme Court in *Mapp v. Ohio*, we were free to determine such an issue under the California decisions setting forth the rules governing police investigations and arrests. In view of the holding in that case that the Fourteenth Amendment requires state courts to exclude unconstitutionally obtained evidence, we must determine at the outset whether the federal rules governing police investigations and arrests have superseded our own. There are significant differences between the respective rules that are relevant to this case.

DISCUSSION

In *Henry v. United States*, the United States Supreme Court held that an arrest occurs when an automobile is stopped during the course of a criminal investigation, and if the officer does not have reasonable cause to arrest the occupant at that time, the arrest is unlawful. Anything the officer learns as a result of stopping the automobile is inadmissible in evidence and cannot justify a search. In this state, however, we have consistently held that circumstances short of probable cause to make an arrest may still justify an officer's stopping pedestrians or motorists on the streets for questioning. If the circumstances warrant it, he may in self-protection request a suspect to alight from an automobile or to submit to a superficial search for concealed weapons. Should the investigation then reveal probable cause to make an arrest, the officer may arrest the suspect and conduct a reasonable incidental search.

The *Mapp* case did not determine whether or not the states must follow all the federal rules.

A state rule governing police procedure is not unconstitutional merely because it permits conduct in which a federal officer may not lawfully engage. The Fourth itself sets forth no more than the basic outlines of lawful law enforcement. It becomes meaningful in specific situations only by reference to the common law and statutory law governing the issuance of warrants, the authority of officers, and the power to arrest. Illegally obtained evidence may be excluded by the federal courts for various reasons. It may be excluded because it was obtained in a way that could not constitutionally be authorized. It may be excluded because it was obtained in violation of a federal statute or a common-law rule or a state rule applicable to federal officers. It may be excluded by virtue of the Supreme Court's monitorship of the federal administration of criminal justice.

The United States Supreme Court has not interpreted the Fourth Amendment as requiring that court to day down as a matter of constitutional law precise rules of police conduct. Indeed, its rule allowing a search by a federal officer without a warrant as incident to a lawful arrest permits reference to state law to determine the validity of the arrest. Accordingly, before a state rule governing police conduct may be struck down, it must appear that neither Congress nor a state legislature could authorize it. If a state adopts rules of police conduct consistent with the requirements of the Fourth Amendment and if its officers follow those rules, they do not act unreasonably within the meaning of the amendment although different rules may govern federal officers.

We do not believe that our rule permitting temporary detention for questioning conflicts with the Fourth Amendment. It strikes a balance between a person's interest in immunity from police interference and the community's interest in law enforcement. It wards off pressure to equate reasonable cause to investigate with reasonable cause to arrest, thus protecting the innocent from the risk of arrest when no more than reasonable investigation is justified.

It remains to determine whether the search in this case complied with the rules of this state. The arresting officer testified that he arrested defendant and Zauzig shortly before 2 a.m. about 20 minutes after he had gone to a market on San Fernando Road where a robbery had just been reported. He was told by other officers at the market that the robber was a fairly tall white man of large build with dark hair who was wearing a red sweater and armed with a .45 automatic. The officer searched the area on foot for about 10 minutes and then returned to his car to search a wider area. While driving west on Providencia about six blocks from the market he saw a station wagon coming toward him with two persons in it. The driver appeared to be a large white man with dark hair wearing a red sweater or jacket. The officer saw the station wagon turn south on San Fernando toward the market, and he turned south into an alley and then west at the next street. He then saw the station wagon turn west from San Fernando on the same street and followed it. The station wagon went to the end of the street where it came to a deadend, made a U-turn, and proceeded back toward San Fernando. The officer circled a block to his right and turned south on San Fernando. He was then a block or two behind the station wagon, which was traveling south on San Fernando at about 25 or 30 miles per hour. The officer overtook the station wagon and observed the passenger "bend forward in the seat, forward and down and raise back up." He turned on his red light, the station wagon pulled over and stopped, and the officer parked behind it. He radioed his location to headquarters and requested a backup car for assistance. Meanwhile Zauzig got out of the driver's seat of the station wagon and walked to the officer's car. The officer asked Zauzig where he was going, and Zauzig told him he was going home to Glendale, that he was more or less lost, and had been driving up and down sidestreets looking for the freeway. He showed the officer his driver's license. The assisting officers arrived, and the officers and Zauzig walked to the station wagon. Defendant was sitting in the right front seat and got out on request. The arresting officer looked under the right front seat and on the floorboards and saw an overnight bag stuffed under the right front seat. He pulled it out, unzipped it, and saw four screw drivers, a flashlight, a pair of canvas gloves and two socks. One sock was knotted at the top and was filled with something that jingled. When he took the bag out of the car, the officer asked Zauzig what it was, and Zauzig told him that it was his basketball equipment. The officer asked what was in the sock, and Zauzig told him that he had some dimes. The officer opened the sock and found nickels, dimes, and quarters. He arrested Zauzig and defendant on suspicion of burglary. The officer also testified that there was nothing in his conversation with Zauzig that would indicate that he had perpetrated a robbery other than that he acted a bit friendly. The movements of the car were such that it was obvious that the occupants were either trying to evade the officer or were confused and did not know the area very well. His purpose in examining the bag was the "possibility of a gun being there." After he had talked to Zauzig and defendant he was satisfied that they had not been involved in the robbery.

It was not unreasonable for the officer to stop Zauzig's car for investigation and to take reasonable precautions for his own safety. He did not have probable cause, however, to arrest Zauzig for robbery. There could have been more than one tall white man with dark hair wearing a red sweater abroad at night in such a metropolitan area. Although Zauzig was in the vicinity of the robbery, he was not observed until about 20 minutes after it occurred when he was driving toward the scene of the crime, not away from it. The officer had no information that the robber had an automobile or a confederate. The erratic route of the car and defendant's movement in the seat were at most suspicious circumstances. The officer's investigation elicited identification upon request and a story consistent with the movements of the car and the officer's own assessment of those movements. Both occupants were out of the car away from any weapons that might have been concealed therein. Instead of interrogating Zauzig and defendant with respect to the robbery or requesting them to accompany the officers the few blocks to the market for possible identification, the officer elected to rummage through closed baggage found in the car in the hope of turning up evidence that might connect Zauzig with the robbery. That search exceeded the bounds of reasonable investigation. It was not justified by probable cause to make an arrest, and it cannot be justified by what it turned up.

The order is affirmed.

*****

CONCLUSION

In *Mapp v. Ohio* the Supreme Court applied the exclusionary rule to the states, such that illegally obtained evidence would be inadmissible against defendants in state courts. Prior to that the federal exclusionary rule only applied to federal officers. The California Supreme Court in *Mickelson*, decided only a year after *Mapp*, was especially sensitive to the U.S. Supreme Court's decision, but then noted that federal law left plenty of room for states to leave their own impressions. In this case it did not believe that allowing police to investigate someone shy of an arrest would violate federal law.

REVIEW

1. What was the initial basis for stopping defendant's vehicle? Was this probable cause or something shy of probable cause?

2. What sorts of behavior by the officer qualified as an "investigation." When did the investigation reach its limits and the officer's behavior transgress what is allowed for an investigative detention?

3. The California Supreme Court lays out a rule similar to that in *Terry v. Ohio*. What is the exact nature of this state rule?

4. Why, ultimately, did the court hold for the defendant?

5. The court says that "A state rule governing police procedure is not unconstitutional merely because it permits conduct in which a federal officer may not lawfully engage." What do you suppose it means by this? Don't you think that the opposite is true? Think of the fact that this case was decided in 1963. Of what relevance is that?

Section 2: Stops and the Fourth Amendment

OVERVIEW

In this section we take up the problem of how California courts have evaluated reasonable suspicion for anonymous tips in light of the Supreme Court cases *Alabama v. White* and *Florida v. J.L.* We also examine how courts in this state have dealt with the notion that there is a time limit on detentions—else they become arrests. Both of these analyses are not atypical of other states which have also had to apply general guidelines of the Supreme Courts toward cases occurring within their jurisdiction.

CASES-

I. People v. Saldana, 101 Cal.App.4th 170 (2002)

In *Alabama v. White*, the Supreme Court determined that anonymous tips that have some level of internal consistency and can be at least partially corroborated may give rise to reasonable suspicion for an investigative stop. In *Florida v. J.L.* it provided the limitation that a tip providing a description and a prediction (that, e.g., a man dressed in a certain way and standing at a certain intersection would have a gun), without more, did not justify a stop. The following California case provides a twist that forced the court into determining which of these precedents the facts most adhered to.

*****

Vogel, J.

BACKGROUND

Deputy Sheriff Patrick Larson was on patrol the evening of June 11, 2001. He received a communication at 7:35 p.m. that according to an anonymous tipster calling from a pay phone, a gray Ford Taurus station wagon with a license ending in the numbers 319 was parked in the parking lot of a restaurant at the intersection of San Gabriel and Garvey in the City of Rosemead, and the driver was carrying a gun and a kilo of cocaine. The same report had been made from the same pay phone to the San Gabriel Police Department 30 minutes earlier.

Deputy Larson went to the described parking lot arriving at 7:44 p.m. and observed a Ford Taurus station wagon with a license plate ending in 319. He entered the entire license plate number in the mobile digital terminal of his patrol car and received information including the address and name of the registered owner, who was appellant Jose Saldana. He entered that address in his terminal and received information that a person at that address was wanted on a warrant. The person named in the warrant was Bernardo Ruiz Moreno, described as born on August 20, 1973, six feet three inches tall, weighing 170 pounds. [Appellant was described as in his mid-50's, about five feet six inches tall.] The warrant was a $7,500 misdemeanor warrant under [Penal Code section prohibiting falsely identifying oneself to a peace officer.]

No one was in or around the parked station wagon, so Deputy Larson waited in the parking lot of another restaurant across Garvey Avenue. About 8:45 p.m. he observed appellant exit the restaurant and enter the station wagon. Deputy Larson followed appellant. Before stopping appellant he requested backup assistance because of the report of a gun.

With the assistance of other units a stop and "felony extraction" were initiated. This involves stopping all other traffic and ordering the driver out of the vehicle at gunpoint. Appellant was directed to stop the station wagon, throw the keys out, get out, back up with his hands in the air, and get down on his knees. Usually the suspect is handcuffed. This procedure was used in this case because of the probability appellant had a gun in the car. Appellant was frisked for weapons but none was found on his person. Deputy Larson asked appellant's name and he replied Jose Saldana. Through a Spanish-speaking officer appellant was asked if there was a gun in the car; he replied, "No, I don't even own one at home." Appellant was asked whether the deputies could search his station wagon and he replied yes.

As soon as Deputy Larson opened the station wagon door, he smelled the strong odor of marijuana. He found a plastic trash bag containing marijuana under the rear-facing seat of the station wagon. He also found a plastic baggie of methamphetamine. He did not find a gun. Deputy Larson arrested appellant. At booking at the sheriff's station appellant had a large quantity of cash on his person.

DISCUSSION

The trial court found appellant was properly detained based on the information available to Deputy Larson, and appellant's consent obtained during the lawful detention validated the search of the station wagon. We independently review the question of law whether the undisputed facts, or facts found by the trial court upon conflicting substantial evidence, show the search and seizure were unconstitutional.

The United States Supreme Court has recently spoken on the issue of when a detention may be justified by an anonymous tip. The court held "an anonymous tip that a person is carrying a gun is, without more, [not] sufficient to justify a police officer's stop and frisk of that person." *(Florida v. J.L.)* (hereafter J.L.). The facts in that case were: an anonymous telephone caller told the police that a young Black male standing at a particular bus stop and wearing a plaid shirt was carrying a gun. Officers responding to the scene saw three young Black males at the bus stop, one wearing a plaid shirt. The men engaged in no suspicious conduct. The officers approached the plaid-shirted suspect, ordered him to put his hands up, and frisked him; they found a gun in his pocket.

The Supreme Court held the gun was inadmissible. "[T]he officers' suspicion that J.L. was carrying a weapon arose not from any observations of their own but solely from a call made from an unknown location by an unknown caller. Unlike a tip from a known informant whose reputation can be assessed and who can be held responsible if her allegations turn out to be fabricated, ... 'an anonymous tip alone seldom demonstrates the informant's basis of knowledge or veracity,' ..." Recognizing that in some situations an anonymous tip, suitably corroborated, may exhibit " 'sufficient indicia of reliability to provide reasonable suspicion to make the investigatory stop' " the court found no such indicia there."All the police had to go on in this case was the bare report of an unknown, unaccountable informant who neither explained how he knew about the gun nor supplied any basis for believing he had inside information about J.L." The fact the tip was "corroborated" as to the "subject's readily observable location and appearance" was insufficient, because this did not show the tipster had knowledge about the concealed criminal activity.

The court distinguished (its prior case where an anonymous tip had sufficient indicia of reliability and was sufficiently corroborated to authorize an investigatory stop. (*Alabama v. White*) [anonymous telephone tip that the defendant would leave a certain address at a certain time in a certain vehicle and would go to a certain location with a brown attaché case containing cocaine was corroborated by police observations of the defendant leaving the first location in the described vehicle and driving to the second location; corroboration of the informant's predictions of defendant's future behavior demonstrated the informant had special familiarity with the defendant's affairs; this was sufficient to support an investigatory stop as distinguished from an arrest on probable cause, because reasonable suspicion for a stop may be based on information of lesser quality and quantity].) The *J.L.* court cautioned, as to *White*, "Standing alone, the tip [in *White*] would not have justified a [detention]. [Citation.] Only after police observation showed that the informant had accurately predicted the woman's movements, we explained, did it become reasonable to think the tipster had inside knowledge about the suspect and therefore to credit his assertion about the cocaine.... Although the Court held that the suspicion in *White* became reasonable after police surveillance, we regarded the case as borderline. Knowledge about a person's future movements indicates some familiarity with that person's affairs, but having such knowledge does not necessarily imply that the informant knows, in particular, whether that person is carrying hidden contraband."

This case is like *J.L.* There was an anonymous telephone tip. The tip contained no internal indicia of the basis for or reliability of the informant's information. The tip did not include predictive information that could be corroborated by observation. The observed corroboration that a vehicle fitting the description was indeed present at the described location did not corroborate the criminal element of the tip that the station wagon contained a gun or cocaine. Appellant's observed conduct of exiting the restaurant, entering the station wagon, and driving away was not suspicious.

The additional factor here, discovery of the outstanding warrant, did not corroborate the anonymous tip, for it had no logical tendency to prove that the current driver of the station wagon was currently in possession of a gun or cocaine. The warrant was not for the registered owner of the station wagon, appellant, but for a person with another name. It was four years old. The only nexus between the warrant and the station wagon was an address. The available information showed only that a person with a different name than the registered owner had the same address four years ago as the currently registered owner and was apparently still wanted for a four-year-old misdemeanor. The existence of the warrant cannot be regarded as corroboration of the anonymous tip.

Even assuming that discovery of the warrant provided an independent ground to *stop appellant's vehicle* to determine whether the driver was possibly the person wanted on the warrant, that possibility was dispelled immediately after the stop. The warrant was for Bernardo Ruiz Moreno, born on August 20, 1973 (i.e., not quite 28 years old at the time of this seizure and search in June 2001), six feet three inches tall, weighing 170 pounds. Appellant was in his mid-50's, about five feet six inches tall. Appellant was asked his name and answered Jose Saldana, not Bernardo Ruiz Moreno.

As observed by the trial court, this case cannot be treated as if it were a traffic stop on an outstanding warrant followed by a polite request for consent to search the vehicle. The deputies at all times treated appellant as if the anonymous tip were true. Deputy Larson did not stop appellant until backup units arrived. Then a "felony extraction" was initiated. Appellant was ordered out at gunpoint, down on his knees and (assuming the usual procedure was followed) handcuffed. This was not a mere detention for determination of identity to match an outstanding warrant. We conclude this case is not distinguishable from *J.L.* The "felony extraction" stop that led directly to the search of the vehicle and seizure of the evidence was not justified, because the anonymous tip was uncorroborated by any observations or information available to the deputies. Appellant's consent obtained during the illegal detention is tainted by the illegality.

Because appellant's motion to suppress evidence was erroneously denied, the judgment must be reversed and appellant must be given the opportunity to withdraw his guilty plea.

The judgment is reversed.

*****

CONCLUSION

In *Saldano*, the tip seemed to be similar to that in *J.L.*, but the police became aware of a warrant existing on a person at the address at which the vehicle in the tip was registered to. But the California Court of Appeal for the 2nd District held that since the warrant did not tend to corroborate the anonymous tip, it was irrelevant for purposes of validating the stop, and since the evidence was a product of the detention it would be inadmissible.

REVIEW

1. Was the court correct in deciding the warrant to be irrelevant? Does it matter what the warrant was for?

2. Since the traffic stop was determined to be illegal, step back to the officer's frame of mind, while observing the car in the parking lot. Was there any other tactic the officer could have employed without involving an illegal stop?

II. People v. Russell, 81 Cal.App.4th 96 (2000)

In *United States v. Sharpe* the Supreme Court refused to apply a bright-line time rule for when a detention becomes too long and violates the "reasonable in scope" requirement for Terry stops. Instead it held that it is "appropriate to examine whether the police diligently pursued a means of investigation that was likely to confirm or dispel their suspicions quickly, during which time it was necessary to detain the defendant." Consider the next case in terms of whether officers met this test.

*****

Sims, J.

BACKGROUND

At about 7:00 a.m. on February 28, 1998, California Highway Patrol Officer Joseph Lapthorne was patrolling Interstate 5 in Shasta County when he observed a black Ford Taurus traveling northbound at a speed of 53 to 58 miles per hour in an area where the speed limit was 65 miles per hour. The Taurus repeatedly drifted around within its lane and sometimes out of its lane. The officer followed for about three miles, during which he ran a check on the license plate, which apparently did not reveal any problems. He then initiated a traffic stop.

Officer Lapthorne had been an officer for 15 years and had received extensive training in drug interdiction. As the officer approached the car, he smelled an "overwhelmingly strong" odor, and in his experience such masking odors were used to mask the odor of drugs.

The driver of the vehicle, Burks, immediately volunteered, without being asked, that the odor was from a Vicks tablet he was taking for a cold. Though there was a package of Vicks in the car, in the officer's opinion the odor he smelled was not Vicks. When asked for identification, Burks produced a California driver's license bearing the name Larry Johnson. Burks said he could not produce the vehicle registration because the car did not belong to him. Defendant Russell then said the car belonged to his niece.

Although nothing in Burks's manner or speech suggested intoxication, the officer observed Burks's eyes were red and watery, suggesting he had been drinking or was sleepy. The officer also made observations which in their totality suggested drug activity, including: the overwhelming odor (frequently used to mask drugs); the driver's unsolicited claim that the odor was a Vicks tablet (suggesting possible drug paranoia); the registered owner of the car was not present (a ploy used by drug traffickers to try to create confusion as to who is responsible for drugs found in the car); one of the occupants was wearing a pager, and there was a cellular phone in the car; there were worn screws on the dashboard and the upholstery did not appear to be the original, suggesting the vehicle may have been disassembled; and the occupants were two men, from Los Angeles, where large quantities of drugs are brought into the country, and were headed north, apparently having driven through the night.

The officer had Burks get out of the car and walk back to the patrol car, in order to investigate the possibility he was not fit to be driving or was involved in drug trafficking activity. No field sobriety test was performed. The officer concluded Burks's red eyes and slow gait were attributable to a cold.

Burks was nervous and hesitant in giving answers. He said he and his passenger were brothers and were on their way to a weekend vacation in Portland, where they were not planning on visiting anyone. The officer knew Portland to be a major distribution area for illegal drugs. Burks said he was cold and sick, so the officer asked if he wanted to sit in the patrol car. Burks sat in the back seat of the patrol car, and the officer closed the door (which could not be opened from the inside). Burks was not handcuffed or placed under arrest, but the officer testified Burks was not free to leave.

The officer then spoke with the passenger, Russell, who said he was Burks's brother and who produced a California driver's license in the name of Robert Bangston. Russell said he and Burks were going to visit Russell's niece in Portland (contrary to Burks's assertion they were not going to see friends or family in Portland), but Russell could not provide an address or phone number for his niece in Portland. Russell first said he and Burks lived in Los Angeles, then said they lived in Portland and Los

Angeles. When asked how they came into possession of the car, Russell initially said his niece had delivered it to him in Los Angeles. He later said Burks and his niece had driven the car to Los Angeles, and the niece had flown back to Portland. Russell said he was responsible for the car and its contents. The entire conversation with Russell lasted approximately three to five minutes, during which Russell was nervous and evasive. The officer had a strong suspicion of drug activity and did not consider Russell free to leave.

The officer asked Russell for consent to search the vehicle, and Russell gave consent. The officer had Russell sit in the back of the patrol car with Burks. Russell was not handcuffed or placed under arrest, but was not free to leave. As Russell entered the patrol car, Burks became upset and asked why he had been stopped and why the car was being searched.

The officer searched the car and found a locked non-factory-manufactured compartment between the rear seat and trunk wall. Defendants were placed under arrest for possession of a false compartment designed for storing controlled substances in a vehicle. The arrest occurred at about 7:25 a.m., approximately 25 minutes after the officer's first verbal contact with defendants.

The locked compartment was later broken open with a crowbar, and revealed guns, two large bricks of cocaine, numerous wax-type Glade air fresheners, and a towel smeared with wax air freshener.

DISCUSSION

Defendants argue the consent to search the car was invalid because it was the product of an unreasonably prolonged detention. We disagree.

An investigatory stop exceeds constitutional bounds when extended beyond what is reasonably necessary under the circumstances that made its initiation permissible. Circumstances which develop during a detention may provide reasonable suspicion to prolong the detention. There is no set time limit for a permissible investigative stop; the question is whether the police diligently pursued a means of investigation reasonably designed to confirm or dispel their suspicions quickly.

Here, defendants suggest there was no reason to stop them, because there was no contention that the erratic driving constituted a traffic violation. However, the erratic driving justified the stop to determine whether the driver was intoxicated.

Defendants argue that any concern the driver was drunk or sleepy were immediately dispelled when the officer spoke to Burks, who spoke coherently and produced his driver's license without difficulty; hence the detention should have ended at that point. However, defendants ignore the evidence that the officer still had reason to question the driver's fitness to drive, because the driver's eyes were red and watery. Although the driver said he had a cold, the officer was not required to accept that statement without further inquiry.

Although the officer concluded the red eyes were attributable to a cold after watching the driver walk back to the patrol car, by that time the officer had received further information giving cause for suspicion concerning drug activity .

Thus, when the officer first approached the car, he noticed an overwhelming masking odor. Although the driver asserted the odor came from a Vicks tablet, the officer testified he noticed the odor as he approached the bumper of the vehicle from behind, the odor was overwhelming, and in the officer's opinion the odor was not Vicks.

Defendants argue many innocent people use air fresheners. However, here the odor was overwhelming from outside the vehicle. Contrary to defendants' position, the odor, together with the other circumstances (e.g., absence of car owner, presence of pager and cell phone, dashboard screw indicating possible removal, etc.) justified investigation of possible drug activity before the officer concluded Burks was fit to drive. On top of all the other circumstances, Burks's nervousness and hesitancy in answering questions gave further basis for suspicion, justifying the questioning of Russell, whose evasiveness and inconsistent answers gave even more grounds for suspicion.

That the officer admitted he investigated the possibility of drug trafficking with every traffic stop does not assist defendants. That could merely mean the officer kept alert for signs of possible drug activity. In any event, the overwhelming masking odor, together with the other circumstances, justified the drug inquiry in this case.

Defendants argue the detention was unreasonably prolonged because the officer had no reason to be concerned about the car being stolen, in that he had already done a vehicle check before stopping them. However, though the car had not been reported stolen, there were still grounds for suspicion, because defendants claimed to have borrowed the car from someone whose address or phone number they did not know, for a long trip to Portland where, according to one defendant, they were going to visit the car owner (despite not knowing her address), and according to the other defendant, they were not going to visit anyone.

We conclude there was no unreasonably prolonged detention in this case.

*****

CONCLUSION

The court's analysis into whether a detention is unreasonable in scope, with respect to its overall length, looks at each phase of the detention and whether it justifies the next phase of the detention. As long as each each phase is logically consistent with previous phases, courts are reluctant to declare that a detention has turned into an arrest because some time limit threshold has been reached.

REVIEW

1.   Can officers stop a car for erratic violation that is not technically a violation of the motor vehicle code? If so, why can they legally do so?

2.   Did defendants' characteristics fit a drug courier profile? What aspects fit this profile? What Supreme Court case justifies use of such a profile to make a detention?

3.   If this stop were to last for an hour, would this be too long? What about three hours? Should there be a bright-line rule for such detentions, or is the Supreme Court's approach the best one, in your opinion?

Section 3: Special Situation Stops

OVERVIEW

According to the Supreme Court, officers can order passengers out of stopped vehicles even without articulable suspicion, can detain suspects for length time periods (such as a day) at international borders without the detention becoming an arrest, and can stop people at a roadblocks to see if they are intoxicated, without having any initial individualized suspicion. In this section we look at how one California court has approached a question left unanswered by the Supreme Court in *Maryland v. Wilson,* 117 S.Ct. 882 (1997).

CASES-

I. People v. Cartwright, 72 Cal.App.4th 1362 (1999)

The Supreme Court has said that police officers may order passengers out of cars but did not make it clear whether this meant that they were "seized." Under certain circumstances, a declaration as to whether the passenger becomes seized at the point of being ordered from the car becomes crucial to the passenger's motion to suppress evidence. This is the issue raised in *Cartwright.*

*****

Bedsworth, J.

BACKGROUND

Officer Dean Michael of the Huntington Beach Police ran a check on the registration of a car in which Misty Anne Cartwright was a passenger. Although the vehicle displayed a current tag, computer records indicated the tag had not been issued for the license plate to which it was attached. Suspecting a violation of [vehicle code section prohibiting unlawful license plates] Michael pulled the car over and asked the driver, Phillip Showalter, for his license and registration. Showalter told the officer his name but was unable to produce any identification or registration for the car. Michael asked Cartwright who she was, and she gave him her name along with some sort of "identification paper."

Michael ran a computer check on the names, then asked Showalter to get out of the car. While complying, Showalter volunteered he was on parole and informed the officer the car belonged to someone else-although he did not know the person's last name. Any experienced officer hearing this frequently used but almost literally incredible tale- provided by a driver who had no identification, no proof of registration, and a car with tags which Department of Motor Vehicles records showed did not belong to it- would have entertained a robust suspicion the car was stolen. And Michael did. He requested Showalter's permission to search the car for evidence of ownership, and Showalter told him to go ahead, denying there was anything illegal in the car. Michael had Showalter sit on the curb and asked Cartwright to step out so he could conduct his search.

Michael never told Cartwright she was obliged to remain at the scene, but he did ask her the driver's name, to see if she would give him a different one than Showalter had. He also asked her whether there was anything illegal in the car. In contrast to Showalter, Cartwright said there was. She told Michael someone had borrowed her purse and left some methamphetamine inside.

Michael asked if it would be okay for him to retrieve it, and Cartwright said it would. Michael *then* directed Cartwright to have a seat on the curb next to Showalter. Along with the methamphetamine, Michael found a spoon, a digital scale, a notebook containing pay-owe sheets, and about 25 clear plastic bags of the type commonly used to package methamphetamine for sale. Cartwright eventually admitted these things were hers and was placed under arrest.

The contact, from its inception to the point at which methamphetamine and drug paraphernalia were discovered, lasted about 10 minutes. It took place in the neighborhood in which Cartwright had been living, and the car contained her belongings, which Showalter was helping her move.

Cartwright pled guilty to possessing methamphetamine for sale and was placed on probation. Cartwright contends she was subjected to an illegally prolonged detention which tainted the consent leading to discovery of the contraband secreted in her purse. Without expressly arguing the point, she grounds her contention on the premise that she was detained by virtue of the traffic stop conducted on the car in which she was riding. We reject that premise and conclude Cartwright was not seized within the meaning of the Fourth Amendment until she was told to have a seat on the curb and she complied.

DISCUSSION

In *Wilson*, a passenger was ordered out of the car in which he was sitting after an officer observed he was sweating and extremely nervous. As Wilson exited the vehicle, a quantity of crack cocaine fell to the ground, and he was placed under arrest.

In holding that officers are entitled to order passengers out of a car as a matter of course, the majority recognized that when a traffic stop occurs, "There is probable cause to believe that the driver has committed a minor vehicular offense, but there is no such reason to stop or detain the passengers. By noting the absence of any objective justification to detain passengers in cars stopped for traffic violations, however, the court obviously did *not* mean to imply that passengers are routinely subjected to illegal seizures. We believe it was saying passengers are not "detained" as the law uses that term.

It is settled that a Fourth Amendment seizure occurs only when an officer intentionally applies hands-on, physical restraint to a suspect or initiates a show of authority to which a reasonable innocent person would feel compelled to and to which the suspect actually *does* submit for reasons that are solely related to the official show of authority.

When the siren and the light on top of a police car are turned on, it is the driver's attention the officer is hoping to capture-not the passenger's. The passenger has typically done nothing wrong and has no power to respond to the police directive. His or her presence in the car is merely fortuitous. The driver is the one the officer is seeking to restrain, and the driver is the one who, by stopping the car, submits to the officer's assertion of authority. The passenger simply has no say in the matter. Without submission by the person to whom the show of authority is directed, no Fourth Amendment seizure can occur absent the imposition of some physical restraint. The fact a passenger is stopped "as a practical matter thus has no Fourth Amendment significance.

Consistent with this analysis, the dissenting justices in *Wilson* observed, any "intrusion on the passengers' liberty occasioned by the initial stop of the vehicle ... was a necessary by-product of the lawful detention of the driver. But the passengers had not yet been seized at the time the car was pulled over, any more than a traffic jam caused by construction or other state-imposed delay not directed at a particular individual constitutes a seizure of that person." While the majority took pains to answer the points raised in the dissent which conflicted with its opinion, it made no attempt to disabuse the dissenters of their view on this particular point-and the reason for that choice seems manifest: They were right.

A typical traffic stop, such as the one occurring here, does not by itself implicate the Fourth Amendment rights of a passenger in the stopped vehicle.

The determination Cartwright was not detained by virtue of the traffic stop does not complete our inquiry. It remains for us to determine whether Michael did or said anything during the traffic stop which would constitute a show of authority that would compel a reasonable innocent person to submit. Further, we must decide whether the discovery of contraband in her purse was the product of any such seizure. We conclude Cartwright was seized only *after* divulging she possessed methamphetamine. Consequently, discovery of the contraband was not the product of a Fourth Amendment seizure, and suppression would not have been appropriate.

After Officer Michael made contact with the driver and found he had no license or registration in his possession, he *asked* Cartwright if she had any identification. Because nothing in the content or form of the question imparted any compulsion to comply, there is no basis for finding Cartwright was under the kind of restraint associated with a Fourth Amendment detention. It is now well established that a mere request for identification does *not* transmogrify a contact into a Fourth Amendment seizure. And her decision to cooperate by producing some sort of identification paper appears to have been wholly consensual.

Next, Michael *asked* Cartwright to step out of the car so he could conduct the search Showalter had authorized. Again, a mere request, as opposed to a command directing the person's movements, does not constitute a Fourth Amendment restraint. And Cartwright was certainly not seized within the meaning of the Fourth Amendment simply because Officer Michael asked her the name of the driver and whether the car contained anything illegal.

Rather, it appears to us that no Fourth Amendment seizure occurred until Officer Michael responded to Cartwright's admission that she was in possession of methamphetamine by *directing* her to sit on the curb and she complied. By then, she had already given consent to search her purse. Thus, her consent could not have been the product of a detention.

From the moment he asked her to step out of the vehicle until the moment she revealed her purse contained methamphetamine, Officer Michael did nothing and said nothing to prevent Cartwright from leaving, and she made no attempt or request to do so. As she explained to the magistrate during the suppression hearing, although the car was stopped in her neighborhood, she stayed with it because she had property inside that Showalter was helping her move. Thus, while she could have terminated the encounter with the officer by simply walking away and leaving Showalter to his own devices, Cartwright chose to stay with the car and answer the officer's questions. [O]fficer Michael said and did nothing to communicate to Cartwright, much less to an objectively reasonable innocent person, that she was obliged to stay with the car or answer his questions.

[W]e are convinced Cartwright's encounter with Officer Michael, until she was told to sit on the curb, was one with which the Fourth Amendment is not concerned.

While we are all familiar with the sinking feeling a driver experiences upon seeing police lights in the rearview mirror, few of us sense impending doom when we are in the passenger seat. The passenger is not a participant in the stop, but an observer. And we are confident few feel fettered by the driver's problems. We therefore conclude Cartwright's detention was not unduly prolonged because she was not detained until there was probable cause to arrest her.

The motion to suppress was properly denied.

*****

CONCLUSION

Cartwright argued that the officer improperly prolonged the detention of the driver (presumably by changing the focus of the stop from license plate verification to something else). She contended that once the officer asked her to step out of the car she was "seized" and since this was a product of an illegally prolonged detention anything the seizure produced as evidence would be admissible, including the methamphetamine resulting from a consent search. However, the court held that the seizure did not occur until after her confession and consent search, when she was ordered to the curb. Therefore, regardless of whether the driver's detention was illegal, the evidence against her was not a product of an illegal detention since she had not yet been seized at the time of its discovery.

REVIEW

1.   After this opinion, do you think there is a difference between an officer asking a passenger to get out of a car and ordering the passenger out of the car? Does *Cartwright* only apply to the former?

2.   How can a passenger benefit from a driver's illegal detention?

3.   Was there any decent evidence in this case that the driver's detention was illegally prolonged? If not, why did the court not simply dismiss the defendant's argument on this basis?

Section 4. Frisks and the Fourth Amendment

OVERVIEW

Frisks raise two questions. First, what constitutes the basis for a frisk, once an officer has made a stop? And second, during the course of a frisk, how invasive is the officer entitled to be? Rather than providing full-length cases in this section, we present two fact scenarios, from two California cases involving frisks. The reader is invited to read the scenarios and form conclusions about the validity of the frisks. Next we'll see how the judges in each case ruled.

CASE COMPARISON EXERCISE: FRISKS

Case I: People v. Dickey, 21 Cal.App.4th 952 (1994)

At approximately 3:40 p.m. on June 28, 1992, Deputy Sheriff Kenneth Conway of the San Luis Obispo County Sheriff's Department (the deputy) was on routine patrol with his partner. He was driving his black and white patrol vehicle on a one-lane dirt road extension of Illinois Avenue in rural Nipomo.

41

He saw a 1977 El Camino which was stopped in the roadway with its engine running. The driver appeared to make "... furtive movements, moving around in the driver's seat."

The deputy approached the driver, appellant herein, and asked him what he was doing parked in the middle of the road. Appellant replied that he was just admiring the view of the valley and sand dunes below.

When asked for identification, appellant truthfully identified himself as Warren Dickey but could not produce written identification or a driver's license. Neither could the passenger. Both were ordered to alight from the El Camino and did so. The deputy ascertained via the police radio that the car was registered to appellant. Appellant, however, was unable to produce the registration certificate for the vehicle. He said that the registration papers might be in a backpack located in the car but the backpack was not his.

The deputy twice requested permission to search the car. Appellant twice refused. The deputy admitted that he was "angry" with appellant and told appellant so. He testified that appellant "... was just wasting time or trying to put things off." He told appellant he would just look for items in plain view in the car to justify the search. He was unable to find anything in plain view. Appellant and the passenger denied ownership of the backpack but appellant gave the deputy permission to search it.

The deputy retrieved the backpack, opened it, and saw a toothbrush and a film canister. The film canister contained powder which he believed to be baking soda, a cutting agent for narcotics. Appellant said that he used the powder to brush his teeth. The deputy testified that after he found the "cut," he wanted to search the car.

The deputy asked appellant and the passenger to accompany him to the rear of the vehicle. Appellant was nervous and sweating despite the fact that it was a cool day. The deputy conducted a patdown search of appellant for weapons. He testified that even though appellant was not "aggressive" he "... potentially may have been armed." He explained his rationale for the "pat-down" as follows: "At that time I was conducting a further investigation and so I patted him down for my safety and if I found something like contraband or something, I could possibly search the vehicle and I wasn't going to turn my back on two guys even with a partner."

The deputy felt no hard objects but did feel a soft object. He testified: "The consistency and feel of the bulge led me to believe that it might be a controlled substance." He amplified his testimony as follows: "I felt the bulge, and it felt not round, but elongated and it had a texture or just a good feeling to it, and I just squeezed from the outside of it and felt it was a plastic-felt like plastic or felt like a plastic baggie with something in it."

The deputy reached into appellant's pocket and retrieved a baggie containing less than one-half ounce of marijuana and a baggie containing 3.19 grams of cocaine.

Case II: People v. Avila, 58 Cal.App.4th 1069 (1997)

On May 16, 1995, at approximately 4:30 p.m., Officer Jones saw defendant, Gilbert Avila, walking across a parking lot. The officer observed defendant littering. Moreover, the officer noted that defendant's manner while littering was "suspicious." Defendant first walked to the passenger side of a truck, then to the driver's side, then back to the front of the truck with his hand directly in front of his body. Finally, he dropped a white envelope from his waist.

Officer Jones contacted defendant while defendant was standing in the open driver's side door of the truck. The officer told defendant that he had observed him littering, and asked defendant for identification. Defendant provided a driver's license in the name of Joseph Vargas. While the officer was talking to defendant, he observed what appeared to be two containers of alcohol on the front seat of the truck. From where the officer was standing, he could not tell if they were full or empty.

Next, the officer observed "a long black metal object" that was similar to a "Mag" flashlight, approximately eight to ten inches from defendant's left hand, behind defendant in the truck. The officer became concerned for his safety, and inquired as to the nature of the object. Without turning around, defendant said that he did not know what the object was. Defendant further stated that the truck did not belong to him, but belonged to a friend of his. Defendant stated that he had illegal alcohol in the truck, but that he did not have any weapons.

The officer told defendant to walk to the back of the truck. Defendant complied, and when he reached the rear of the truck he "assumed the position" without being asked to. The officer then conducted a patdown search of defendant's person for weapons.

While patting down defendant, the officer felt a bulky and somewhat hard object at defendant's ankle. The officer asked what the object was and defendant's reply was unclear. The officer repeated his question and defendant said, " 'It is meth.' " After finding two more bulges, the officer handcuffed defendant and removed three baggies of methamphetamine. Defendant was placed under arrest, and later more methamphetamine and a gun were found in his vehicle.

ANALYSIS

In case one, the court (Yegan, J., writing) held that the initial frisk was unreasonable, and even if it had been legitimate, the scope of the frisk was unreasonable. The proper test, it said, was whether all factors considered singly or in combination would lead an officer to reasonably believe that a weapon might be used against him or her. In this case, the defendant had no ID, refused a consent search, was nervous and sweating, and had baking soda in a canister. This did not constitute reasonable belief that a weapon might be involved, said the court. Furthermore, even if it had constituted such belief, the officer had no right to remove the "soft object" he found on the defendant, since it was not "immediately apparent" it was a weapon.

In case two, the court (Hollenhorst, J., writing) found first that the officer did have reason to frisk, in light of the defendant's acting suspiciously, dropping an envelope, appearing intoxicated, and residing closely to a metal object. Second, the scope of the search was permissible, because although the methamphetamine was a soft object, the officer did not initially remove it—instead he asked what it was, and the defendant replied that it was meth. This "confession" provided probable cause to arrest the defendant, and so removing the object was justified as a search incident to arrest (see Chapter Six).

REVIEW

1.   What is the difference between the tests determining whether a Terry stop is legitimate and whether a frisk pursuant to such a stop is legitimate?

2.   When can police search deeper than the outer layers of clothing?

CHAPTER FIVE

Seizures of Persons: Arrest

In this chapter we examine arrests. An arrest is more intrusive and restraining than a *Terry* stop and consequently requires a higher objective basis: probable cause. An arrest may be effectuated immediately, or in some instances, a *Terry* stop may become an arrest once the scope of the stop has been exceeded (for example, too much time passes, or the officers move the suspect, further constraining his or her liberty). Arrests can be made with or without warrants, depending on the circumstances. Arrests in public are guided by one set of standards, dealing mostly with information known to police officers; arrests in one's private home by another set, informed by arrest warrants, and at times without warrants if there are exigent circumstances. Full custodial arrests for minor vehicle code misdemeanors are allowed in California (as well as by federal law) and are made pursuant to officer discretion.

Section 1. Definition of Arrest

OVERVIEW

An arrest, as defined in California Penal Code section 834, is "taking a person into custody, in a case and in the manner authorized by law. An arrest may be made by a peace officer or by a private person." Section 835 elaborates: "An arrest is made by an actual restraint of the person, or by submission to the custody of an officer. The person arrested may be subjected to such restraint as is reasonable for his arrest and detention." Arrest, thus, involves two aspects: the taking of a person into custody, and actual restraint or submission to custody. Note that the second feature (actual restraint) is in keeping with the Supreme Court's decision in *California v. Hodari*, 499 U.S. 621 (1991), in that the seizure (or arrest) of a fleeing person cannot occur until the person is actually stopped.

Section 2: Reasonable Arrest

OVERVIEW

Whether magistrates are determining if it is appropriate to issue arrest warrants, or if officers are making on-the-spot decision to arrest, probable cause is the necessary basis for these arrests. The first case we'll look at in this section is *People v. Rosales*, which applies the "totality of circumstances" test to determining whether probable cause exists. Remember, if an arrest is invalid, anything achieved pursuant to the arrest (such as evidence in a search incident-to-arrest) may be suppressed.

Warrantless arrests in a person's home are forbidden by the Fourth Amendment to the U.S. Constitution as well as by article I, section 13 of the California Constitution. This was established by a leading Supreme Court case, *Payton v. New York*, 445 U.S. 573 (1980). There is exception to this general rule, though, when exigent circumstances are present. The Supreme Court hasn't been too helpful in forming bright line rules for these circumstances, but has pointed to federal circuit court guidelines. We'll see how the California Supreme Court has applied the exigent circumstances exception in *People v. Williams*.

The following statutes provide some overview of California's approach to arrests. Penal Code section 817(a) deals with issuance of arrest warrants by magistrates; section 836 applies to officers making arrests; and section 840 provides for appropriate times-of-day for arrests.

Penal Code Section 817. Probable cause; declarations; warrants; issuance; form; certificate of service

(a)(1) When a declaration of probable cause is made by a peace officer of this state, in accordance with subdivision (b) or (c), the magistrate, if, and only if, satisfied from the declaration that there exists probable cause that the offense described in the declaration has been committed and that the defendant described therein has committed the offense, shall issue a warrant of probable cause for the arrest of the defendant.

Penal Code Section 836. Arrest with and without warrant; citizen's arrest by domestic victim; protective or restraining order; assault or battery upon spouse, etc.; concealed weapon offense

(a) A peace officer may arrest a person in obedience to a warrant, or, pursuant to the authority granted to him or her by Chapter 4.5) of Title 3 of Part 2, without a warrant, may arrest a person whenever any of the following circumstances occur:

(1) The officer has probable cause to believe that the person to be arrested has committed a public offense in the officer's presence.

(2) The person arrested has committed a felony, although not in the officer's presence.

(3) The officer has probable cause to believe that the person to be arrested has committed a felony, whether or not a felony, in fact, has been committed.

(b) Any time a peace officer is called out on a domestic violence call, it shall be mandatory that the officer make a good faith effort to inform the victim of his or her right to make a citizen's arrest. This information shall include advising the victim how to safely execute the arrest.

(c)(1) When a peace officer is responding to a call alleging a violation of a domestic violence protective or restraining order issued under [various code provisions] or of a domestic violence protective or restraining order issued by the court of another state, tribe, or territory and the peace officer has probable cause to believe that the person against whom the order is issued has notice of the order and has committed an act in violation of the order, the officer shall make a lawful arrest of the person without a warrant and take that person into custody whether or not the violation occurred in the presence of the arresting officer. The officer shall, as soon as possible after the arrest, confirm with the appropriate authorities or the Domestic Violence Protection Order Registry that a true copy of the protective order has been registered, unless the victim provides the officer with a copy of the protective order.

(2) The person against whom a protective order has been issued shall be deemed to have notice of the order if the victim presents to the officer proof of service of the order, the officer confirms with the appropriate authorities that a true copy of the proof of service is on file, or the person against whom the protective order was issued was present at the protective order hearing or was informed by a peace officer of the contents of the protective order.

(3) In situations where mutual protective orders have been issued, liability for arrest under this subdivision applies only to those persons who are reasonably believed to have been the primary aggressor. In those situations, prior to making an arrest under this subdivision, the peace officer shall make reasonable efforts to identify, and may arrest, the primary aggressor involved in the incident. The primary aggressor is the person determined to be the most significant, rather than the first, aggressor. In identifying the primary aggressor, an officer shall consider (A) the intent of the law to protect victims of domestic violence from continuing abuse, (B) the threats creating fear of physical injury, (C) the history of domestic violence between the persons involved, and (D) whether either person involved acted in self-defense.

(d) Notwithstanding paragraph (1) of subdivision (a), if a suspect commits an assault or battery upon a current or former spouse, fiancé, fiancée, a current or former cohabitant, a person with whom the suspect currently is having or has previously had an engagement or dating relationship, person with whom the suspect has parented a child, or is presumed to have parented a child pursuant to the Uniform Parentage Act, a child of the suspect, a child whose parentage by the suspect is the subject of an action under the Uniform Parentage Act, a child of a person in one of the above categories, any other person related to the suspect by consanguinity or affinity within the second degree, or any person who is 65 years of age or older and who is related to the suspect by blood or legal guardianship a peace officer may arrest the suspect without a warrant where both of the following circumstances apply:

(1) The peace officer has probable cause to believe that the person to be arrested has committed the assault or battery, whether or not it has in fact been committed.

(2) The peace officer makes the arrest as soon as probable cause arises to believe that the person to be arrested has committed the assault or battery, whether or not it has in fact been committed.

Penal Code Section 840. Time of arrest; felony; misdemeanor

An arrest for the commission of a felony may be made on any day and at any time of the day or night. An arrest for the commission of a misdemeanor or an infraction cannot be made between the hours of 10 o'clock p.m. of any day and 6 o'clock a.m. of the succeeding day, unless:

(1) The arrest is made without a warrant [Sections 836, 837].

(2) The arrest is made in a public place.

(3) The arrest is made when the person is in custody pursuant to another lawful arrest.

(4) The arrest is made pursuant to a warrant which, for good cause shown, directs that it may be served at any time of the day or night.

As the preceding statutes show, arrests can be made by warrant when a magistrate has issued a warrant (section 817). Arrests can also be made without a warrant under the circumstances laid out in section 836. This section also describes the circumstances under which California police officers are supposed to make arrests in domestic violence situations. Section 840 delineates when daytime arrests must be made, compared to when nighttime arrests are permitted.

Officers making arrests in California are authorized to use force to make an arrest when the suspect flees or forcibly resists, but the amount of force they use is subject to the constraints imposed by the Supreme Court in *Graham v. Connor*, 490 U.S. 386 (1989). Unreasonable force violates the suspect's Fourth Amendment rights.

CASES-

I. People v. Rosales, 192 Cal.App.3d 759 (1987)
Penal Code Section 836(3)

In *Illinois v. Gates*, 462 U.S. 213 (1983), the Supreme Court rejected the two-prong *Aguilar-Spinelli* rule for testing whether an anonymous informant's information results in probable cause, and substituted a "totality of the circumstances" approach. This is the approach California courts take in evaluating whether probable cause exists, in general (the test is not limited to anonymous informant information). The court in *Rosales* provides a nice application of this test.

Epstein, J.

BACKGROUND

South Los and Elm Street are two rival gangs operating in the South Gate and Gardena areas of Los Angeles County. Two of the victims in this case, Albert Estrada and Robert Gutierrez, were members of the South Los gang. They lived with the other two victims, Leticia and Rosa Hernandez (sisters), at the home of George Hernandez on Indiana Avenue in South Gate.

Most of the other principals in the case were members of the Elm Street gang. That gang had sponsored a dance in Gardena on August 27, 1983, which apparently was attended by members of both gangs. A fight broke out toward the end of the evening. Members of the Elm Street gang held South Los responsible for the fight, and relations between the two groups were tense.

The next day, three members of the Elm Street gang visited George Hernandez at his home. They told him of the shooting at the dance, that they knew Estrada and Gutierrez were living there, and that they had better move to a new location.

The record does not reveal whether this warning was transmitted to Estrada or Gutierrez; however, the record indicates they were still living at the Hernandez residence on August 30, 1983, when the criminal assaults at issue in this case occurred.

Defendants were together that evening at Rosales's home with two women. Both men were members of the Elm Street gang, and one of them asked Darrin Montalvo to come over. When he arrived, Mayfield claimed to have been stabbed at the dance, and said that he was seeking revenge. The three men and two women got into Montalvo's blue Camaro and drove to the neighborhood of the Hernandez residence.

They arrived in the neighborhood at about 10 p.m., just as Estrada, Gutierrez and the Hernandez sisters were driving home. The cars passed in opposite directions. Mayfield identified Estrada as a member of the South Los gang, and directed Montalvo to stop his car, and put it into reverse in an effort to catch up with the other car. Montalvo tried to comply, but the maneuver was unsuccessful.

At Rosales's suggestion, they then drove to Eva Ortega's apartment. Ms. Ortega's boyfriend, Javier Rodriguez, was at the apartment. He, too, was a member of the Elm Street gang. After a short conversation between Mayfield and Rodriguez, the four men (defendants Mayfield and Rosales, and Rodriguez and Montalvo) drove to Rodriguez's home. Rodriguez went inside and returned with a shotgun and shells, which he gave to Rosales. Rosales loaded the shotgun, and climbed into the bed of a black pickup truck owned by Rodriguez. The other three were seated in the cab, with Rodriguez driving, Mayfield sitting on the right passenger side, and Montalvo in the middle.

As they drove off, Mayfield told Rosales that he would "give you the signal when to fire." The black pickup slowed as it approached the Hernandez residence. As it did, Mayfield told Rosales to "[g]o for it. Fire." Rosales fired the shotgun and reported, "I think I hit 'em."

He had shot Rosa Hernandez in the abdomen, inflicting a fatal wound. Estrada was hit in the left calf. Leticia Hernandez and Albert Gutierrez were not injured.

The four men went to a woman's house, then left that location, proceeding on 93rd Street, where they saw a Highway Patrol vehicle. Rodriguez stopped the pickup, and asked everyone to get out. The others did so, Rosales taking the shotgun with him.

In the meantime, South Gate police had responded to the shooting. Leticia told one of the interrogating officers that she recognized the black pickup truck as looking exactly like a vehicle owned by a member of the Elm Street gang named Shorty. ("Shorty" is the nickname of Javier Rodriguez, who owned the pickup.) A radio bulletin was put out for the vehicle.

The Highway Patrol officers had stopped the truck about 11:45 p.m. for equipment violations, and they identified it as the vehicle described in the radio bulletin.

The officers found spent shell casings in the bed of the truck. The truck was impounded. Later, it was identified by Leticia Hernandez as the vehicle used in the drive-by shooting. Still later, a series of latent fingerprints was removed. These fingerprints matched prints from Montalvo, Rodriguez, Mayfield and Rosales.

Montalvo fled to Mexico the next day. He turned himself in to the police some three weeks later. He originally was arrested for murder, but the juvenile delinquency proceeding against him was later resolved when he admitted having committed an act of voluntary manslaughter. He was placed on summary probation, and was promised that he would receive no further punishment in the case if he testified truthfully.

Mayfield, Rosales and Rodriguez were arrested on the day after the shooting. Rodriguez's case is not before us, and Mayfield raises no issue about his arrest. Rosales, however, argues that the police lacked probable cause to arrest him, and that the fingerprint evidence obtained as a result of the arrest must be suppressed.

DISCUSSION

Rosales was arrested without a warrant. The only product of the arrest that was used against him at trial is a set of fingerprints taken during the booking process. Rosales moved to suppress all fingerprint evidence on the ground that the arrest was not supported by probable cause to justify a strong suspicion of culpability in the shooting. The People argued that the arrest was supported by sufficient probable cause and that, even if it were not, the fingerprint linkage would inevitably have been discovered. The trial court denied the motion to suppress. We affirm the trial court's ruling.

It is the general rule that the evidentiary fruits of an illegal arrest must be suppressed upon the proper application of the arrested person.

A warrantless arrest is authorized and legal "[whenever] [the arresting officer] has reasonable cause to believe that the person to be arrested has committed a felony, whether or not a felony has in fact been committed." [Penal Code 836(3)]. "Reasonable or probable cause for an arrest has been the subject of much judicial scrutiny and decision. There is no exact formula for the determination of reasonableness. Each case must be decided on its own facts and circumstances [citations] - and on the total atmosphere of the case. [Citations.] Reasonable cause has been generally defined to be such a state of facts as would lead a man of ordinary care and prudence to believe and conscientiously entertain an honest and strong suspicion that the person is guilty of a crime. [Citations.] Probable cause has also been defined as having more evidence for than against; supported by evidence which inclines the mind to believe, but leaves some room for doubt. [Citations.] It is not limited to evidence that would be admissible at the trial on the issue of guilt. [Citation.] The test is not whether the evidence upon which the officer acts in making the arrest is sufficient to convict but only whether the person should stand trial. [Citation.]"

The reasonableness of the officer's subjective belief is tested by an objective standard. That standard cannot be applied with mathematical precision, or according to a set formula. Instead, "each case must be decided on the *totality of facts and circumstances* at the time an arrest is made."

We examine the probable cause issue in this case with these principles in mind.

Rosales was arrested at his home by Detective Robert Mayer, of the South Gate Police Department. Detective Mayer was especially knowledgeable about gangs operating in the area of his department, including the two gangs involved in this case. He had all of the information that had been given to the investigating officers by the victims of the shooting. He therefore knew that the shooting was probably perpetrated by members of the Elm Street gang who were seeking revenge against members of the South Los gang for the fracas at the dance in Gardena a few nights before. He also knew that members of the Elm Street gang were aware of the fact that two South Los members were living at the Hernandez residence on Indiana Street.

Detective Mayer also listened to a tape recording of an anonymous telephone call received at the South Gate Police Department on the morning after the shooting. The caller mentioned she had been inside "the house at the time of the shooting, that being the house on Indiana," i.e., the Hernandez residence. Continuing, the caller said that Rodriguez (who, at that time, was the only person under arrest) was not the only one involved. She said that Mayfield and Big Tudy (Rosales's nickname) also were involved, Big Tudy was the shooter, both were members of the Elm Street gang, and Big Tudy lived on Iowa Street. Because she knew both Mayfield and Big Tudy, she feared she would be in a "lot of trouble" with them if she revealed her identity. Finally, the caller said Big Tudy knew that Rodriguez would not say anything to the police and "is going to take the rap," but that Big Tudy was about to leave for Texas.

Detective Mayer knew that Big Tudy was Rosales's nickname. He was familiar with Rosales by reputation and knew his younger brother ("Little Tudy").

Raymond Lilley, a South Gate Police Department sergeant, was better acquainted with Rosales. Lilley was an expert on local gangs and had followed Rosales's career since 1974 when Rosales was allegedly involved in a high school stabbing. He knew that Rosales had fled to Texas several years before, when he was wanted for armed robbery. He also knew that Rosales had returned and had assumed a leadership position in the Elm Street gang. He related all of this to Detective Mayer.

Detective Galbreath, the investigating officer, Lilley and Mayer all thought it was likely that Rosales would flee to Texas, if he had not done so already.

Mayer went to Little Tudy's home, hoping to find Rosales. While driving by the house, Mayer saw Little Tudy pull up. Knowing that he had been seen by Little Tudy, Mayer stopped to make contact. At that time, he saw Rosales standing in the front yard. Rosales looked in Mayer's direction, and immediately ran into the house. Mayer called for backup on a hand-held radio, and Little Tudy yelled to his brother that the officer knew he was there. Rosales emerged from the house and was arrested.

The Attorney General agrees that uncorroborated information of an anonymous nonvictim witness is not a sufficient basis to provide probable cause to arrest. But, he argues, there is corroboration in this case, in the officers' expert knowledge of Rosales's past criminal activities, his membership in the Elm Street gang, and his previous flight to Texas.

The weight that may be given to information received from an anonymous informant was extensively considered in *Illinois v. Gates*. *Gates* is best known for its rejection of the two-prong *Aguilar-Spinelli* rule for testing the adequacy of a search warrant declaration that is based on information supplied by an anonymous informant. *Gates* replaced that test with a totality-of-the- circumstances approach. It found that approach to be "far more consistent with [the court's] prior treatment of probable cause than is any rigid demand that specific 'tests' be satisfied by every informant's tip. Perhaps the central teaching of our decisions bearing on the probable-cause standard is that it is a 'practical, nontechnical conception.' [Citation.]" "[It] is a fluid concept - turning on the assessment of probabilities in particular factual contexts - not readily, or even usefully, reduced to a neat set of legal rules. Informants' tips doubtless come in many shapes and sizes from many different types of persons. ..." And even in cases in which the informant's motives may be doubted, "his explicit and detailed description of alleged wrongdoing, along with a statement that the event was observed firsthand, entitles his tip to greater weight than might otherwise be the case."

California has applied a totality-of-the- circumstances approach to test probable cause for an arrest, as well. We see no reason why the full *Gates* rationale, including its discussion of the weight to be given information from an anonymous informant, should not be as fully applicable to the question of probable cause to support an arrest as it is to a search. That, in fact, appears to be its application in federal cases.

In this case, the anonymous telephone caller possessed a wealth of specific information about the shooting. She knew the identity of the respective gangs involved and of their enmity, how the shooting occurred, and when it occurred; she recognized the shooter (Rosales) and one of his accomplices (Mayfield); she knew that each was a member of the Elm Street gang; and she knew where Rosales lived. Finally, she knew that Rosales was planning to flee to Texas. The caller also explained how she happened to know all of this: she was acquainted with the defendants and she was inside the home at the location of the shooting when it occurred.

By the time that Detective Mayer arrested Rosales, he knew that much of the caller's information already had been corroborated. The shooting had occurred as described; defendants were members of a gang that was out for revenge against a rival gang of which two of the victims were members; the drive-by shooting occurred at their residence; and Rosales had fled to Texas once before in order to avoid prosecution in California.

Finally, when Detective Mayer appeared at the Rosales residence, Rosales saw Mayer and immediately ran inside his house. His flight, under these circumstances, is a further basis to suspect his guilt.

Added to the corroborating information obtained from the field investigation, Rosales's flight at the sight of a detective, and the detectives' knowledge of gang behavior in the area the informant's detailed statement provided "a state of facts as would lead a man of ordinary care and prudence to believe and conscientiously entertain an honest and strong suspicion" that Rosales was guilty of a crime. Hence, there was probable cause for the arrest, and the motion to suppress was properly denied.

*****

CONCLUSION

The court upheld the legality of Rosales' arrest, applying the totality of circumstances approach adopted by the Supreme Court in *Illinois v. Gates*. Although both that case and this case involve anonymous informants, California courts consider the totality of circumstances approach to apply generally to probable cause determinations.

REVIEW

1. Why was Rosales trying so hard to have his arrest determined invalid? Hint: What was the fruit of the poisonous tree and how would it help him if it could be eliminated?

2. What is the California approach to determining probable cause, according to this court?

3. What were all the factors that justified Rosales' arrest?

II. People v. Williams, 48 Cal.3d 1112 (1989)

California follows what is known locally as the *Payton-Ramey* rule. Barring exigent circumstances, arrests can only be made in a private home (including private dwellings of non-defendants) with a warrant. *People v. Ramey*, 16 Cal.3d (1976) set this rule as the standard in California several years before the U.S. Supreme Court set it in *Payton*. But what are exigent circumstances? The following case deals with that issue.

*****

Kaufman, J.

BACKGROUND

[The following comes from the prosecution's case.]

Defendant and his brother were indicted in Placer County for the rape, robbery, kidnapping, kidnapping for purposes of robbery and murder of Heather Mead. Both men were also charged with burglary. Special circumstances of murder committed during the commission or attempted commission of rape, robbery, kidnapping, kidnapping for purposes of robbery and burglary were alleged, as were allegations of having been armed with and of having personally used a firearm during the commission of the offenses.

The trial court denied a joint pretrial motion for change of venue. The trials were subsequently severed and defendant was tried first. During the jury selection, defendant renewed his motion for change of venue. The trial court again denied the motion. The jury returned guilty verdicts on all counts and found true all the special circumstance and most of the enhancement allegations. The jury fixed the penalty at death. Appeal is automatic.

On June 12, 1980, at approximately 5:20 a.m., the lifeless body of a young woman, Heather Mead, age 22, was found on Industrial Boulevard near Roseville in Placer County. She had been shot five times. An autopsy revealed that Mead had sustained three gunshot wounds to the head, one to the abdomen and one to the thigh. At least two of the shots had been fired from a distance of three to five feet. The time of death was estimated to have been between 3 and 4 that morning. Based on the location of the wounds, the amount of blood and the presence of the expended bullets, the investigating officer, Detective Johnnie Smith of the Placer County Sheriff's Department, concluded that Mead had been shot at that location.

The autopsy also revealed that Mead had engaged in sexual intercourse within two to twenty-four hours prior to her death, and that she had been either a virgin or sexually inexperienced.

Mead was a resident of Roseville in Placer County. During the week preceding her death, however, she had been house-sitting for her vacationing aunt and uncle, Fred and Bettie Graham, at their residence on Roble Way in the North Highlands section of Sacramento.

On the evening of June 10, the day before the murder, Mead had dinner with her fiance, Bruce Pfeiffer. Pfeiffer testified that he left her that evening at the Graham residence and returned to the naval base where he was stationed. He stated that during the four and one-half years he had known Mead, they had never engaged in sexual intercourse.

Later that evening, Mead went to Jeffrey Kearney's residence and spent the night there. Kearney testified that he and Mead had been close friends but, like Pfeiffer, denied that they had ever had sexual intercourse. Before Mead left for work the next morning, June 11, she arranged to meet Kearney that evening at a bar called the Blue Lantern in Roseville. The meeting would never take place.

Mead worked as a "gofer" for Atteberry and Associates, an engineering and consulting firm in Roseville owned by her aunt, Susan Atteberry. Mead's aunt and uncle, Fred and Bettie Graham, also worked for Atteberry and Associates. On June 11, 1980, Mead was told she could leave work about 4 p.m. She informed a coworker that she planned to meet Kearney that evening.

On the same day, about 1:30 p.m., Kevin McGruder was driving to his home in the North Highlands section of Sacramento when he saw defendant, an acquaintance from high school, walking on the street. McGruder gave defendant a ride to his (McGruder's) house, which was located on Roble Way, next door to the Grahams' residence. Upon their arrival, McGruder and defendant heard shouting and went into the backyard where they encountered Mrs. Gahan, the neighbor who lived on the other side of the Grahams. Mrs. Gahan was upset because the Grahams' dogs were running loose. She told McGruder that the Grahams were not at home (McGruder recalled that she said they were "on vacation") and that she was concerned because the dogs were unattended. Defendant was present during this conversation. Shortly thereafter, the two men separated.

Later that evening, McGruder was driving home from work when he saw defendant's brother, Fredrick Williams, at a neighborhood Circle K store. He stopped and gave Fredrick a ride to his (McGruder's) home. When they arrived, McGruder observed Fredrick put on a pair of black gloves and walk across the street to a park. McGruder noted a white Chevrolet Impala parked in the Grahams' driveway. He had seen it there before. The car belonged to Heather Mead. The time was approximately 12:30 a.m.

At approximately 1:15 a.m., McGruder was in his bedroom watching television when he heard a sound like glass breaking from the direction of the Graham residence. A minute or two later, he heard a voice which he recognized as defendant's saying "stop crying" and words which sounded like the number

"86." In an earlier statement to the police and in his preliminary hearing testimony, McGruder was far less certain that it was defendant's voice or that these were the precise words which he heard. In any event, McGruder called the Sacramento Sheriff's office at approximately 1:45 a.m. to report a disturbance next door. A few minutes later, two patrol cars arrived. Either through misinformation or a misunderstanding, however, the officers believed that the caller (McGruder) lived at 6835 Roble Way, which was in fact the Graham residence, and that the disturbance was at 6839 Roble Way, the Gahan residence. The officers observed some lights on and a figure, whom they took to be the caller, peering from a window of the Graham residence. A white Impala was parked in the driveway. The officers checked and "cleared" the Gahan residence and departed at approximately 2:08 a.m.

Approximately two hours later, about 4 a.m., Tammy French, defendant's girlfriend, received a telephone call from defendant at her residence in Marysville. Defendant told her that he was at a liquor store around the corner and that he was coming over. He said that he had left some items on the porch and asked her to take them inside. Ms. French went outside and found a jewelry box, gloves, gun holsters, a mask, a stethoscope, and two knives. As she was placing these in a bag, she saw defendant walking toward the house carrying a CB radio. Ms. French and defendant took the items upstairs. She noted that defendant appeared to have been recently sweating.

Defendant told Ms. French that a friend, Art Johnson, had driven him to Marysville (defendant did not own a car). He had a gun, which he unloaded, and explained that he had "found" or stolen it. Defendant stated that he intended to sell some of the jewelry and either sell or otherwise dispose of the gun.

Later that morning, June 12, 1980, defendant left for Sacramento. He took the gun and shoulder holster with him. At approximately 11 a.m., Kenneth Mitchell received a telephone call from defendant. Defendant asked if he wanted to buy a gun. Mitchell stated that he did and the two arranged a meeting at the home of Tony Armstrong, a mutual friend, in North Highlands. Mitchell purchased the gun (a .38-caliber pistol), a holster and some shells for $25. When defendant returned to Marysville that night, he told French that he had disposed of the gun.

Two days later, during the early morning hours of June 14, Mitchell was running from the Birdcage apartments in Sacramento, where he had been stealing "in-dashes" from parked vehicles, when he "lost" the gun that he had purchased from defendant. Later that morning, a newspaper delivery boy found the gun and turned it over to the Sacramento Sheriff's department. It was later determined to be the gun that fired the bullets recovered from Heather Mead's body. Fred Graham confirmed that the weapon in question was among the items that had been stolen from his residence.

On June 13, the day after the murder, the police found Mead's car parked one to two blocks from the residence of defendant's girlfriend, Tammy French. Defendant was arrested that evening at Ms. French's apartment. A CB radio identified as having come from Mead's vehicle, a key to Mead's car, Mead's prescription eyeglasses, several pieces of jewelry with the Grahams' name on them, and a Texaco credit card issued to Atteberry and Associates were recovered from the French residence.

Forensic evidence relating to hair, semen and fingerprints found at the various crime scenes was introduced at trial. Of the 10 or so hairs found in Mead's left hand, the state's expert testified that none could have come from defendant or his brother. However, Negroid hairs found on Mead's navel, pubic area and breast, and on the bed sheet recovered from Mead's bedroom in the Graham residence had characteristics similar to that of defendant and his brother. The experts were generally unable to say whether the hairs were more similar to one brother or the other.

54

Tests to determine blood type and secretor status were conducted on defendant and his brother; the blood types of Ms. Mead, Jeff Kearney, Bruce Pfeiffer and a third friend of the victim, Rod Zeller, were also determined. Further tests were performed to determine each of the foregoing individuals' phosphoglucomutase (PGM) grouping. The state's expert criminalist, Michael Saggs, testified that he ran similar tests on seminal material found on vaginal and vulva swabs taken from the victim, as well as on blood and seminal stains found on Mead's panties and on the bedsheet in Mead's bedroom. Based on these tests, Saggs concluded that defendant could not be eliminated as having had sexual intercourse with Mead, although it was also impossible to state categorically that neither defendant's brother nor the other persons tested had deposited semen.

Julita Fong, a pathologist who testified for defendant, challenged Saggs's conclusions. Contrary to Saggs, Dr. Fong stated it was not possible to conclude unequivocally that the seminal material on the panties and the vaginal swabs was consistent with defendant's secretor or PGM status. Dr. Fong conceded, however, that her conclusions were based upon photographs of Saggs's test results, and would have been stronger if based upon an independent analysis of the samples.

Evidence was also presented that defendant's fingerprints were found on a note in Mead's vehicle, and on a Stoney Ridge Enterprises business card found in the Graham residence.

[The following comes from the record of the motion to suppress hearing.]

Inspector Smith inspected the body of the victim shortly after it was discovered in the early morning hours of June 12, 1980. He observed a spent slug and bullet fragments at the scene and concluded that the victim had been shot at that location, possibly by a .38-caliber handgun. Relatives of the victim were contacted who informed Smith that she had been house-sitting for her aunt and uncle, the Grahams, in Sacramento. Officers questioned neighbors of the Grahams, including Kevin McGruder, that day as well as the next, June 13, 1980. From McGruder the police learned that defendant might have known the Grahams were on vacation, that McGruder had driven defendant's brother to the vicinity of the Graham residence, had heard defendant's voice inside the house within hours of the murder, and had called the police to report a disturbance.

On the evening of June 12, Inspector Smith learned from Fred Graham, who had just returned from holiday, that a .38-caliber revolver was among the items stolen from the residence. The following morning, June 13, 1980, Inspector Smith learned that the victim's car had been located in Marysville. Field questioning continued through the afternoon, including a follow-up interview with McGruder. About 5:30 p.m., Inspector Smith attempted to contact defendant, who lived with his parents about three-tenths of a mile from the Graham residence. Smith was then told by defendant's mother that she had not seen defendant since midnight of June 11, just hours before the murder. Mrs. Williams directed Smith to another residence where defendant had stayed in the past. The individuals at this location informed Smith that defendant had a girlfriend in Marysville, Tammy French. Smith then went to Marysville on the evening of June 13 and learned that the victim's car was parked within one to two blocks of French's residence. In Marysville, Smith rendezvoused with officers from the Sacramento County sheriff's office, who had simultaneously been putting together an affidavit for an arrest warrant based upon defendant's alleged involvement in two Sacramento burglaries a month earlier.

The officers then went to French's residence, knocked on the front door which was a common door to three apartments, and were permitted entry by a young child into a common foyer. They immediately observed defendant peer over a balcony from upstairs and run into an apartment. The officers gave chase, located defendant in the dining room and placed him under arrest. Smith then asked Ms. French if they could speak in private. She led him into the bedroom, where he observed a CB radio on the floor and the other stolen property which defendant had left there the day before.

55

DISCUSSION

Defendant contends that the trial court erred in denying his motion to suppress evidence, based on his claim that the arrest was unlawful and therefore that all of the evidence seized at the time should be suppressed. He charges illegality on two theories. First, he contends that his arrest on a Sacramento County burglary arrest warrant was invalid because it was allegedly obtained as a pretext to obtain evidence pertinent to the homicide, because the affidavit in support of the arrest warrant failed to establish probable cause, and because the affiant made false and misleading statements. Alternatively, defendant contends that the police lacked independent probable cause to arrest for the homicide.

The trial court ruled that the arrest was legal, both because the burglary warrant was valid and because there was probable cause to arrest for the homicide.

"As a general matter, '[a] peace officer may arrest a person without a warrant whenever he has reasonable cause to believe that the person arrested has committed a felony.' [Citations.] However, ... article I, section 13 , of the California Constitution and the Fourth Amendment of the federal Constitution prohibit warrantless arrests within the home, even upon probable cause, in the absence of exigent circumstances. The same constitutional protection extends to individuals sought to be arrested in someone else's private dwelling.

"'[E]xigent circumstances' means an emergency situation requiring swift action to prevent imminent danger to life or serious damage to property, or to forestall the imminent escape of a suspect or destruction of evidence. There is no ready litmus test for determining whether such circumstances exist, and in each case the claim of an extraordinary situation must be measured by the facts known to the officers." Although the United States Supreme Court has not fully delineated the scope of the exigent circumstances exception, it has recognized the seminal case of *Dorman v. United States* as "a leading federal case defining exigent circumstances ..." in a warrantless arrest situation.

Dorman found the following factors relevant to a determination of exigent circumstances: "First, that a grave offense is involved, particularly one that is a crime of violence ... [¶] Second, ... that the suspect is reasonably believed to be armed. Delay in arrest of an armed felon may well increase danger to the community ... [¶] Third, that there exists ... a clear showing of probable cause ... [¶] Fourth, strong reason to believe that the suspect is in the premises being entered. [¶] Fifth, a likelihood that the suspect will escape if not swiftly apprehended. [¶] Sixth, the circumstance that the entry, though not consented, is made peaceably." Both federal and California cases have found exigency where there was a threat that delay would result in the destruction of evidence.

All of the foregoing factors justified, indeed compelled, the warrantless arrest in this case. The crimes were vicious and violent. The suspect was quite clearly armed. The police had obtained trustworthy information pointing to defendant as one of the perpetrators. The proximity of the victim's car clearly suggested defendant's presence in the apartment, and also made flight a realistic possibility. The entry was peaceable. Moreover, the possibility that defendant might have learned from friends or family that the police were looking for him and might, as a result, dispose of any blood- stained clothing, stolen property or the murder weapon made arrest all the more urgent.

There was no unjustified delay by the investigating officers during which time an arrest warrant for the homicide could have been obtained. Inspector Smith's field investigation had been progressing steadily from the morning of the murder, on June 12, to the early evening of the 13th. At that point, as Inspector Smith testified, "everything [was] starting to ... come together." Viewed as a whole, the circumstances confronting the officers were more than sufficiently urgent to justify a warrantless arrest of defendant in his girlfriend's apartment for the rape, robbery and homicide.

In view of the foregoing conclusion, we need not address defendant's alternative contention concerning the validity of the burglary arrest warrant.

The judgment of conviction is reversed [on other grounds].

*****

CONCLUSION

Although the court held against the defendant's claim that the warrantless arrest was illegal, holding instead that there were valid exigent circumstances, it ultimately reversed the conviction because it believed the defendant should have received the change of venue asked for at time of the trial (see Chapter Thirteen for discussion of change of venue motions).

REVIEW

1.   What evidence was the product of the defendant's arrest?

2.   What factors does the court borrow from Dorman to consider whether exigent circumstances against? Are all of these legitimate considerations, in your opinion?

3.   Do you agree with the court that all factors were met in this case?

Section 3: After the Arrest

OVERVIEW

Officers having probable cause that a felony was committed almost invariably make a full custodial arrest if they have met the statutory obligations. Misdemeanor suspects are given more leeway. For some types of misdemeanors, such as crimes against persons or driving under the influence, an arrest is probable. But what if the offense is deemed fairly trivial by most people, such as failing to put on a seatbelt? Recall that the Supreme Court held in *Atwater v. City of Lago Vista*, 532 U.S. 318 (2001) that as long as an offense is a crime for which arrest is authorized, if police have the option to cite and release or to arrest, they can always in their discretion choose the latter. California has taken this approach for some time. Most cases causing controversy arise during various vehicle violations. California courts have held that in minor vehicle code violations officers have discretion in determining when to effectuate full custodial arrests. *E.g., People v. Monroe*, 12 Cal.App.4th 1174 (1993).

CHAPTER SIX

Searches for Evidence

The validity of searches for evidence is one of the most important concepts in the law of criminal procedure, for if within this domain defendants' arguments about the impropriety of police procedures are successful, the end result is often the suppression of crucial prosecution materials that may result in reversal of convictions. The general rule is that search warrants are necessary before police can conduct a search, but there are many exceptions to the rule, as we shall see. In this chapter we first examine the requirements of a search warrant, and second, we turn to the exceptions to the warrant requirement. We are traversing the second step of the three-tiered analytical strategy discussed previously, where step one is to determine if the police action was a search in the first place, step two is to determine if the search was reasonable, and step three is to determine whether the evidence from an unreasonable search should be excluded.

Section 1. Searches with Warrants

OVERVIEW

Penal Code sections 1525 and 1531 lay out the basic elements of the warrant requirement in California, which mirrors the federal requirement. Warrants must withstand three criteria. They must describe the items to be seized with particularity, such that the police cannot go on a "treasure hunt." They must be based on a sworn declaration of probable cause (usually by the law enforcement officers seeking the warrant). And they must be served in a reasonable manner, meaning that in most circumstances police must knock and announce themselves prior to entry. Note in Penal Code section 1531, forced entry is authorized if after announcement the police are refused entry. Also note the requirement in section 1525 that applications for search warrant require the requester to specify that the place to be searched is controlled by an attorney, doctor, therapist, or clergyman. This is necessary because there are rules of confidentiality of evidence between members of these occupations and their clients that may affect what may and may not be seized by the police.

> **Penal Code Section 1525. Issuance; probable cause; supporting affidavits; contents of application**
>
> A search warrant cannot be issued but upon probable cause, supported by affidavit, naming or describing the person to be searched or searched for, and particularly describing the property, thing, or things and the place to be searched.
>
> The application shall specify when applicable, that the place to be searched is in the possession or under the control of an attorney, physician, psychotherapist or clergyman.

Penal Code Section 1531. Execution; authority to break in after admittance refused

OFFICER MAY BREAK OPEN DOOR, ETC., TO EXECUTE WARRANT. The officer may break open any outer or inner door or window of a house, or any part of a house, or anything therein, to execute the warrant, if, after notice of his authority and purpose, he is refused admittance.

CASES-

I. People v. Hulland, 110 Cal.App.4th 1646 (2003)

Search warrants must be based on probable cause. What if an officer has probable cause to search a place, but waits too long to do so? At what point does evidence satisfying probable cause become "stale" such that a warrant based on it is invalid?

*****

Perren, J.

BACKGROUND

On November 15, 2001, Pasadena Police Officer Kevin Jackson sought and obtained a warrant to search two residences and two automobiles purportedly belonging to Hulland. The affidavit in support of the warrant stated that in September the officer had been contacted by a confidential reliable informant (CRI) who told him that Hulland was dealing marijuana. A Department of Motor Vehicles (DMV) records check verified the CRI's statement that Hulland lived in an apartment on Crenshaw Boulevard in Los Angeles. The affiant also stated that the records reflected an address for Hulland on Don Ricardo Drive. The attached DMV printout reflects, however, that a Ricky *Holland* resides at the Don Ricardo Drive address.

The CRI agreed to participate in a controlled purchase of marijuana from Hulland. Between September 21 and 30, the CRI called Hulland's cell phone and ordered marijuana. Hulland agreed to deliver the marijuana to the CRI at a parking lot in Pasadena. Officer Jackson drove the CRI to the parking lot. Hulland drove next to the driver's side window and handed the officer a sweatshirt wrapped around an unspecified amount of marijuana. In exchange, the officer gave Hulland an unspecified amount of money. The officer removed the marijuana and returned the sweatshirt to Hulland.

On October 9, Officers Jackson and Medrano conducted surveillance of both the Crenshaw Boulevard and Don Ricardo Drive addresses. Officer Medrano observed Hulland as he left the apartment building on Crenshaw Boulevard and got into the car he had used to deliver the marijuana. Officer Jackson observed a Mercedes Benz parked at the Don Ricardo Drive address that was purportedly registered to Hulland. According to the officer's affidavit, the CRI had verified that Hulland drove a green Mercedes. As the DMV printout indicated, however, the Mercedes was registered to a Ricky *Holland* who resided at the Don Ricardo Drive address.

After the controlled buy, Officer Jackson made several attempts to contact Hulland by calling his cell phone and pager. Both numbers had been disconnected. Based on his experience, Officer Jackson believed that Hulland had changed his cellular and pager numbers in an effort to avoid apprehension. Officer Jackson also stated in his affidavit that on October 12, an agent of the United States Postal Inspectors Office told him that a "Ricky Hulland" was currently receiving mail at both the Crenshaw Boulevard and Don Ricardo Drive addresses.

Officer Jackson stated that in his opinion "[g]iven the large quantity of marijuana that Hulland sold and transported, it is my belief that he continues to traffic in large quantity narcotics." The officer based his opinion on his six years of experience as a police officer, the past eleven months of which were under assignment in a special section that investigates mid-to-major level, drug-related crimes. The officer also stated his belief that the police surveillance and postal inspector's apparent confirmation that Hulland received mail at both the Crenshaw Boulevard and the Don Ricardo Drive addresses provided probable cause to believe that Hulland resided at both addresses.

Officer Jackson and other officers served the search warrant at the Crenshaw Boulevard address on November 15. During the search, they seized approximately 110.97 grams of marijuana, 10.97 grams of rock cocaine, $3,800 in cash, a handgun, a shotgun, a scale, and zip lock baggies. When Officer Jackson attempted to serve the warrant at the Don Ricardo Drive address, he discovered that a Ricky *Holland* resided there and that the Mercedes identified in the search warrant was registered to him.

On April 10, 2002, Hulland moved to quash the warrant and to suppress the seized evidence on the ground that the information supporting the finding of probable cause was stale. The trial court agreed that the information was stale because the warrant was not issued until at least 52 days after the controlled buy.

In support of the prosecution's contention that the warrant was executed in good faith, Officer Jackson testified that, in his opinion, the information in the warrant was not stale because he had purchased "just under a pound" of marijuana from Hulland and believed that an individual selling such a large amount of marijuana would still be dealing the drug less than two months later. The officer also testified that his delay in seeking the warrant was due to his continuing efforts to confirm that Hulland lived at both addresses. The officer did not indicate what those efforts were, however, nor did he provide any explanation for the 52-day delay. He also stated he had continued calling Hulland's disconnected numbers to determine whether they were only temporarily disconnected. He further testified that he had spelled Hulland's name for the postal inspector prior to receiving the purported confirmation that Hulland lived at the Don Ricardo Drive address. He failed, however, to explain the discrepancy between the CRI's purported representation that Hulland drove the green Mercedes identified in the search warrant and the fact that the vehicle was actually registered to the individual named *Holland* who resided at the Don Ricardo Drive address and that no green Mercedes was ever linked to Hulland.

The court concluded that Officer Jackson had executed the warrant in good faith, and accordingly denied the motion to suppress. The court reasoned: "I certainly can't fault the police officer from [*sic*] believing that if he bought some drugs from the individual then went back 52 and 57 days later, with a search warrant, I can't fault him for searching for drugs where the seller resides."

DISCUSSION

[First, the court discussed standard of review, indicating that they accept the trial court's factual findings but exercise independent judgment on the legal issues.]

60

The trial court found that the warrant under which Officer Jackson searched Hulland's residence was not supported by probable cause because it was based on stale information. Information that is remote in time may be deemed stale and thus unworthy of consideration in determining whether an affidavit for a search warrant is supported by probable cause. Such information is deemed stale unless it consists of facts so closely related to the time of the issuance of the warrant that it justifies a finding of probable cause at that time. The question of staleness turns on the facts of each particular case. If circumstances would justify a person of ordinary prudence to conclude that an activity had continued to the present time, then the passage of time will not render the information stale.

It is undisputed that the probable cause determination in this case was dependent on the information leading to and including the controlled buy. The relevant inquiry is thus whether Officer Jackson held an objectively reasonable belief that this information had not grown stale by the time he sought and obtained the warrant. Although there is no bright line rule indicating when information becomes stale, delays of more than four weeks are generally considered insufficient to demonstrate present probable cause. For example, a delay of 34 days between a controlled sale of heroin and the officer's affidavit for the search warrant has been held insufficient to establish present probable cause. Longer delays are justified only where there is evidence of an activity continuing over a long period of time or the nature of the activity is such as to justify the inference that it will continue until the time of the search.

Respondent does not challenge the trial court's finding that the controlled buy of marijuana from Hulland had grown stale by the time the warrant was issued. This implicit concession of the staleness issue is well taken. There was no information before the magistrate regarding any prior or subsequent criminal activity by Hulland, nor any evidence of such activity ever taking place at his residence. Although evidence of drug dealing may be sufficient by itself to furnish probable cause to search the defendant's residence nothing about the nature of the transaction here supports an inference that Hulland continued to sell marijuana until the time of the search, much less that he would be keeping the drugs at his residence . This conclusion is buttressed by the fact that the controlled buy took place in a parking lot in a different city. Thus, the trial court was correct in concluding that the warrant was not supported by probable cause in that it was based on information that had grown stale by the time the warrant was issued.

[The court spent the remainder of the case discussing whether the officer had relied in good faith on a facially invalid warrant, concluding that the officer could not reasonably have believed the warrant to be valid.]

The judgment is reversed with instructions to the trial court to enter an order granting Hulland's motion to suppress.

*****

CONCLUSION

It was stipulated by the state in this case that the warrant was facially invalid because the evidence was stale. The court's discussion of staleness thus was not at controversy, but we included it here to provide the reader with an understanding of the staleness concept. The court went on to discuss the good faith exception in conjunction with stale evidence. We will address the good faith rule in a later chapter.

REVIEW

1. What was the sole basis for the search warrant?

2. How long was the delay in seeking the search warrant? How long do California courts say constitutes a reasonable delay beyond which evidence will be stale?

3. Does it matter that the officer didn't specify a reason for the delay? Can you think of any reasons for the delay that would make the search warrant more valid?

4. What do you think of the officer's reasoning that a sale of such a large amount of marijuana means that the suspect was still likely to be involved in dealing drugs several weeks later?

Section 2: Searches without Warrants

OVERVIEW

Officers can still conduct searches of persons and places without a warrant, under a number of circumstances, or exceptions. One of the most prevalent is the search-incident-to-arrest, established in *Chimel v. California*, 395 U.S. 752 (1969). The Supreme Court held that upon validly arresting an individual, officers can search the person and the immediately "grabbable distance." The purpose is to protect the officers in case the individual is armed or has immediate access to weapons or destructible evidence. In *New York v. Belton,* 453 U.S. 454 (1981) the Court held that upon arresting a driver of a car, the entire passenger compartment of the car could be searched pursuant to *Chimel*, even if the driver was no longer in the vehicle. The search-incident-to-arrest exception is very broad. One of the only major limitations the Supreme Court has laid down recently, in *Knowles v. Iowa*, 525 U.S. 113 (1998) is that officers cannot search individuals who have only been cited with infractions and not arrested. Searches-incident-to-arrest can be conducted before, during, or after the arrest, as long as probable cause to arrest had arisen prior to the search.

When an individual consents to a search this is also classified as an exception to the warrant requirement. Consent must be made voluntarily and knowingly, but it is not crucial that the person be told of the right to withhold consent. The test for voluntariness is designated as "totality of circumstances" in the leading Supreme Court case *Schneckloth v. Bustamonte*, 412 U.S. 218 (1973). The scope of the consent relates to what a reasonable officer should have understood the scope to be, not upon the subjective understanding of the citizen. Third parties can consent to searches of another if they have authority to consent or if the officer reasonably believed they had authority.

Vehicle searches are another exception to the warrant requirement. Because vehicles can be readily moved, the Supreme Court held in *Carroll v. United States*, 267 U.S. 132 (1925) that if probable cause exists to search a car, a search may be conducted without a warrant. The search should be limited to the areas that could possibly contain the material on which probable cause is based. If probable cause exists that a container has contraband and the container is put in a vehicle, the officers may search the container without a warrant because when the vehicle is driven off, the container will be transported as well.

Finally, searches may be conducted under certain circumstances without warrants if exigent considerations exist, including potential for destruction of crucial evidence, hot pursuit of dangerous persons, and potential for danger to communities, such as when a bomb may exist in a private place for which the police lack a warrant but need to access immediately.

California sticks to federal law regarding exceptions to search warrants, but this means that it is constantly interpreting the federal case law, which often has gaps and doesn't clearly apply to each possible fact scenario. Below we discuss two such cases, one relating to search-incident-to-arrest and one relating to the exigent circumstances exception.

CASES-

I. People v. Ingham, 5 Cal.App.4th 326 (1992)

In this first case we address an interesting and rather confusing search-incident-to-arrest, a case that limits the exception.

*****

Best, P.J.

BACKGROUND

Defendant, Peggy Ingham, was charged with possession of methamphetamine for sale. The trial court ordered all evidence suppressed and discharged defendant. Thereafter, the district attorney filed this appeal.

After being told an anonymous source had implicated defendant's residence in drug sales, Officer Charles Maxwell asked Officer Marianne Mollring to serve a $2,000 traffic warrant on defendant. Officer Mollring was told about the drug allegation and was instructed to bring in defendant.

Officer Mollring, assisted by Officer Rodriguez, went to defendant's house and knocked on the door. Defendant answered but denied being Peggy Ingham. Rather, defendant said she was Peggy's sister and did not have any identification. Defendant then went inside to look for something with her name on it and the officers followed. In the meantime, Officer Mollring radioed dispatch and requested a booking photograph of Peggy Ingham be brought out.

When the photograph arrived, Officer Mollring told defendant she was under arrest. Defendant asked if she could get something out of her purse and was given permission to do so. The purse was located on the living room floor near a wall. Officer Mollring followed defendant as she walked over to the purse and watched defendant take out a large clutch wallet. When defendant opened the wallet, Officer Mollring saw a California driver's license inside. Defendant then took another small wallet out of her purse and tucked it into her bra. Defendant put the large clutch wallet back in the purse and left the purse on the floor. The purse was so "stuffed" with items it would not close and consequently, the clutch wallet was sticking out of it. Officer Mollring then handcuffed defendant and took both her and her purse to the patrol car. Officer Mollring testified she took the purse because the wallet had identification in it and the wallet was in the purse.

During the trip to the police station defendant became ill and an ambulance was called. Officer Maxwell was notified of their arrival. While in the sally port of the jail, Officer Mollring removed the purse from the patrol car and began searching it on the trunk of her car. Officer Maxwell was present during this search and removed certain items from the purse. An envelope containing narcotics was found in the purse.

A search warrant for defendant's house was issued based primarily on the contraband found in the purse. Pursuant to this warrant, narcotics and pay-owe sheets were seized.

DISCUSSION

"It is settled Fourth Amendment doctrine that a police officer may, incident to a lawful arrest, conduct a contemporaneous warrantless search of the arrestee's person and of the area into which the arrestee might reach to retrieve a weapon or destroy evidence." Such searches may be made whether or not there is probable cause to believe the arrestee may have a weapon or is about to destroy evidence. "The potential dangers lurking in all custodial arrests make warrantless searches of items within the 'immediate control' area reasonable without requiring the arresting officer to calculate the probability that weapons or destructible evidence may be involved. [Citations.] However, warrantless searches of luggage or other property seized at the time of an arrest cannot be justified as incident to that arrest either if the 'search is remote in time or place from the arrest,' [citation], or no exigency exists." Once law enforcement officers have reduced personal property not immediately associated with the person of the arrestee to their exclusive control, and there is no longer any danger the arrestee might gain access to the property to seize a weapon or destroy evidence, a search of that property is no longer an incident of the arrest.

Here, the property at issue is defendant's purse. The " 'search incident to arrest' rule has been interpreted to include a woman's purse as a normal extension of the person subject to search as an item 'customarily carried by an arrested person ... [and] within the area of her immediate control.' " Further, so long as the purse is in use by the arrestee at the time of her arrest, it does not need to be on her person at that moment to be subject to search.

Thus, here, a search of defendant's purse at the time of her arrest would have been justified as incident to the arrest. The purse was in use by defendant and was located on the floor of the room where the arrest took place, i.e., within the area of her immediate control. It is of no consequence that the police officers were apparently not concerned about defendant either obtaining a weapon from the purse or destroying evidence in the purse. A search is not invalidated so long as the circumstances, viewed objectively, justify the action.

However, the search was not conducted until defendant arrived at the police station. In this situation *United States v. Chadwick, supra,* requires a search warrant for personal property "not immediately associated with the person of the arrestee" which has been reduced to the officers' exclusive control. Nevertheless, other courts have held a purse could be lawfully searched without a warrant at the police station because a purse is regarded as an extension of the person for purposes of search. The person of an arrestee can be searched either at the place of arrest or at the police station.

Purse searches at the police station have also been upheld as part of the booking process. It is not inconsistent with the Fourth Amendment and therefore not unreasonable for police to conduct an inventory search as part of the booking procedure. " 'At the station house, it is entirely proper for police to remove and list or inventory property found on the person or in the possession of an arrested person who

64

is to be jailed.' " The reasonableness of the governmental activity is not controlled by the existence of alternative " ' "less intrusive " ' " means.

Generally, in the cases where the booking search of a purse has been upheld, the purse has been in the defendant's possession at the time of the arrest and the location of the arrest has not been conducive to leaving the purse behind. One exception is *People v. Bullwinkle* [where] the defendant was arrested in her home and the police took custody of her purse. The purse was later searched at the station as part of the booking process. The appellate court upheld this search noting that booking searches have traditionally been thought to extend to a purse. However, the defendant voluntarily took the purse to the station. The court commented that defendant, "knowing that she was about to be taken to jail, chose to take her purse. She had no reasonable expectation that she could take it to jail without its contents being examined." Thus, in *Bullwinkle,* by the defendant's choice, the purse was "immediately associated" with her person.

In contrast here, defendant did not choose to take her purse to jail. Rather, she removed what she wanted to take with her from the purse and thus essentially "disassociated" herself from it. Consequently, the purse should not be considered an extension of defendant's person at the time of her arrest. Further, since defendant was arrested in her home, the purse could have been safely left behind. Nevertheless, the police officers picked up the purse and took it to the station. Thus, the search of the purse at the station cannot be justified as either incident to her arrest or part of the booking procedure.

Probable cause to search a purse at the scene of the arrest can also justify a later search at the police station. In *People v. Decker* the court held since there was probable cause to search the defendant's purse for contraband at the scene of the arrest, the fact the purse was not searched until it was brought back to the police station was irrelevant.

Here, the trial court concluded the officers would have been justified in taking the large wallet containing defendant's identification, but they did not have probable cause to take the purse. The trial court found the wallet was "very big" and, in fact, would not fit into the purse. Defendant could not close the purse.

Based on these facts, the trial court's determination there was no justification for taking the purse is correct. Officer Mollring saw defendant's driver's license in the wallet. The wallet was a large, discrete item which did not even fit inside the "container," i.e., the purse. It was the driver's license the officers wanted to seize to show defendant had falsely represented her identity. Further, defendant admitted she was Peggy Ingham before she was arrested. Since there was no probable cause to search the purse at the time of the arrest, the search at the police station cannot be justified on a probable cause theory.

In sum, the search of defendant's purse at the police station does not fit within any of the exceptions to the warrant requirement. Defendant's actions with respect to the purse support the conclusion the purse was not an extension of her person at the time it was searched. Thus, the search at the station cannot be justified either as incident to the arrest or as a booking search. Further, there was no probable cause to search the purse itself. Thus, the trial court properly suppressed the evidence found inside the purse.

[The court then rejected a claim based on good-faith exception to the exclusionary rule.]

The order suppressing evidence is affirmed.

*****

CONCLUSION

The court held most notably that if the police had searched the purse at time of the arrest, it would have been a legal search-incident-to-arrest, but because they took the purse with them and searched it later it was not proper. This is an excellent example of how law enforcement officers would be better served by boning up on the law of criminal procedure! Still, many times it is difficult to predict in advance how a court will rule on a particular scenario. For police officers, it is best to err on the conservative side (in this case, search the purse immediately, knowing that the search will qualify under the exception).

REVIEW

1. Of what relevance is it that the defendant withdrew what she wanted from the purse and case the rest of the purse aside?

2. Is it relevant that her driver's license was sticking out of the purse and the purse wouldn't close? If so, how?

3. How does the ruling of this case square with the purposes of the search-incident-to-arrest exception?

II. People v. Bullock, 226 Cal.App.3d 380 (1990)

When proper exigent circumstances exist, officers may conduct a search without a warrant. In the next case, this "search" involved returning a drug dealer's pager calls.

*****

Scotland, J.

BACKGROUND

On May 23, 1988, Officer Wells of the Stockton Police Department's narcotics division received information that an employee of a local motel had observed a bag containing marijuana and white powder appearing to be cocaine in room 115. According to the employee, the room was registered to a person named Calvin Hatton. The employee also indicated that one of the room's occupants had taken the bag of suspected drugs and placed it in an Oldsmobile, the license number of which the employee provided to the police department. Officer Wells ran a Department of Motor Vehicles (DMV) check on the Oldsmobile and Hatton, obtained his description, and learned that Hatton was the registered owner of the vehicle. DMV also reported that Hatton's driver's license was suspended.

While other officers began the process of obtaining a search warrant for Hatton, his car and room 115, Wells went to the motel and began watching the Oldsmobile. After approximately 45 minutes, an individual matching Hatton's description and another person, later identified as defendant, got into the Oldsmobile and drove off.

Wells followed and radioed for assistance. At Wells's request, a patrol unit stopped the Oldsmobile, and Hatton was placed under arrest for driving with a suspended license. The passenger identified himself as defendant, and a warrant check revealed that two arrest warrants had been issued for his apprehension. Defendant was arrested pursuant to the warrants, and a search of his person revealed an electronic pager clipped to his belt and $526 cash in his pants pockets.

After an officer arrived with the search warrant, Wells searched the Oldsmobile. He found a paper bag under a blanket in the middle of the front seat. Inside the bag were three zip-lock baggies containing rock cocaine, two baggies containing marijuana, a sixth baggie containing a mixture of cocaine base in marijuana, and another baggie which held "numerous smaller empty zip-lock bindles."

During the hour it took Wells to complete the arrest report and booking procedure, defendant's pager signalled on at least 20 occasions that it had received messages. Based upon his training and experience in drug investigations, Wells knew that pagers are commonly used by drug dealers to facilitate the sale of controlled substances "via customers phoning up requesting an amount and naming a location for delivery." Realizing that the incoming calls might be of evidentiary value, Wells retrieved the callers' numbers by pushing a button which caused the numbers to be displayed on a screen on top of the pager. Some of the numbers appeared to be in code; others were regular seven-digit phone numbers. Wells called the telephone numbers. Three or four of the individuals who answered requested the delivery of cocaine. A typical request asked for a "twenty dollar rock."

An employee of the paging company testified that each of its subscribers is assigned a dedicated telephone number which he or she provides to persons wishing to contact the subscriber. To leave a message, a person calls that number, waits for a recorded message directing him or her to enter a numerical message, and then enters an identifying code number or a telephone number where the caller can be reached. When the pager receives a message, it will beep or vibrate. At the push of a button, the caller's code number or telephone number will appear on its display screen. Messages intended for a particular pager cannot be received by other units unless they are specially programmed to do so. Persons listening to a radio tuned to the frequency used by the pagers would not hear spoken messages but might hear the tones produced by the caller's touch-tone telephone. The pager seized from defendant had a memory that could store a maximum of four messages for retrieval at a later time.

DISCUSSION

Defendant correctly contends that the officer's activation of the pager's display mechanism constituted a "search" within the meaning of the federal and state Constitutions.

[The court notes that it was a search because defendant had a reasonable expectation of privacy in the information recorded in his pager, since the numbers weren't in plain view and unlike voice messages could not be heard by the public.]

[D]efendant does not claim that Officer Wells lacked probable cause to intrude upon defendant's reasonable expectation of privacy. Wells, an expert in the investigation of drug trafficking, knew that illicit drugs had been seen in a room which the officer reasonably could believe was occupied by defendant. Moreover, the drugs were later seized from a vehicle in which defendant was riding. Based upon the quantity and packaging of the drugs, the additional empty bindles, the large amount of cash found on defendant, and the pager-an instrument commonly used in selling illegal drugs-Wells had probable cause to believe that defendant was engaged in drug trafficking. Accordingly, Wells properly seized the pager as an instrument used in the commission of the crimes for which defendant was arrested. Thereafter, each time the pager signalled it had received a message, Wells had ample reason to believe that the incoming call was related to defendant's criminal activity. Thus, he had probable cause to search the beeper by activating the numerical display screen to obtain the message.

Nevertheless, defendant contends that the search could not be conducted without a warrant. Recognizing that the existence of exigent circumstances may excuse the warrant requirement he claims that no exigency existed here. At this point, we must part company with defendant.

Defendant relies on *United States v. Chadwick*. However, that case does not support his argument. In *Chadwick*, federal agents made a warrantless seizure of a footlocker which they had probable cause to believe contained illegal drugs. Thereafter, they transported the footlocker to a federal building where it was opened and marijuana was discovered. In finding the search unlawful, the Supreme Court, inter alia, rejected the prosecution's claim that the footlocker's mobility justified dispensing with the warrant requirement. The court reasoned that once federal agents had seized the footlocker and transported it to headquarters under their exclusive control, there was no risk that the evidence could be destroyed or lost during the time it would take agents to obtain a search warrant.

Such was not the case here. Every activation of defendant's pager by an incoming call signalled a reasonable likelihood that the message was for the purpose of ordering drugs. Thus, each call constituted potentially incriminating evidence against defendant. In addition, each message was evidence of a new offense, attempted possession of controlled substances by another offender whom Officer Wells had the authority to apprehend. Contrary to defendant's claim, the evidence established that a danger existed that the incoming telephone numbers would be lost unless quickly retrieved by the officer. As the prosecutor argued in opposition to the motion to suppress: "With information coming across the pager, if you don't activate it then and retrieve the information, you are not going to be able to get it. So certainly an exigency of circumstances [exists]. You can't just wait and 24 hours later have the same information."

Defendant stresses the fact that the pager could store incoming calls. Thus, he implies that the prosecution made no showing that any delay to obtain a warrant would result in the destruction of evidence. We disagree. The pager could store a maximum of four telephone numbers; yet, at least twenty were received during the booking process. Necessarily, some of those numbers would have been lost had the officer not timely retrieved them.

More importantly, in our view a reasonable, well-trained officer should not be expected to know the storage capacities, if any, of all the pagers on the market. Even if the officer were aware that the pager had some storage capacity, given the uncertainty of how many calls might come in, he should not be required to gamble on whether, due to the pager's limited memory capacity, any of the stored information may be lost during the time it would take to obtain a search warrant. The very real possibility that the evidence might be lost if not timely retrieved created an exigent circumstance necessitating the officer's immediate action. Given this exigency, Officer Wells was justified in immediately retrieving the numbers without first obtaining a search warrant.

Assuming an officer were aware that a pager had an unlimited ability to store incoming telephone numbers, the immediate retrieval of incoming messages would be justified by another exigency: the need to return the calls in a timely manner while the callers were likely to be present at the numbers they had indicated. When reasonable cause exists to suspect that the callers might be seeking to acquire drugs, an officer reasonably could believe that their need to buy drugs was acute and that they might turn to other sources if their calls were not promptly returned. Thus, any delay in returning the calls could result in the loss of evidence of illegal drug activity.

Since exigent circumstances permitted Officer Wells to dispense with the warrant requirement, the trial court properly denied defendant's motion to suppress.

The judgment is affirmed.

CONCLUSION

The court held first that activating a pager constituted a "search" under the Fourth Amendment and therefore must be held to be reasonable. Since the officer failed to get a search warrant before searching defendant's property (the pager), an exigent circumstances must exist. The danger of losing evidence cropping up during each "beep" constituted such a danger, according the court, rendering the search of the pager reasonable under the circumstances.

REVIEW

1. Why could the pager not be searched as a search-incident-to-arrest?

2. Why does the defendant bring up the point that the pager could store calls? What is the state's response?

CHAPTER SEVEN

Special-Needs Searches

OVERVIEW

In this chapter we consider special-needs searches, also termed "administrative searches." The driving motivation behind these searches is not necessarily criminal investigation, but a range of other needs, usually relating to maintaining order and protecting the public. These needs are balanced with concerns for individual privacy. Examples of types of administrative searches are:

- Inspection of housing
- Inspection of businesses
- Welfare inspections
- Fire inspections
- Border searches
- Sobriety checkpoints
- Routine license and registration inspections
- Airport searches
- Searches of students
- Parole searches
- Probation searches
- Hospital testing

Administrative searches are usually held to implicate the Fourth Amendment, but require a standard of proof that is somewhat less than probable cause (e.g., reasonable suspicion). In the leading case of *Camara v. Municipal Court*, 387 U.S. 523, the U.S. Supreme Court addressed these searches in the context of housing inspections, laying out a balancing test that involves the consideration of whether the type of search (1) is historically accepted by the public and judiciary, (2) is necessary to accomplish acceptable results, and (3) only minimally invades privacy.

The following statutes are samples of legal rules of for two types of administrative searches: searches of students, and searches of parolees. Education Code section 49050 limits the intrusiveness of searches by school employees, and Penal Code section 3067 delineates the conditions for special-needs searches of parolees.

Education Code Section 49050. Prohibited searches

No school employee shall conduct a search that involves:

(a) Conducting a body cavity search of a pupil manually or with an instrument.

(b) Removing or arranging any or all of the clothing of a pupil to permit

70

a visual inspection of the underclothing, breast, buttocks, or genitalia of the pupil.

Penal Code Section 3067. Search or seizure; written agreement; application; intent

(a) Any inmate who is eligible for release on parole pursuant to this chapter shall agree in writing to be subject to search or seizure by a parole officer or other peace officer at any time of the day or night, with or without a search warrant and with or without cause.

(b) Any inmate who does not comply with the provision of subdivision (a) shall lose worktime credit and shall not be released until he or she either complies with the provision of subdivision (a) or has no remaining worktime credit, whichever occurs earlier.

CASES-

I. In re Randy G., 26 Cal.4th 556 (2001)

School searches are held to the standard of "reasonable suspicion" just as in a *Terry* stop. But what about detentions that lead to searches—what level of proof is necessary for detentions occurring in schools? The California Supreme Court addressed this in the following case.

*****

Baxter, J.

BACKGROUND

A petition filed alleged that the 14-year-old minor had violated the penal code by possessing a knife with a locking blade on school grounds. Prior to the jurisdictional hearing, the minor moved to suppress evidence of the knife, asserting that its discovery during a consent search had been tainted by the preceding illegal detention in violation of the Fourth Amendment. Moving him from the classroom into the hallway for questioning was, he claimed, an unreasonable detention because there was no articulable basis for a reasonable suspicion that he had engaged or was engaging in the proscribed activity, i.e., violation of a criminal statute or school rule. The motion was denied, after which the petition was sustained. The minor was declared a ward of the court and placed on probation.

The evidence offered at the hearing on the motion to suppress reflects the following:

Cathy Worthy, a campus security officer at the public high school attended by the minor, testified that during "passing time," approximately 9:00 a.m. on March 16, 1999, she was between "C building and A auditorium." As she came around one of two large pillars in that area, she observed the minor and a friend in an area of the campus in which students are not permitted to congregate. When the minor saw Worthy, he "fixed his pocket very nervously." Some of the lining of the left pocket was still sticking out. Worthy asked the two if they needed anything and instructed them to go to class. The minor finished fixing his pocket and went back to class. Worthy followed them to see where they were going because the minor acted "very paranoid and nervous." She then notified her supervisor and at his direction summoned another security officer.

When the two officers went to the classroom, Worthy asked the minor if she could see him outside. Once in the hallway, Worthy asked the minor if he had anything on him. He replied "no" and repeated that denial when asked again. The second officer asked the minor for consent to search his bag. The minor consented, and replied "no" again to Worthy's repeated question whether he had anything on him. The second officer then asked the minor for permission to do a patdown search. Worthy asked if it was okay, and the minor replied "yes." A patdown search by the other officer revealed a knife, later found to have a locking blade, in the minor's left pocket.

During the 10 minutes the minor was in the hallway being questioned by Worthy before the consent to search was given, he was not free to leave.

Commenting that the officer had engaged in "good security work" based on the minor's looking nervous or paranoid and adjusting his pocket upon seeing her, the judge denied the motion to suppress.

On appeal from the order declaring him a ward of the court, the minor repeated the arguments made in support of his motion to exclude the knife-i.e., that because the campus security officer had lacked reasonable suspicion of criminal activity or violation of a school rule, the detention violated his right to be free of unreasonable searches and seizures guaranteed by the Fourth Amendment, and that his consent to search was a product of that unlawful detention. The Court of Appeal agreed with the minor that the standard to be applied was whether "the detaining officer has reasonable suspicion that the person to be detained has been, is, or is about to be engaged in criminal activity" or is about to engage in a violation of those school rules that exist for the protection of other students attending school or for the preservation of order at the school. The *Frederick B.* court had adapted its standard for judging the lawfulness of a *detention* of a student from [two Supreme Court cases], both of which involved the *search* of a student. Applying that standard (as expanded to include school rules and regulations designed for the protection of students or the preservation of order), the Court of Appeal held that the detention of the minor was reasonable. The minor's violation of a school rule, together with his nervous fixing of the protruding lining of his pocket, gave rise to reasonable suspicion sufficient to justify a detention for the purpose of asking questions about the conduct the security officer had observed.

In this court, the minor contends that no articulable facts supported a reasonable suspicion of misconduct. The People argue that the reasonable- suspicion standard does not apply to a detention of a student by a school official on school grounds.

DISCUSSION

According to the minor, the question presented here is whether the circumstances outlined above "made the security officer aware of sufficient ' articulable facts' to warrant reasonable suspicion that [the minor] was committing a crime, or violating a rule designed to protect other students or to maintain order in the school, thereby justifying his detention for investigation of the offense." He contends that the absence of facts supporting reasonable suspicion rendered his detention invalid under the Fourth Amendment, requiring suppression of the locking-blade knife found in his pocket.

To decide whether relevant evidence obtained by assertedly unlawful means must be excluded, we look exclusively to whether its suppression is required by the United States Constitution.

The first question, then, is whether the minor was detained.). A detention occurs "[o]nly when the officer, by means of physical force or show of authority, has in some way restrained the liberty of a citizen ...." In the general run of cases, where the police have succeeded in apprehending the suspect, there is no dispute that the suspect's liberty has been thereby restrained. After all, in those cases, the defendant, in the absence of the stop, would have been free to continue on his way.

A minor at school, however, can hardly be said to be free to continue on his or her way. "Traditionally at common law, and still today, unemancipated minors lack some of the most fundamental rights of self-determination-including even the right of liberty in its narrow sense, *i.e.*, the right to come and go at will. They are subject, even as to their physical freedom, to the control of their parents or guardians." Although the high court has rejected the notion that public schools, like private schools, exercise only parental power over their students, the power that public schools do exercise is nonetheless "custodial and tutelary, permitting a degree of supervision and control that could not be exercised over free adults."

To begin, minor students are required to be in school. While they are there, the "primary duty of school officials and teachers ... is the education and training of young people. A State has a compelling interest in assuring that the schools meet this responsibility. Without first establishing discipline and maintaining order, teachers cannot begin to educate their students. And apart from education, the school has the obligation to protect pupils from mistreatment by other children, and also to protect teachers themselves from violence by the few students whose conduct in recent years has prompted national concern. California fulfills its obligations by requiring each school board to establish rules and regulations to govern student conduct and discipline and by permitting the local district to establish a police or security department to enforce those rules.

At school, events calling for discipline are frequent occurrences and sometimes require "immediate, effective action." To respond in an appropriate manner, " 'teachers and school administrators must have broad supervisory and disciplinary powers.' " California law, for example, permits principals, teachers, and any other certificated employees to exercise "the same degree of physical control over a pupil that a parent would be legally privileged to exercise ... which in no event shall exceed the amount of physical control reasonably necessary to maintain order, protect property, or protect the health and safety of pupils, or to maintain proper and appropriate conditions conducive to learning."

Encounters on school grounds between students and school personnel are constant and much more varied than those on the street between citizens and law enforcement officers. While at school, a student may be stopped, told to remain in or leave a classroom, directed to go to a particular classroom, given an errand, sent to study hall, called to the office, or held after school. Unlike a citizen on the street, a minor student is "subject to the ordering and direction of teachers and administrators.... [¶] [A student is] not free to roam the halls or to remain in [the] classroom as long as she please[s], even if she behave[s] herself. She [is] deprived of liberty to some degree from the moment she enter[s] school, and no one could suggest a constitutional infringement based on that basic deprivation."

Thus, when a school official stops a student to ask a question, it would appear that the student's liberty has not been restrained over and above the limitations he or she already experiences by attending school. Accordingly, the conduct of school officials in moving students about the classroom or from one classroom to another, sending students to the office, or taking them into the hallway to ask a question would not seem to qualify as a detention as defined by the Fourth Amendment. In the absence of a Fourth Amendment claim, relief, if at all, would come by showing that school officials acted in such an arbitrary manner as to deprive the student of substantive due process in violation of the Fourteenth Amendment.

A number of factors, however, counsel caution before holding that the Fourth Amendment does not apply to the exercise of physical control by school officials over their students. First, we must acknowledge the United States Supreme Court's reluctance to expand the concept of substantive due process. The court has instructed that " '[w]here a particular Amendment provides an explicit textual source of constitutional protection against *a particular sort of government behavior*, that Amendment, not the more generalized notion of substantive due process, must be the guide for analyzing these claims.' " Here, of course, the "particular sort of government behavior" engaged in by school officials would unquestionably constitute a detention *outside* the school setting.

Second, we have employed the Fourth Amendment framework in the analogous circumstances of parole and probation searches, even though it might appear that parolees and probationers have no Fourth Amendment protection against suspicionless searches and seizures. In *Tyrell J.*, for example, we held that a juvenile probationer subject to a valid search condition does not have a *reasonable* expectation of privacy over his or her person or property, which is the " 'touchstone' " of Fourth Amendment analysis. Nonetheless, we rejected the notion that the probationer has no legally cognizable privacy rights at all and permitted the probationer to challenge a search as arbitrary, capricious, or undertaken for harassment. Similarly, in *Reyes*, we held that a parolee subject to a valid search condition does not have "any expectation of privacy 'society is " prepared to recognize as legitimate" ' " yet may still challenge the search as arbitrary, capricious, or undertaken for harassment. By analogy, we might permit a minor student, even though he appears to retain no appreciable liberty on school grounds, to challenge the conduct of school officials as arbitrary, capricious, or harassing under the Fourth Amendment, which, after all, was crafted to " ' "safeguard the privacy and security of individuals against *arbitrary* invasions by governmental officials." ' ..."

Finally, we note that a number of federal cases have (without much analysis) held or assumed that, notwithstanding the considerable restraints on a student's movement by virtue of being at school, conduct by a school official to control that movement is a seizure within the meaning of the Fourth Amendment.

Neither this court nor the Supreme Court has deemed stopping a student on school grounds during school hours, calling a student into the corridor to discuss a school-related matter, or summoning a student to the principal's office for such purposes to be a detention within the meaning of the Fourth Amendment. For the reasons stated above, we would be hesitant to term such conduct a "detention" here. However, we find it unnecessary to decide whether school officials' infringement on the residuum of liberty retained by the student is properly analyzed as a detention under the Fourth Amendment or as a deprivation of substantive due process under the Fourteenth Amendment, for (as we explain below) we discover that the test under either clause is substantially the same-namely, whether the school officials' conduct was arbitrary, capricious, or undertaken for purposes of harassment.

Although individualized suspicion is usually a prerequisite to a constitutional search or seizure, "such suspicion is not an 'irreducible' component of reasonableness." Under the Constitution, the usual prerequisites can be modified when " 'special needs' " render those rules impracticable. Special needs" exist "in the public school context." In *T. L. O.*, for example, the court permitted the on-campus search of a minor student's person, the type of intrusion that ordinarily must be supported by probable cause to believe a violation of the law has occurred, so long as there were reasonable grounds for suspecting the search would uncover evidence of a violation of law or school rules. In *Vernonia*, the court approved drug testing of student-athletes, even in the absence of any individualized suspicion of drug use, based once again on the special needs of the public school context.

Vernonia and *T. L. O.* both involved searches. The issue here is a seizure. Still, the test for assessing the reasonableness of official conduct under the Fourth Amendment is essentially the same: "it is necessary ' first to focus upon the governmental interest which allegedly justifies official intrusion upon the constitutionally protected interests of the private citizen,' for there is 'no ready test for determining reasonableness other than by balancing the need to search [or seize] against the invasion which the search [or seizure] entails.' " Here, "the ' reasonableness' inquiry cannot disregard the schools' custodial and tutelary responsibility for children."

The governmental interest at stake is of the highest order. "[E]ducation is perhaps the most important function of state and local governments." Some modicum of discipline and order is essential if the educational function is to be performed." School personnel, to maintain or promote order, may need to send students into and out of classrooms, define or alter schedules, summon students to the office, or question them in the hall. Yet, as the high court has observed, school officials "are not in the business of investigating violations of the criminal laws ... and otherwise have little occasion to become familiar with the intricacies of this Court's Fourth Amendment jurisprudence." Those officials must be permitted to exercise their broad supervisory and disciplinary powers, without worrying that every encounter with a student will be converted into an opportunity for constitutional review. To allow minor students to challenge each of those decisions, through a motion to suppress or in a civil rights action under, as lacking articulable facts supporting reasonable suspicion would make a mockery of school discipline and order.

On the other hand, the intrusion on the minor student is trivial since, as stated, the minor is not free to move about during the school day. If the school can require the minor's presence on campus during school hours, attendance at assigned classes during their scheduled meeting times, appearance at assemblies in the auditorium, and participation in physical education classes out of doors, liberty is scarcely infringed if a school security guard leads the student into the hall to ask questions about a potential rule violation.

In *T. L. O.*, the court balanced the competing interests involving a search of a minor student on school grounds and reduced the quantum of suspicion required from probable cause to reasonable suspicion. The minor argues that the same reasonable-suspicion standard used for school searches should govern the assumed detention here. We disagree. Different interests are implicated by a search than by a seizure, and a seizure is "generally less intrusive" than a search. In recognition of that distinction, the constitutionality of investigative detentions of persons on the streets is already measured by the standard of reasonable suspicion, not probable cause. Were we simply to extend that standard to the school setting, we would have failed utterly to accommodate the special needs existing there. Therefore, we conclude instead that detentions of minor students on school grounds do not offend the Constitution, so long as they are not arbitrary, capricious, or for the purposes of harassment.

Our conclusion finds support in cases from other jurisdictions. In school officials, after learning that police had received an anonymous tip that the minor had a gun, removed the minor from class and brought him to the principal's office. The gun was discovered during a consent search. The minor sought to suppress the gun as the fruit of an unlawful detention. The court assessed the reasonableness of the school officials' conduct in removing the minor from class by balancing the state's substantial interest in maintaining a safe educational environment against the minor's limited control over his person during school hours and concluded that the policy served by *Terry*'s reasonable-suspicion standard does not apply to the detention and questioning of a student by school officials. The court noted, as we have above, that "the mere detention and questioning of a student constitutes a more limited intrusion than a search of his person and effects. Thus, we think it makes no sense to require the same level of suspicion to justify the school officials' actions in each situation." "To require teachers and school officials to have reasonable suspicion before merely questioning a student would destroy the informality of the student teacher relationship, which the United States Supreme Court has respected and preserved. Instead, teachers and school officials would be forced to conduct surveillance, traditionally a law enforcement function, before questioning a student about conduct which poses a serious threat to the safety of the students for whom they are responsible."

The minor has never contended that Worthy acted arbitrarily, capriciously, or in a harassing manner in calling him into the hall. Hence, no Fourth Amendment violation occurred.

Seemingly acknowledging the state's vital interest in establishing and maintaining a safe educational environment, the minor then urges that the reasonable-suspicion standard, even if inapplicable to the conduct of teachers and administrators, should apply to encounters between students and school *security officers*. In holding that the reasonable-suspicion standard remains appropriate for such cases, he reasons, this court will not necessarily be committing itself to that standard "across the whole range of student encounters with teachers, principals, or other personnel." We decline the invitation to distinguish the power of school security officers over students from that of other school personnel, whose authority over student conduct may have been delegated to those officers. The same observation and investigation here could well have been undertaken by a teacher, coach, or even the school principal or vice-principal. If we were to draw the distinction urged by the minor, the extent of a student's rights would depend not on the nature of the asserted infringement but on the happenstance of the status of the employee who observed and investigated the misconduct. Of equal importance, were we to hold that school security officers have less authority to enforce school regulations and investigate misconduct than other school personnel, there would be no reason for a school to employ them or delegate to them duties relating to school safety. Schools would be forced instead to assign certificated or classified personnel to yard and hall monitoring duties, an expenditure of resources schools can ill afford. The title "security officer" is not constitutionally significant. Therefore, we will not interfere in the method by which local school districts assign personnel to monitor school safety.

The judgment of the Court of Appeal is affirmed.

*****

CONCLUSION

The student in this case argued that the legality of his seizure should be governed by reasonable suspicion under the Fourth Amendment and that the security guard lacked such suspicion in stopping him (a stop which resulted in a consent search which turned up a knife). The California Supreme Court wobbled around the question of whether the Fourth Amendment applied, holding that it didn't matter whether the Fourth Amendment or the Fourteenth Amendment's Due Process Clause applied—the result is the same, that the test for a detention of a student on school grounds is okay as long as it is not "arbitrary, capricious, or for the purposes of harassment."

REVIEW

1. What are the arguments for and against the Fourth Amendment being applied to detentions of students in schools?

2. What is the level of proof required for searches of students in schools? Why is this level not required for seizures—what does the court say about the difference between searches and seizures?

3. If reasonable suspicion had applied, do you think the security guard's detention of Randy G. was valid?

4. What are the "special interests" involved in school settings that require lowering the level of proof necessary for invasions of privacy?

CHAPTER EIGHT

Police Interrogations and Confessions

In this chapter we examine one key police and prosecutorial investigative tool: gaining confessions from suspects during interrogations. While confessions are crucial to crime control, allowing police to have unfettered discretion in gaining confessions leads to abuse. This has led the Supreme Court over several decades to put up safeguards, such as the requirement that police read suspects *Miranda* rights prior to custodial interrogation. We'll look first at how shoddy interrogations may lead to false confessions. Then we'll examine the *Miranda* requirements, looking at a case dealing with the meaning of "interrogation" and a case dealing with a rescue exception to the general requirement. Finally we'll discuss what it means to have "waived" *Miranda* rights.

Section 1: The Interrogation and Confession Setting

OVERVIEW

It is commonly believed that people do not falsely confess to something they did not do. After all, why would they? However, false confessions do occur, and for multiple reasons. Some people crave attention, and a false confession puts them in the limelight. Others have psychological conditions resulting in a belief they have done something when they have in fact not. And finally, coercive police interrogations may result in a person confessing to something they know they did not do, or perhaps via such interrogations they come to believe they did something that they are innocent of.

Consider the incredible case of the murder of Stephanie Crowe, in Escondido, outside of San Diego. The 12-year-old was murdered in her house in 1998, brutally stabbed nine times. The Escondido police investigation immediately turned toward family members, since they believed it was an inside job. Another possibility was a local transient who had been in trouble for accosting other similarly-aged girls, and had been in the neighborhood recently peeping in windows, but they disregarded this avenue. Instead, they turned to coercive interrogation tactics directed at Stephanie's brother Michael and his friends, working toward a conspiracy theory where Michael and his friend Aaron killed Stephanie with their friend Josh's knife. During these so-called "confessions" police relied on a number of heavily coercive tactics, including sleep-deprivation, lying to the juveniles (e.g., telling Michael that Stephanie's blood was found in his bedroom), and using an unproven voice stress machine to repeatedly claim that the boys were lying. In the case of Michael, he was interrogated for hours on end without his parents being informed. Michael became so confused he eventually decided he must have done it, that there was a "bad Michael" (as the police told him there must be) that was responsible—he just didn't remember how he did it. Josh was told he would take the fall for his friends' actions, and he eventually constructed a scenario in which his friends were responsible. The investigation began with the assumption the boys were responsible, based on extreme interrogation practices, and all subsequent forensic evidence was gathered under this theory—the possibility that the transient, Richard Tuite, was responsible was ignored, since it wasn't consistent with their theory.

In the end, the forensic evidence gathered did not support the prosecution's theory very well, but the prosecution still had partial confessional evidence to be presented at trial (some parts of the confessions were disallowed as violating *Miranda*) and the prevailing sentiment in the area was that the boys had done it. On the eve of the trial, due to efforts by one of the defense attorneys, blood was finally matched from Tuitte's clothing and Stephanie's DNA: a direct hit, Stephanie's blood was on Tuitte's garments. As this book is in publication, Tuitte is on trial for the murder of Stephanie Crowe. How can police tactics lead to false confessions? Put yourself in the shoes of a confused 12-year-old who is put in a small room without his parents for hour upon hour and bombarded by hostile questioning by police officers, told scores of lies, and threatened that his days of freedom are over, and try to imagine the possibilities. In the following sections we explore the laws that try to safeguard these practices. For more information on the Stephanie Crowe case, visit the San Diego Union-Tribune's special report on the case, at www.signonsandiego.com/news/reports/crowe.

Section 2: Miranda v. Arizona

OVERVIEW

By now you are probably familiar with the guts of the *Miranda* decision. The warnings include suspects' right to remain silent, that anything said may be held against them, that they are entitled to an attorney, and that if they cannot afford an attorney one will be provided for them. Statements taken in violation of these warnings cannot be introduced as evidence against their guilt (but may be used to impeach their credibility if they take the stand). Most of the controversy in this area deals with what is interrogation (officers' words that should be known would elicit an incriminating response about the crime in question), what is custody (an inherently coercive atmosphere where the suspect doesn't feel free to leave) and what is a valid waiver (a knowing and voluntary one). We'll discuss two California cases in this section—one dealing with the interrogation question and one with a unique exception to the general rule, involving the rescue of a defendant by an officer.

CASES-

I. People v. Morris, 192 Cal.App.3d 380 (1987)

*****

Hamlin, J.

BACKGROUND

Defendant and his brother, Richard Dean Morris, were jointly charged with the 1984 murder of Cindy Marie Morris, their sister-in-law. Following a separate jury trial of defendant, he was convicted as charged. Defendant appeals from the ensuing judgment sentencing him to prison for a term of 25 years to life.

On appeal, defendant contends his conviction must be reversed because the trial court erred prejudicially in admitting evidence of his statements during renewed booking interrogation and in instructing the jury. We disagree for the reasons stated below and affirm the judgment.

Paramedic Donald Campbell was dispatched to 5316 Ninth Street in Keyes about 6:30 a.m. on October 6, 1984. Upon entering the house Campbell found a female body, later identified as 22-year-old Cindy Morris, lying in a bed and covered up to the neck. The body was cool to the touch and showed signs of bruising on the neck and face.

At about noon that same day, Dr. William Ernoehazy performed an autopsy and determined strangulation by hand caused Cindy's death. He also opined that numerous abrasions and contusions of Cindy's face and neck occurred as the result of at least three separate applications of force.

The day before Cindy's death, Cindy's mother observed that defendant appeared to be very angry with Cindy; after defendant said something to Cindy, she appeared nervous and told her mother she was having trouble with defendant. Moreover, in the weeks preceding the death and during conversations at which both defendant and Rick were present, defendant's sister, Bonnie Rose Lankford, heard remarks that she could "bank on" Cindy's death and also overheard a conversation about a drug which could not be detected in a victim's system. Bonnie believed her brothers were angry with Cindy because Cindy did not want them around Randy. Bonnie heard defendant say that he would like to kill "that bitch"; defendant thought Cindy was a bad influence on Randy and also claimed that Cindy was going out with other men.

Bonnie's boyfriend, Danny Doster, had also heard defendant talking about Cindy "going out on" Randy. Additionally defendant had asked Doster on several occasions prior to Cindy's death if Doster could get them some pills which they could use to kill Cindy. Like Bonnie, Doster was told he could "bank on" Cindy's death, and defendant offered Doster a thousand dollars to keep his mouth shut. Doster did not take defendant's threats seriously since defendant and Rick were always "running their mouths," i.e., threatening to do something to someone.

A second sister of defendant, Rick, and Randy, Susan Marie Kreiter, and Kreiter's husband, Douglas, testified under grants of immunity about the false alibi they furnished defendant at his request. When defendant and Rick first arrived at the Kreiter residence on October 6, 1984, defendant told Susan that he had killed Cindy and that he and Rick needed an alibi. Susan said both were dirty and sweaty and seemed nervous, pale, and shaky. Once joined by Douglas Kreiter, defendant related in detail the story of Cindy's death, telling the Kreiters how Cindy had struggled from the bedroom to the kitchen and then back into the bedroom. Rick told the Kreiters he watched defendant's back and at one time helped defendant hold Cindy down. When Cindy screamed, defendant put a pillow over her face to muffle the sound, and defendant told Susan he had kept socks on his hands during the killing to conceal fingerprints. He said he thought Cindy was dead at one point, but she sat up in bed and he had to 'redo " it. After the second strangling, defendant checked Cindy's pulse twice to be sure that she was dead before leaving the house. Defendant told Susan he had killed Cindy because she was mistreating Randy by stealing money from him, going out on him, and neglecting their daughter and because Cindy had told Randy to tell defendant and Rick to stay away.

Defendant asked Susan to tell the police that he and Rick had stayed at her house that night and had left town following a fight with their sister Bonnie. Defendant told the Kreiters he would give them in exchange for the alibi $10,000 (per Susan) or $5,000 (per Douglas) from the $20,000 he was supposed to get for killing Cindy. Several witnesses testified that defendant was to get $20,000 of the insurance proceeds, Rick was to get $10,000 for his participation, and Randy would keep the remainder. However, the Kreiters told defendant they did not want the money. Defendant told Susan that Randy was supposed to be jogging at the time of the killing but came home too soon and had to be sent out again. Defendant told Randy to be sure to be seen. Randy, dressed in a jogging suit, did in fact stop by at a neighbor's house about 6 a.m. on October 6, where he had a cup of coffee. The neighbor, Charles Gibson, knew Randy but testified he had never seen Randy out jogging before nor had Randy ever stopped by Gibson's house at that early hour.

Shortly after this discussion about their need for an alibi, defendant and Douglas Kreiter went to the store, and defendant told Kreiter the killing had been hard, and he had not realized she would fight as she did.

Both Susan and Douglas Kreiter initially gave police the false alibi which defendant had requested, stories which both Kreiters recanted when threatened with prosecution. Both Kreiters confirmed, however, that when defendant learned on the day of the killing that Randy had been arrested, defendant wanted to turn himself in but was dissuaded by family members. Apparently it was not clear whether Randy had been, in fact, arrested or whether he had merely been taken to the hospital.

Defendant also made incriminating statements to Timothy Leroy Martin which were overheard by Martin's girlfriend Lori Kaufman. Both Martin and Kaufman testified; defendant explained to Martin that he had killed Cindy by strangling her and left the body covered in order to keep it warm. Rick admitted he was involved in the killing by helping to hold Cindy down. Explaining his motivation, defendant said Cindy was "bringing Randy down by not keeping house and that general type of stuff," and defendant also told Martin he was supposed to get $20,000 of the insurance proceeds, while Rick got $10,000 and Randy kept the rest. Defendant had supplied drugs, primarily methamphetamine and marijuana, to both Martin and Kaufman, as well as most of the other non-law-enforcement witnesses in this case; many of these witnesses testified they might well have been under the influence of one or more of these drugs at the time they heard or engaged in those conversations to which they testified. Two additional statements by defendant were introduced into evidence, one of which, that made to a police officer, Gary Dean Wilkerson, is the focus of defendant's first issue on appeal and need not be reiterated here. However, Leland Cupp testified he was present in a holding cell at the Stanislaus County Municipal Court when he overheard defendant say to Rick and to other men, "'The bitch sat up and I had to kill her again,'" and "'It's not the first time she's done this. She's nothing but a whore.'"

Defendant took the stand in his own defense and testified that he had known Cindy for some time prior to her marriage to Randy. The relationship was not a friendly one, and defendant acknowledged some disagreements with Cindy because of her reluctance to let Randy associate with him and with Rick. Defendant claimed he never had words directly with Cindy, but asked Randy to speak to her about it. Defendant also admitted that during the three months prior to Cindy's death he had made statements that he would like to kill her but was not serious when he made the statements. For the year preceding her death, defendant had used methamphetamine on a daily basis, maintaining about a $300 per day habit which he financed by selling drugs to others. Defendant also smoked marijuana every day and used heroin to "come down" from prolonged methamphetamine use.

Defendant had been using methamphetamine for the week preceding Cindy's death and had gone without sleep for most of that time. On the night of the killing, defendant argued with his sister Bonnie and then went to a park near his parents' home with Rick where the two smoked marijuana and Rick tried to calm defendant down. Rick went home after about an hour and a half, and defendant went to visit a friend to look for drugs. About 6 a.m. defendant arrived at Randy and Cindy's house where he told Cindy he had come to collect some money that Randy owed him. When Cindy told defendant Randy would not pay him and started "mean mouthing" defendant and threatening to tell Randy defendant had made advances to her, defendant slapped Cindy. When Cindy lunged at him, defendant grabbed her and strangled her. Defendant claimed he did not know what was going through his mind at the time, that he was just mad at Cindy and had not gone to their residence with any intention of killing her.

81

At the hearing to determine the admissibility of defendant's testimony, Officer Wilkerson testified he had already completed the booking process and placed defendant in a holding cell when he, Wilkerson, remembered he had forgotten to place an identifying wrist bracelet on defendant. Consequently Wilkerson removed defendant from the holding cell and noted that defendant, who had been upset, nervous, and crying during the booking process, was somewhat calmed down. Wilkerson then asked defendant, "if we should anticipate any type of problem with his being there in jail." When defendant replied, "'I don't think so,'" Wilkerson went on and asked defendant "' Who are you accused of killing?'" Defendant "cried a little bit and then he stated, 'My brother, Randy Morris, was in last October for it.' And 'I never did anything like this before - I killed my sister-in-law.'" Defendant was "still very shaken up, very nervous." Wilkerson was unequivocal in his testimony that these questions were asked of defendant solely for the purpose of jail security and not to elicit information from defendant that might be used against him. Wilkerson defined jail security as his suspicion that "there might be some problem with the person that he was accused of killing having relatives or close friends in the jail or could be some type of retaliation." Wilkerson testified this is a procedure normally conducted when someone is about to be jailed for a serious offense such as murder or violent assault.

DISCUSSION

In rejecting defendant's contention that the statements were obtained in violation of his *Miranda* rights and therefore were inadmissible at trial, the trial court held that:

"The Court: It would appear that based on the cases that the People have cited in their trial brief on this issue, questions asked during the booking process and not done for interrogation which elicit gratuitous type answers, are not considered to be interrogation and can be admissible in spite of their failure of a Miranda warning or Defendant requesting his rights under Miranda.

"Here the two questions asked, 'Would there be any trouble, yes or no,' that certainly didn't call for any type of incriminating answer. The question, 'Who are you accused of killing,' that would not call for an incriminating answer. Accordingly, based on the law as set forth in the cases just cited by the Court, and the nature of the questions asked, the Court will admit the testimony."

We believe the trial court's conclusion is erroneous under the standard announced by the United States Supreme Court in *Rhode Island* v. *Innis, supra.* Even the first question asked by Officer Wilkerson, i.e., whether jail personnel should anticipate any "trouble" in connection with defendant's incarceration, given the context of possible retaliation by members of the victim's family or the victim's friends, goes well beyond the type of neutral questioning permissible in a booking interview. Moreover, when defendant answered equivocally and Wilkerson pursued the matter, asking defendant who defendant had been accused of killing, it seems obvious that this is the type of police conduct which "the police should know [is] reasonably likely to elicit an incriminating response from the suspect."

The standard here is not what the police absolutely know; it is what they *should* know is *reasonably* likely to elicit an incriminating response from a suspect. As the court in *Rhode Island* v. *Innis* made clear, the focus in this inquiry is not on objective proof that the police were intending to elicit an incriminating response; rather the focus is on the subjective perceptions of the suspect. It is much too narrow a reading of *Rhode Island v. Innis* to conclude that simply phrasing a question addressed to a criminal suspect in terms of "accusation" removes the question from the realm of those which the police should reasonably expect to produce an incriminating response. This conclusion is certainly amplified when personal characteristics of the suspect are taken into consideration; a suspect who is visibly upset and, in fact, crying, as was defendant in the instant case, is less likely to appreciate the subtlety in a question such as the one here under consideration.

The focus of our analysis is *not* what the police may lawfully ask a criminal suspect to ensure jail security. The police may ask whatever the needs of jail security dictate. However, when the police know or should know that such an inquiry is reasonably likely to elicit an incriminating response from the suspect, the suspect's responses are not admissible against him in a subsequent criminal proceeding unless the initial inquiry has been preceded by *Miranda* admonishments. A police officer's concerns for jail security, encompassing the safety of the suspect, can be triggered by a variety of factors, some of which would have nothing to do with the offense underlying the suspect's incarceration and, as importantly, could only be explored by inquiring of the defendant himself. Thus a suspect who is booked into jail wearing tattoos or other indicia of gang affiliation might alert the booking officer to the possibility of gang-related violence; the quickest way for the officer to resolve such concern is to ask the suspect whether jail personnel should anticipate any trouble in this regard once the suspect becomes housed in the jail. So long as the offense for which the suspect is in custody is not itself gang-related, there is no reason the officer should foresee the question will elicit an incriminating response. In such a circumstance, an incriminating response is not the product of affirmative police conduct and would be admissible in the absence of *Miranda* warnings.

The difference in the instant case is the direct and recognized link between the booking officer's inquiry and the crime for which defendant had been arrested and was in custody. Conceding that jail personnel may have legitimate concerns about a suspect's safety vis-a-vis revenge or retaliation, the police obviously have a victim in mind when they arrest a suspect on suspicion of murder or some other assaultive crime. In most cases a booking officer concerned with jail security need not interrogate a suspect to determine the alleged victim since this information is, or certainly should be, obtainable from the arrest report or from the arresting officer. While the facts in this case do not suggest the questions were anything more than ill-advised, i.e., there is no evidence of affirmative subterfuge or deceit, permitting the police to elicit and use potentially incriminating unMirandized statements from a criminal suspect under the rubric of jail security would critically undermine the important safeguards established in *Miranda*.

The People's response that defendant waived his *Miranda* rights cannot be considered by this court because this theory was not presented to the trial court. The rule precluding reliance on a new theory on appeal seems particularly apt in this case. The People point to a stipulation entered on the record during the rebuttal testimony of Detective Mac Reece who arrested defendant and "read him what is called his *Miranda* admonition and that the Defendant indicated he understood those rights and was willing to talk with Detective Reece." However, the People ignore earlier evidence that defendant subsequently invoked his right to remain silent and was only then transported to the jail facility where the booking procedure took place. This latter evidence was never formalized as a stipulation because the trial court properly ruled it would permit no evidence that defendant had invoked his right to remain silent. Consequently, it would be unfair to permit the People to rely upon a stipulation clearly taken out of context to defeat defendant's argument that the interrogation discussed above was improper.

[The Court goes on to conclude that even though Wilkerson's questioning of Morris was an interrogation, the admission of this testimony did not require reversal, because his response was an admission of responsibility not a confession of the elements of the crime, and there was sufficient independent evidence against him.]

*****

CONCLUSION

The court in this case focuses on applying *Rhode Island v. Innis* to the facts, and notes that the crux behind whether the booking question was an interrogation is whether the officer *should have known* that the question would elicit an incriminating response. It is important for the reader to understand that unless the defense can show that the outcome of the trial would have been different if the admission hadn't been let into evidence, then the error is harmless and no reversal of the conviction will result.

REVIEW

1. Does it matter what the officer's intentions were when asking the question "Who are you accused of killing?

2. Was the first question asked the defendant, about whether there should be any problem with his being in jail there, considered interrogation? What's the key difference between the two questions?

II. People v. Stevenson

In *New York v. Quarles*, 467 U.S. 649 (1984), the Supreme Court carved out a public safety exception to the Miranda requirements, where the warnings are not necessary if the questioning involves the immediate need to protect the public from danger. In that case there was evidence that the suspect knew where a firearm was, and the police wanted to find the weapon before anyone could be hurt by it. In the following case, a California court deals with the interesting question of whether this exception applies when it is the suspect himself who is in danger.

*****

Baron, J.

BACKGROUND

Deputy Sheriff Richard Schlegel testified that he was on routine patrol in a high-narcotics area of Los Angeles County on June 1, 1995, about 12:30 a.m., when he first observed appellant Jeffrey Andre Stevenson. Appellant also saw Deputy Schlegel and as the deputy approached appellant, appellant turned and walked rapidly away while, at the same time, placing something in his mouth. As appellant lifted his hand to his mouth, Deputy Schlegel saw a rock of cocaine drop to the ground. Deputy Schlegel arrested appellant, recovered the cocaine, looked in appellant's mouth and observed a white residue in appellant's mouth. It looked to the deputy as if appellant had chewed up cocaine.

Concerned about a possible overdose, Deputy Schlegel immediately transported appellant to a local hospital where he was treated by emergency room physician Dr. Brian Harris. In Dr. Harris's opinion, appellant was at risk of acute myocardial infarction and hemorrhagic stroke. Appellant became combative when the doctor attempted to pump his stomach. Both Deputy Schlegel and Dr. Harris repeatedly asked appellant if he had ingested narcotics. Appellant continually denied ingesting any controlled substances but eventually, after being informed of the risk of coronary artery disease and myocardial infarction, appellant reluctantly admitted he had swallowed six to eight pieces of rock cocaine. As a result, Dr. Harris again attempted to pump appellant's stomach, but aborted the procedure when appellant vomited macerated fragments of what could have been cocaine and seemed in no further danger of an overdose.

Appellant and his friends, Lavell Austin and Anthony Breland, testified appellant had just left a liquor store when he was arrested by Deputy Schlegel for no apparent reason; they did not see appellant with any cocaine and the officer did not find any after searching the area. Appellant denied possessing or ingesting cocaine or anything else prior to his arrest. He denied that Deputy Schlegel took him to the hospital immediately. They stopped at the police station for five to ten minutes on the way. He also denied telling Deputy Schlegel or Dr. Harris that he swallowed cocaine. Appellant admitted he had been convicted of selling cocaine in 1988 and commercial burglary in 1992; since then he has not used, possessed or sold cocaine and has worked as an in- home nurse.

The jury convicted appellant of possession of a controlled substance. This appeal followed.

DISCUSSION

Appellant contends that the trial court erred in refusing to suppress evidence of his admission that he had swallowed six to eight pieces of cocaine because he had not been advised of his *Miranda* before Deputy Schlegel and Dr. Harris questioned him at the hospital. Appellant recognizes that the "public safety" and "rescue" exceptions to *Miranda* hold that "[w]hile life hangs in the balance, there is no room to require admonitions concerning the right to counsel and to remain silent." However, appellant argues the emergency doctrine only applies when the life of a victim, an officer, or the public-at-large is at risk. Appellant reasons that "... the need for answers to questions in a situation posing a threat to the public safety outweighs the need for the prophylactic rule protecting the Fifth Amendment's privilege against self-incrimination" but, "the need for answers to questions in a situation posing a threat to a defendant's own safety does not." Thus, according to appellant, "[w]here the police believe that a defendant's own safety is threatened, they should not be permitted to decide for defendant whether that possible threat justifies an incursion upon his own privilege against self-incrimination; the defendant can ... make that decision for himself after being properly *Mirandized*." We find this argument untenable.

"[T]he two basics of the *Miranda* opinion relevant here are (1) its assumption that the purpose of custodial interrogation is to further criminal prosecution, and (2) its public policy to outlaw police misconduct relating to the third degree. Neither point is central to the question of police conduct in emergencies, where the primary objective of police action is to save human life." (People v. Riddle).

The scope and elements of what constitutes a valid instance of exigent circumstances were well defined in the *Riddle* case. There, the wife of a burglary victim was missing. The police took the burglary suspect into custody and initially asked him questions about the whereabouts of the missing woman without first advising him of his *Miranda* rights. This was held not to be error. *Riddle* determined that when the possibility of saving the life of a missing victim exists, noncoercive questions may be asked of a suspect in custody, even though the answers to the questions may incriminate the suspect. In reaching this decision, the court relied in part on the United States Supreme Court's decision in *Mincey v. Arizona* which stated: " ' "The need to protect or preserve life or avoid serious injury is justification for what would otherwise be illegal absent exigency or emergency." ' [Citation.]".) The *Riddle* court then set forth requirements which it deemed sufficient to excuse noncompliance with *Miranda*: "1. Urgency of need in that no other course of action promises relief; [¶] 2. The possibility of saving human life by rescuing a person whose life is in danger; [¶] 3. Rescue as the primary purpose and motive of the interrogators." (*Id.* at p. 576.)

The court in *People v. McDermond* applied the *Riddle* rescue doctrine in a situation where it was a noncustodial murder suspect whose life was in danger. The suspect had repeatedly stressed in letters to the sheriff's department and to the press his intent "not to be taken alive." In order to induce the suspect to surrender, the police made false promises and representations to the suspect that they wanted to help not punish him which resulted in a telephone call from the suspect in which he confessed to the murder of his mother and brother. In holding the suspect's confession admissible, *McDermand* pointed out that " '... an interrogation concerning "rescue" might ordinarily have the dual purpose of both rescue and incrimination, but so long as the developed facts show the motive behind the interrogation to be *primarily* that of rescue, the interrogation is justifiable despite an apparent *Miranda* violation.' [Citation.]"

In our view, this case also falls within the purview of the rescue doctrine and we are satisfied that all three *Riddle* requirements are present. The deputy had a reasonable belief that appellant had consumed cocaine based upon seeing appellant place his hand to his mouth, the recovery of the rock of cocaine which dropped from appellant's hand as his hand went to his mouth, and the white residue in his mouth. Deputy Schlegel had learned at the sheriff's academy that cardiac arrest and death can result from a cocaine overdose. Unsure of the quantity of cocaine and concerned that appellant had taken an overdose, the deputy questioned appellant about the amount of cocaine he had ingested. Appellant denied consuming cocaine, but the deputy thought otherwise. Deputy Schlegel testified that he felt he had an "obligation and responsibility" to make sure that appellant was treated if appellant had, in fact, consumed any narcotics. Thus, for medical reasons, the deputy did not want to book appellant and place him in custody at the station. Instead, he took appellant to the hospital.

At the hospital, Deputy Schlegel informed Dr. Harris that he believed appellant had consumed cocaine. Dr. Harris testified that when appellant was received at the hospital, his heart rate was very elevated, he was anxious, very diaphoretic, sweating, and appeared to be emotional. In the doctor's opinion, appellant's elevated heart rate and other aspects of the physical exam put him at risk for acute myocardial infarction and hemorrhagic stroke. The doctor had seen cardiovascular disease and death and hemorrhagic stroke with people who had ingested small amounts of cocaine. However, other substances also cause a patient to exhibit appellant's symptoms. The doctor attempted to initiate a number of diagnostic modalities to determine which substance appellant ingested, including gastric lavage or pumping his stomach which requires placing an oral gastric tube into his stomach to remove the substances so they could be sent to the lab for analysis. But appellant became combative and would not allow any of the procedures. Thus, the doctor could only rely on "history." Accordingly, both the doctor and the officer inquired many times of appellant if he had ingested any controlled substances that evening. Finally, after explaining to appellant the risk of coronary artery disease and myocardial infarction, appellant reluctantly said he had swallowed some rocks of cocaine.

On the facts we have outlined, we see no rational reason to exclude appellant from the reaches of the rescue doctrine. When a life is in danger, the law should make no distinctions. Accordingly, when it is the arrestee's life which is in jeopardy, the police are equally justified in asking questions directed toward providing life-saving medical treatment to the arrestee without first warning the arrestee that his answers can be used against him in a court of law. The *Miranda* advisement was meant to protect an accused from the loss of his right to silence, not from the loss of his life. The doctrinal underpinnings of *Miranda* do not require us to exclude appellant's statement, thus penalizing the deputy for asking the very questions which were the most crucial to the effort to provide appellant with medical treatment.

The judgment is affirmed.

*****

CONCLUSION

The Court allowed the admission of Stevenson's statement that he had swallowed rock cocaine, because it held that the questions were asked in order to possibly save his life. The doctrine it relied on is a derivation of the public safety exception, called the rescue doctrine.

REVIEW

1.   What does it matter if the six to eight rocks were admitted or not, since one rock was recovered at the scene?

2.   What is the difference between the public safety and rescue exceptions?

3.   Do you believe suspects should have the right to decide whether to be "rescued" or not if their responses to questions aimed at their safety may be used against them later?

Section 3: The Waiver of Rights to Counsel and to Remain Silent

OVERVIEW

About 80% of suspects waive their rights, but they can still argue that they did not know what the rights were or that they were giving them up, or that they didn't voluntarily waive them (rather, they waived them from coercion or a promise of leniency). Such claims are difficult to show, however. A separate question is whether, after rights have been waived, the police still acquire a confession that is not voluntary. If they do, this may be a violation of the 14th Amendment's Due Process Clause. The test is whether the "totality of circumstances" show that the police used coercion and the coercion caused the incriminating statements.

What about the case of Michael Crowe and his friends? How should it be evaluated whether their confessions were voluntary? In both the federal system and California, prosecutors must show confessions to be voluntary by preponderance of the evidence, which is a fairly easy burden of proof to demonstrate. In the case *In re Aven S.*, 1 Cal.App.4th 69 (1991), a juvenile argued that in the case of minors, voluntariness should be held to a higher standard of proof, because minors are impacted by coercive interrogation more significantly than adults. The court rejected this claim, holding instead that age can be one of the many factors used in evaluating the "totality of circumstances" of voluntariness.

CHAPTER NINE

Identification Procedures

Police and prosecutors rely heavily on the use of eyewitness identification, both during investigation, to identify suspects, and during trial, to infer guilt beyond reasonable doubt. Eyewitness identification is sometimes controversial, though, since mistakes do occur, as perception, memory, suggestion, and recall all contribute to inaccuracies. One only has to look so far as the Innocence Project (which works toward the release of convicts of serious crimes whom it believes are innocent) to gain a sense of the number of errors made in identification—the primary reason innocent people are in prison for murder is faulty eyewitness identification. Yet, because it is such an enormously powerful and necessary tool, the Supreme Court takes a lenient approach to the admissibility of identifications.

Section 1: The Constitution and Identification Procedures

OVERVIEW

Three primary types of eyewitness identification are used: lineups, showups, and photo identifications. The first involves showing a sequence or series of individuals similar to the suspect's description (along with the suspect), and allowing the witness to "pick" the suspect from the array. This occurs in a controlled setting (usually a police station). The second occurs more often in the field—a typical example is driving a witness past a potential suspect and asking the witness if that person is whom he or she saw participate in the crime. The third involves showing the witness photographs and asking the witness to identify whether the perpetrator appears in any. False positives occur when witnesses pick a person who is not responsible; false negatives occur when witnesses fail to pick someone who was responsible. Although these procedures vary in terms of accuracy, the Supreme Court has held them all to the same test in terms of their excludability from evidence. Under *Simmons v. United States*, 390 U.S. 377 (1968) the procedure must first be determined to have been impermissibly suggestive, and second, the suggestive procedure must have created a very substantial likelihood of misidentification. The first prong can often be satisfied, but the second is difficult to overcome. Even if a pretrial identification is thrown out, the witness may still be able to identify the defendant in court.

In this section we will discuss two cases. The first is a sample application of the *Simmons* rule with a twist—the defendant argued that the suggestive pretrial photo identification tainted the in-court identification. Second, we'll look at an interesting case involving the use eyewitness identification based on hypnosis. Two statutes are relevant. Evidence Code 1238 specifies a hearsay exception for witness identification. If an exception were not created, when a witness testifies about her earlier identification of the defendant in one of the identification procedures would be inadmissible hearsay evidence since she did not make the identification in court. But the Federal Rules of Evidence and all state rules contain an exception to allow such identifications into testimony. The second statute, Evidence Code 795, is California's approach to the admission of testimony by witnesses who have been hypnotized.

Evidence Code Section 1238. Prior identification

Evidence of a statement previously made by a witness is not made inadmissible by the hearsay rule if the statement would have been admissible if made by him while testifying and:

(a) The statement is an identification of a party or another as a person who participated in a crime or other occurrence;

(b) The statement was made at a time when the crime or other occurrence was fresh in the witness' memory; and

(c) The evidence of the statement is offered after the witness testifies that he made the identification and that it was a true reflection of his opinion at that time.

Evidence Code Section 795. Testimony of hypnosis subject; admissibility; conditions

(a) The testimony of a witness is not inadmissible in a criminal proceeding by reason of the fact that the witness has previously undergone hypnosis for the purpose of recalling events which are the subject of the witness' testimony, if all of the following conditions are met:

(1) The testimony is limited to those matters which the witness recalled and related prior to the hypnosis.

(2) The substance of the prehypnotic memory was preserved in written, audiotape, or videotape form prior to the hypnosis.

(3) The hypnosis was conducted in accordance with all of the following procedures:

(A) A written record was made prior to hypnosis documenting the subject's description of the event, and information which was provided to the hypnotist concerning the subject matter of the hypnosis.

(B) The subject gave informed consent to the hypnosis.

(C) The hypnosis session, including the pre- and post-hypnosis interviews, was videotape recorded for subsequent review.

(D) The hypnosis was performed by a licensed medical doctor, psychologist, licensed clinical social worker, or a licensed marriage and family therapist experienced in the use of hypnosis and independent of and not in the presence of law enforcement, the prosecution, or the defense.

(4) Prior to admission of the testimony, the court holds a hearing at which the proponent of the evidence proves by clear and convincing

evidence that the hypnosis did not so affect the witness as to render the witness' prehypnosis recollection unreliable or to substantially impair the ability to cross-examine the witness concerning the witness' prehypnosis recollection. At the hearing, each side shall have the right to present expert testimony and to cross-examine witnesses.

(b) Nothing in this section shall be construed to limit the ability of a party to attack the credibility of a witness who has undergone hypnosis, or to limit other legal grounds to admit or exclude the testimony of that witness.

CASES-

I. People v. Contreras, 17 Cal.App.4th 813 (1993)

In this first case a photo identification procedure was used that the defendant-appellant claims tainted the victim's in-court identification of him.

*****

Thaxter, J.

BACKGROUND

Following trial by jury, appellant Ruben Contreras was found guilty of first degree murder with special circumstances, attempted murder, conspiracy to commit robbery and two counts of robbery.

On appeal, Contreras contends the court erred when it denied his pretrial motion to suppress evidence that the surviving victim identified him, claiming that the identification was tainted by impermissibly suggestive photographic procedures.

On March 30, 1989, Alvaro Lopez and Guadalupe Sanchez agreed to assist Jose Casares in a cocaine sale. Casares was a known cocaine dealer. Lopez met Casares when the two were in jail together. Sanchez lived with Lopez and Lopez's sister, Hidalia Lopez, who was Sanchez's common law wife.

On March 30, Lopez and Sanchez drove Hidalia's car to Elvira Haro's residence. Haro was caring for Lopez's twins, one of whom was ill. Lopez needed money to buy medicine for the sick child. They left, intending to go to Lopez's uncle's house. On the way they met Casares. According to Lopez, Sanchez agreed to buy Casares three ounces of cocaine and deliver it to Casares's home. Lopez denied being a drug dealer, but the two men did purchase cocaine. Sanchez placed it under the seat of the car.

Between 6:30 and 7 p.m., Lopez and Sanchez arrived at Casares's residence. Casares and appellant got into the backseat of Hidalia's car. Sanchez was driving and Lopez was in the front passenger seat. The group drove to the location where Casares supposedly had a friend who wanted to buy drugs. The friend had company, however, and no sale was made. Then Casares told Sanchez to drive to an area on Avenue 328 near Road 127 where the group was to wait.

After the car stopped, Casares ordered Sanchez to give him the cocaine. Sanchez handed the cocaine to Casares in the backseat. Casares then shot Sanchez in the head at close range, killing him.

Casares yelled to appellant to cut Lopez's throat. A struggle ensued. Lopez was shot in the arm by Casares and stabbed numerous times by appellant. Lopez was able to exit the car but the attack continued. Lopez was stabbed approximately 14 times. Finally, Lopez fell on the ground near the back of the car. Casares fired at Lopez but missed. Casares and appellant then dumped Sanchez's body and drove off. Witnesses summoned help and Lopez miraculously survived. Those who witnessed the crime were unable to positively identify the assailants. They all agreed the assailants were young adult Mexican males, but their descriptions varied somewhat as to height, weight and build.

Lopez initially failed to identify his assailants. He was shown two photographic lineups, one including Casares's picture and one including appellant's, but made no identification. The investigating officer saw Lopez react to Casares's photo and told Lopez's wife that he thought Lopez was being untruthful in saying he did not recognize his assailants in the photographs. He also told her that two suspects were in custody. After speaking with his wife, while still hospitalized, Lopez picked Casares from a photo lineup but did not identify appellant. He also failed to identify appellant when shown a single photo of appellant by the deputy district attorney two days before the preliminary hearing. Lopez identified appellant at the preliminary hearing when appellant was sitting at counsel table next to Casares. At trial, Lopez said he was sure appellant was his assailant. Lopez admitted he lied when he first told officers he did not recognize Casares in the photo lineup. He said his motive in lying was his desire to "get revenge" once released from the hospital. He not only recognized Casares's picture, he knew him.

DISCUSSION

Appellant contends the pretrial identification procedures used by law enforcement were unduly suggestive and as a result, Lopez's in-court identification of appellant should have been suppressed. Appellant argues the identification procedures were unduly suggestive in two ways. First, he contends that when Lopez failed to identify his assailants when first shown the "mug" showup in the hospital, Detective Morales, by his conduct and statements, impermissibly suggested to Lopez that his assailants were pictured in the photos presented. Second, appellant argues it was impermissibly suggestive to show Lopez a single photo of appellant shortly before the preliminary hearing. According to appellant, these suggestive procedures resulted in the in-court identification of appellant as the assailant.

A pretrial identification procedure violates a defendant's due process rights if it is so impermissibly suggestive that it creates a very substantial likelihood of irreparable misidentification. The defendant bears the burden of proving unfairness as a "demonstrable reality," not just speculation. (*Simmons v. United States*)

On review we must consider the totality of the circumstances to determine whether the identification procedure was unconstitutionally suggestive. We must resolve all evidentiary conflicts in favor of the trial court's findings and uphold them if supported by substantial evidence.

In denying appellant's motion to suppress evidence that Lopez identified appellant as his assailant, the trial court expressly rejected Lopez's explanations of why he had not identified appellant until the preliminary hearing. The trial court considered the circumstances under which Lopez was attacked and concluded Lopez did not have ample opportunity to see his assailant so he could later identify him. The court concluded Lopez's in-court identification was highly suspect, but not because of the procedures used by the police. The trial court surmised Lopez's in-court identification was based solely on the fact that both suspects were seated at counsel table and Lopez knew Casares was one of the assailants. The court further concluded that its doubts about Lopez's veracity and its suspicions regarding the in-court identification were not sufficient grounds to suppress the identification evidence. Because the issue revolved around Lopez's credibility, the court ruled that all circumstances surrounding the identification should be submitted to the jury.

As we read the court's ruling, the court did not expressly determine whether the identification procedures used here were impermissibly suggestive. Instead, the court seems to have moved directly to the question of whether the in-court identification of appellant resulted from such procedures. The court concluded it did not.

Appellant's complaint about Morales's conduct and statements when he showed Lopez the "mug" lineup in the hospital is groundless. Telling a witness suspects are in custody or questioning a witness further if the officer believes the witness actually recognized someone in the lineup is not impermissible. The officer did nothing improper when he showed the "mug" lineup to Lopez in the hospital.

The more difficult question involves the single photograph of appellant later shown to Lopez. Numerous cases have condemned the use of a single photo identification procedure.

Although the trial court did not make an express finding on whether the pretrial photographic procedures were suggestive, it is clear from the record that they were. After Lopez had failed to identify appellant from the photo lineup, the deputy district attorney showed him a single photo of Contreras two days before the preliminary hearing and asked if Lopez could identify him as his assailant. Lopez had been told there were two individuals in custody and knew Casares was one of them—he knew the police wanted Lopez to identify the other. The picture was a clear photo of appellant. The procedure could only suggest to Lopez that the police believed Contreras to be the other assailant.

Merely concluding that the pretrial procedures were suggestive does not end the analysis, however. In *Manson v. Brathwaite* the United States Supreme Court, weighing various interests involved in such cases, rejected a strict exclusionary rule whenever an identification follows suggestive photographic procedures. The court stated that the proper standard "is that of fairness as required by the Due Process Clause of the Fourteenth Amendment."

Accordingly, numerous cases have found no due process violation from the admission of evidence of identifications made either at the time of or subsequent to a single photo showup. As this court has noted, no identification procedure can be completely insulated from suggestion.

The classic statement applicable to such cases was made by the United States Supreme Court in *Simmons v. United States*. "... [W]e hold that each case must be considered on its own facts, and that convictions based on eyewitness identification at trial following a pretrial identification by photograph will be set aside on that ground only if the photographic identification procedure was so impermissibly suggestive as to give rise to a very substantial likelihood of irreparable misidentification."

The high court's language ("as to give rise to") suggests that due process interests are affected only when there is a causal relationship between the photographic procedure and the witness's identification of the defendant. This is most commonly illustrated by cases in which the trial court is convinced that the witness's identification is based on an independent recollection of the assailant, and allows admission of the identification. For instance, in *People v. Edwards*, the victim first saw the defendant through a window at a hospital shortly after she was raped. The defendant was the only person in the room other than a deputy sheriff. Later she saw a single photograph of the defendant on a detective's desk. The trial court allowed her in-court identification because she had ample opportunity to identify her assailant during the assault and was unequivocal when she identified the defendant at trial. The conviction was upheld on appeal.

[The court provided two more examples where photographic procedures were causally connected to the witness's identification—in both examples the identification was admitted.]

The mere fact that a witness is unable to identify a defendant from photographs shown him does not render a subsequent in-court identification inadmissible.

This case is somewhat unique because the trial court expressly found the in-court identification resulted neither from the pretrial photographic procedures nor from Lopez's independent recollection. Instead, the court concluded Lopez was untruthful in his testimony concerning his observations of the assailant and his ability to recognize him, and that the identification was based on Lopez's seeing appellant in court with Casares, whom he had already identified. The court rejected appellant's claim that the in-court identification was a product of the impermissibly suggestive pretrial photographic procedures. Recognizing that its own findings rendered the proffered testimony "unreliable," the trial court went on to explain: "This Court's opinion of Lopez' veracity does not allow a granting of Contreras' motion to suppress. Lopez' veracity about his undisclosed identification of Contreras [sic] photo and his in-court identification goes to the weight of the identification and not to its admissibility. Contreras' motion to suppress Lopez' undisclosed photo identification and in-court identification is denied. The question of Lopez' truthfulness about the identification of Contreras should be fully explored before the jury ...."

We know of no similar case in which the trial court concluded the identification evidence was unreliable for a reason other than the suggestive pretrial procedures. Appellant, however, has not shown us why our approach to the issue here should be different from those in which the trial court finds the identification was based on the witness's independent recollection. In either type of case, the crucial finding is that the identification did not result from the photographic procedures. If the trial court has made findings of fact supported by substantial evidence, we are bound to accept those findings.

The trial court carefully considered Lopez's testimony and concluded Lopez was lying about his ability to identify appellant. The court's finding is supported by the record. Lopez had been anything but forthright with law enforcement from the outset. At the preliminary hearing, Lopez testified he did not recognize appellant in either the photographic showup or when shown the single photograph of defendant because the photographs were dark. As the trial court noted, the photograph of Casares was just as dark and Lopez had no trouble identifying him. Also, the single photograph of appellant was clear and a good likeness of Contreras. Moreover, Lopez failed to identify appellant after his alleged motive for lying to police (the desire to "get revenge" himself) was removed, i.e., after being told two suspects were in custody.

While other reasonable inferences might have been drawn from the evidence presented at the suppression hearing, we cannot say that the inferences drawn by the trial court are unreasonable.

Appellant cites a number of federal cases involving claims of due process violations based on showing a witness a single photograph of the defendant. In several of those cases, however, the appellate court concluded that even though the procedure was impermissibly suggestive, it did not, under the totality of circumstances, create a substantial risk of misidentification at trial. In other cases a due process violation was found, but because each case turns on its own facts, they offer little guidance here.

We do not see any unfairness, certainly none offending constitutional standards, in the court's decision to allow the identification evidence. The jury was made fully aware of the circumstances leading to Lopez's ultimate, in- court identification. The jury heard that Lopez was unable to identify Contreras until seeing him at the preliminary hearing, even though shown pictures of him earlier. The jury saw the photograph of Contreras and could draw its own conclusions about its clarity. It could decide whether Lopez should have been able to identify appellant if he indeed had been the assailant. In addition, the jury had the benefit of testimony from appellant's expert witness, who opined that showing the photographs to Lopez before the preliminary hearing created a substantial likelihood of misidentification.

In short, when the court concluded that Lopez's identification of Contreras was not the result of having been shown the photographs, the identification issue was largely one of credibility. The credibility of a witness's testimony is a question for the jury at trial, not an issue to be resolved in pretrial motions. We conclude that appellant has not shown that admission of the identification evidence resulted in unfairness "as a demonstrable reality."

Judgment affirmed.

*****

CONCLUSION

This case is an excellent example of the hurdles a defendant must go through to have eyewitness identification stricken. In this case the defendant argued that showing the witness a single photo of him directly prior to the preliminary hearing, when the defendant had already failed to identify him from previous photographs, in essence was a subtle push toward the witness to identify him in court as the perpetrator (despite whether he could in fact identify him accurately). The court failed to find a causal connection between the suggestive photo identification and the in-court identification.

REVIEW

1. What did the trial court conclude about Lopez's in-court identification?

2. What is the relevance of the trial courts' conclusion to the appellate court's analysis?

3. The court failed to give examples of cases where suggestive identification procedures did in fact taint in-court testimony. Can you construct any hypothetical scenario that would be suffice?

II. People v. Hayes, 49 Cal.3d 1260 (1989)
California Evidence Code section 795

An interesting question arises when police witnesses are hypnotized in order to enhance their recollection of the events and memory of the suspect's features. In some cases their hypnotized statements may give police information which they can use to subsequently discover further evidence. But does hypnosis significantly change a person, such that their subsequent testimony and identifications is rendered unreliable? And is there a difference in reliability between the witness's testimony that occurs prior to hypnosis and post-hypnosis? These are addressed in the following California Supreme Court case.

94

Eagleson, J.

BACKGROUND

Defendant Louis Victor Hayes was convicted by jury trial of the first degree murder of Rigoberto G. and the robbery, rape, and forcible oral copulation of the deceased victim's wife, Marie G., as well as the burglary of their residence.

Officer Ronald Reed testified that he responded to a report of a shooting in Burlingame at 4:16 a.m. on February 27, 1979. Firemen were already at the scene. He entered the apartment and found Rigoberto G. lying on his back in the front hallway, bleeding profusely from a gunshot wound to the chest. The victim died en route to the hospital.

The deceased's wife Marie was in the kitchen/living room area with her aunt and uncle, who occupied an upstairs apartment. Crying hysterically, she told Reed that two Black male adults had broken into her house, raped her, stole a ring and watch, and upon fleeing had shot her husband.

Marie described the first assailant who entered the apartment (later identified as defendant Hayes) as a Black male in his early 20's, with a "slim" build, approximately 6 feet tall, 160 to 170 pounds, black hair, brown eyes, mustache and possible goatee, wearing dark clothing and a dark, possibly black, watch cap. He was carrying a large black gun approximately four to six inches long, which she believed was a revolver.

Marie described the second assailant who entered the apartment (later identified as Jack Roundtree) as a "black male adult in his twenties, about five-foot-ten, 180 pounds, stocky build, dark clothing and had a ski mask on. He was carrying a small, silver automatic pistol approximately two inches long." In a second statement given a short time later but still prior to being hypnotized, Marie further described the second assailant's "ski mask" as "a dark watch cap, possibly black, that was pulled down over his face with two eyelets cut out and cut out by hand, they were jagged."

At 4:53 a.m., Reed took Marie to Peninsula Hospital for a rape examination. She was then advised that her husband had died en route to the hospital. At approximately 7 a.m., she was taken to the police station and separately interviewed by Officer Reed and Homicide Detective James Eldridge over the next two hours. Reed testified that during this interview Marie related the following account of events:

She and her husband had sexual intercourse and went to bed at 9:15 p.m. She set her alarm clock for 3:30 a.m., as she had to be at work as a waitress at a Burlingame hotel at 5 a.m. She awoke and was dressing when she heard a knock at the front door. Marie glanced at the clock; it was 4 a.m. Her husband was still asleep. She unlocked the front door and opened it "a little" to look outside. Seeing no one, she started closing the door when unmasked "suspect one" appeared and pushed the door in. She described "suspect one" during this interview as a Black male in his early 20's, 6 feet tall, slim build, weighing approximately 160 to 170 pounds, with a mustache and possibly a goatee, wearing dark clothing and a dark colored watch cap, and holding a black gun 4 to 6 inches long.

As "suspect one" entered the apartment Marie yelled for her husband who awoke, sat up in bed, and asked what was going on. "Suspect one" yelled to his confederate to "come on in," whereupon "suspect two" entered the apartment. Marie described "suspect two" during the interview as a Black male, 5 feet 10 or 11 inches tall, 180 pounds, also wearing dark clothing, with a watch cap pulled over his head and eyeholes cut or ripped out around the eyes. He held this "mask" down over his face with his right hand. In his left hand he held a small, silver automatic pistol, approximately two inches long.

"Suspect one" told Marie he "wanted all the money." She replied that she did not have much, and that what she had was in a jar near the couch in the bedroom. He ordered her to get it. She complied, placing a gallon jar of coins on the cabinet next to the doorway, and returned to the bed next to her husband. Marie told Reed she "begged them not to hurt us and told them to take the money and leave us alone.

"Suspect two" then ordered her into the bathroom. She complied. The lights were on and she sat down in a corner near the shower. He closed the door and directed her to sit on the toilet. He pointed his gun at her, unzipped his pants, and ordered her to suck his erect penis, pulling her forward by her shoulder. She closed her eyes and complied.

"Suspect two" then ordered Marie to get up and take off her dress, panties and pantyhose, and forcefully raped her, achieving ejaculation. He ordered her to wipe his penis with a bath towel. She complied, thereafter wrapping the towel around herself and returning to the bedroom where her husband asked what had happened.

The two assailants then started arguing: "suspect two" wanted Marie to start unhooking the stereo, "suspect one" had other plans for her. "Suspect one" next touched her breast, then started pulling at her high school ring, which she removed from her finger and gave to him. He took her husband's wristwatch from the nightstand and placed it in his pocket. He next ordered Marie into the kitchen to get her purse. She complied. He told her he wanted only bills, not coins. She could not find any currency in her purse. He then ordered her to sit on a kitchen chair and exposed his uncircumcised penis. He placed his gun to the left side of her neck and ordered her to "[suck] on it and it better be good." When he achieved an erection, he ordered her to stand on a chair, then changed his mind and told her to lay down on the kitchen floor. "Suspect two," who was standing in the hallway with his gun pointed in the direction of the bedroom, looked into the kitchen to see what "suspect one" was doing. "Suspect one" spread Marie's legs apart, placed the gun against her head and forcibly raped her, stating: "It better be good, better be good."

As she was being raped the second time, Marie heard "suspect two" saying, "Stay in bed, get back in bed." She heard her husband say "No," after which "suspect one" joined "suspect two" in the hallway as he was backing toward the front door. Marie came running out of the kitchen, heard a shot and her husband yell "Marie," then saw him fall to the floor. She did not see which of the two assailants had fired the shot. The two assailants ran out the front door. Marie shoved it closed and telephoned the fire department.

Officer Reed testified that during this interview on the morning of the incident, Marie told him she was certain she could identify the first assailant who entered the apartment: the taller, thinner one who wore no mask.

At trial, Homicide Detective Eldridge recounted the separate statement he took from Marie after Officer Reed had interviewed her. It was his standard practice to have the "primary investigation officer" who was first to arrive on the crime scene interview the victim or witnesses, whereafter he would reinterview them. The record reflects that Marie's statement to Detective Eldridge was virtually identical in all particulars to the statement she gave to Officer Reed.

Marie was then hypnotized within hours of the crimes for the purpose of assisting a police artist in the creation of a composite sketch of the face of her unmasked assailant, and to develop more information regarding the details of the crimes. Further details regarding the hypnotic session are set forth below.

Also on that same day Jack Roundtree was arrested for an unrelated armed robbery. At that time he was wearing a dark blue knit cap with distinctive hand-cut eyeholes. Marie was immediately shown the distinctive "cap mask" and identified it as "identical" to the one worn by her masked assailant the night before.

Although Marie was the principal prosecution witness, there was considerable additional evidence presented in the People's case-in-chief.

[The court then discusses additional circumstantial evidence against the defendant.]

DISCUSSION

In *People v. Shirley* - decided three years after Marie was hypnotized during the investigation of this case - we held that "the testimony of a witness who has undergone hypnosis for the purpose of restoring his memory of the events in issue is inadmissible as to all matters relating to those events, *from the time of the hypnotic session forward*." We further characterized "events in issue" as those that were "the subject of the hypnotic session." In *People v. Guerra*, the rule of *Shirley* was made retroactive to all cases not yet final as of the date *Shirley* was decided. This is such a case.

After furnishing her statements hours after the incident, Marie assisted Belmont police artist Frances Caine in compiling a composite drawing of her unmasked assailant. To facilitate the drawing and develop more information regarding the details of the crime, Detective Eldridge asked Lieutenant James Scales, a police hypnotist, to hypnotize Marie. Marie's session with Caine and Scales was recorded on tape, and a transcription of the recording was admitted in evidence. Scales was told that Marie was a rape victim and had witnessed a shooting; he was not given further details of the crimes. According to Marie, Lieutenant Scales succeeded in relaxing her, but she remained conscious and aware throughout the procedure and did not feel she had been placed in a hypnotic state. Scales told Marie to make any desired changes in the drawing during the hypnotic session. Marie recalled making only minor changes in the appearance of the eyes and hat in the composite drawing of the suspect.

The day following the murder, Marie tentatively selected defendant's photograph from a photographic lineup as the unmasked assailant. One week later she positively identified Hayes at a physical lineup, noting that he no longer had a mustache or goatee and had cut his hair shorter. She positively identified him again at trial.

Under the rule of *Shirley*, Marie's *posthypnotic* testimony, including her posthypnotic lineup and in-court identifications of Hayes, was inadmissible. The error must be deemed prejudicial if we determine it is reasonably probable that a result more favorable to the defendant would have occurred had such testimony not been admitted.

The Attorney General urges that we find the error harmless for several reasons: Marie "never wavered" and was "certain of her facts and her identification"; her description of "suspect one" did not change after the hypnotic session; at the time of the hypnosis neither the hypnotist nor police artist had a suspect in mind and thereby could not have implanted in Marie's mind any suggestion that defendant was a suspect; "[Marie] herself discounted the value of the hypnosis and doubted whether she had ever been hypnotized"; and defendant has not shown he was denied effective cross-examination of Marie.

We reject these urgings under the rule of *Shirley*. Moreover, we need not belabor the point. It is indisputable that Marie had no occasion to identify Hayes until *after* she had been hypnotized. The posthypnotic identification was erroneously admitted under *Shirley*, and since this was the only direct identification of the defendant we conclude it is reasonably probable that the lone surviving victim's positive identification of him as the unmasked assailant helped secure his convictions. We therefore reverse the convictions.

The matter of the admissibility of "prehypnotic evidence" was expressly left open in *Guerra*. We now hold, in accord with a nearly unanimous body of sister-state that a witness who has undergone hypnosis is not barred from testifying to events which the court finds were recalled and related prior to the hypnotic session.

In his concurring opinion in *Guerra*, Justice Kaus succinctly summarized the argument and authorities in support of such an exception to the *Shirley-Guerra* exclusionary rule for prehypnotic evidence. His analysis is instructive:

"To the extent that the *Shirley* decision embodies the principle that testimony 'created' in [a police-conducted] hypnosis session is not sufficiently reliable to be admitted in a criminal trial, I agree that it establishes a rule that goes to the heart of the accuracy of the factfinding process and should be applied retroactively.

"But while I agree that the victim's *hypnotically created* testimony ... was impermissibly admitted and should be excluded on retrial, I would make it clearer than the majority does that *Shirley* should not be applied retroactively to bar the victim from testifying on retrial about facts or memories that the trial court can reasonably determine were *not* created during the hypnosis session. ...

"... [The] police and prosecution have been on notice since *Shirley* was filed of the consequences that flow under that decision if a potential witness is hypnotized. As a result, the *prospective* application of *Shirley's* strict exclusionary rule may not impose substantial, adverse effects on the administration of justice in this state. [Fn. omitted.]

"But the same cannot be said for the *retroactive* application of the decision's prophylactic sanction. We must remember that this is only one of many cases that will be affected by our determination of the appropriate remedy to apply to those witnesses who were hypnotized before *Shirley*. With respect to such cases, there is a special need to ensure that in our zeal to protect the citizenry from the hazards of hypnosis, we do not create a greater injustice by an after-the-fact disqualification of crucial witnesses who have relevant - frequently vital - information that is not tainted by the hypnosis.

"Although it may not be immediately apparent from a reading of the scholarly majority opinion, the recent out-of-state decisions which are most in tune with *Shirley* do *not* support *Shirley's* conclusion that a witness who has been hypnotized may not testify with respect to any subject discussed in the hypnosis session. ... [Virtually] all of the other states that have adopted a ' per se' rule excluding *hypnotically induced testimony, have at the same time expressly declared that a witness is not necessarily barred from testifying to events which the witness recalled and related to others before undergoing hypnosis.*

"These decisions recognize that while there are theoretical objections to even such testimony, the probable reliability and potential importance of the evidence justifies its admission. As the New York Court of Appeals explained: ' A criminal trial for rape or assault would present an odd spectacle if the victim was barred from saying anything, including the fact that the crime occurred, simply because he or she submitted to hypnosis sometime prior to trial to aid the investigation or obtain needed medical treatment. Even in cases dealing with the frailties of eyewitness identification some allowance must be made for [¶] When confronted with suggestive pretrial identification, it has not been found necessary to preclude the witness from making an in-court identification on the basis of recollections prior to the suggestive procedure, if it is found as a fact that he can do so without relying on the improperly made identification .... A similar procedure would seem to be appropriate in cases involving the pretrial use of hypnosis. ...'

"Thus, when the scope of the recent out-of-state decisions is properly understood, it becomes clear that the numerous authorities relied on by the majority to accord retroactive application to *Shirley* do not support the proposition that a witness hypnotized before *Shirley* should be totally barred from testifying at trial. Rather, the cases suggest that such a witness should generally be permitted to testify at trial as to prehypnosis memories so long as there is satisfactory evidence from which the trial court can determine that the witness did in fact recall and relate the statements before undergoing hypnosis.

Our subsequent research has revealed the following additional sister-state and federal circuit court cases postdating *Shirley* and *Guerra* which, like the numerous out-of-state decisions cited by Justice Kaus in *Guerra, except* prehypnotic evidence - i.e., evidence which the hypnotized witness recalled and related prior to undergoing hypnosis - from their respective state and federal circuit rules excluding or restricting the admission of posthypnotic testimony.

In accord with these authorities, we conclude that the defendant should not gain effective immunity from prosecution by a rule that would bar the previously hypnotized victim, without exception, from the witness stand. Accordingly, should the People elect to retry this case, the fact that Marie underwent hypnosis will not bar her from testifying to events which the court finds she recalled and related prior to the hypnotic session, and any other testimony concerning subjects not discussed during her hypnotic session.

Under the standard for admitting prehypnotic evidence generally adopted by the courts of our sister states which have addressed the question, a witness is permitted to testify to events that the trial court finds the witness both recalled and related to others before undergoing hypnosis. In turn, the opposing party is permitted to introduce evidence of the fact and method of the hypnosis, and its potential effects on the witness's recollection.

We adopt this standard as governing the admissibility in California of all prehypnotic evidence predating January 1, 1985 - the effective date of Evidence Code section 795.

We must also determine whether Evidence Code section 795 will apply to any *retrial* of this case.

[For the provisions of this code see the beginning of this section.]

A new statute is generally presumed to operate prospectively absent an express declaration of retroactivity or a clear and compelling implication that the Legislature intended otherwise. We find nothing to overcome that presumption in this case.

We therefore construe the regulatory provisions of Evidence Code section 795 as prospective only; [it] will not apply to retrial of this case. The standard we adopt today shall govern the admissibility of all prehypnotic evidence predating January 1, 1985 - regardless of when such evidence was or may in the future be offered at trial.

In conclusion, evidence of events and descriptions that Marie both recalled and related to police officers prior to undergoing hypnosis, introduced by the prosecution through the testimony of Marie as well as those officers to whom she gave her prehypnotic statements, and any other testimony concerning subjects not discussed during the hypnotic session, will be admissible in any retrial of this case.

The judgment of the Court of Appeal is reversed with directions to reverse the judgment of conviction.

*****

CONCLUSION

The court held that because Marie's identification of the defendant in a photo, in a lineup, and at trial all occurred after the hypnosis, it was inadmissible. Furthermore, because her identification was the only direct (not circumstantial) evidence against him, the conviction must be overturned. However, it also decided that were the prosecutors to retry Hayes, she could be put on the stand and testify about matters prior to the hypnosis, and officers could testify to what she told them prior to hypnosis. Additionally, it held that the set of rules in Evidence Code section 795 did not apply, because it was put into law well after the investigation in this case.

REVIEW

1. What is the reasoning behind distinguishing between pre- and post-hypnotic testimony?

2. Why is it that the decision in Shirley doesn't apply to pre-hypnotic testimony?

3. What decision must prosecutors make following this reversal? What factors will they rely on in making the decision?

4. What safeguards does the Evidence Code supply regarding hypnotic testimony?

Section 2: DNA Profile Identification

OVERVIEW

As with federal law, California law allows DNA evidence to be used to match material from the crime scene with characteristics of the suspect's genetic structure, under the *Kelly-Frye* standard for the admissibility of scientific evidence. However, different California courts have approved of different types of DNA analysis. For an example of the capillary electrophoresis method, see *People v. Henderson*, 107 Cal.App.4th 512 (1999); for an example of the Applied Biosystems 310 genetic analyzer, see *People v. Smith*, 107 Cal.App.4th 646; for an example of the short tandem repeats method, see *People v. Allen*, 72 Cal.Appp.4th 1093; many other examples of different methods exist over the different appellate districts.

CHAPTER TEN

Constitutional Violations: Exclusionary Rule and Entrapment

In this chapter we discuss two very different mechanisms whereby a defendant may use the government's unconstitutional conduct to his or her advantage: suppression of illegal obtained evidence via the exclusionary rule, or acquittal by defense of entrapment. Both involve improper police procedures that do not make the defendant "innocent" but may result in a not guilty finding. One key difference between the two is that the exclusionary rule is part of procedural criminal law whereas entrapment is a defense, which is part of substantive criminal law.

Section 1: The Exclusionary Rule

OVERVIEW

When the government violates the rights afforded to individuals by the Constitution, it means nothing unless there is a remedy. Before the exclusionary rule, there were only weak remedies, such as the right to file complaints against, civilly sue, or attempt to prosecute the government actors. Eventually, though, the federal system adopted the exclusionary rule, prohibiting the use of illegally obtained evidence against the defendant in trial. This was incorporated through the 14th amendment to apply to states in *Mapp v. Ohio*, 367 U.S. 643 (1961). Thus, the modern rule is that illegally obtained evidence is inadmissible in trial as proof of the defendant's guilt; however, for confessions, if a defendant chooses to take the stand in her own defense, the prosecution may still be able to use illegally obtained confessions to impeach the defendant's veracity. Another exception to the exclusionary rule is that if police officers in good faith execute a facially valid warrant that is later determined to be faulty, evidence obtained pursuant to the warrant may still be admissible. This good-faith exception may apply beyond the search warrant example, when officers rely on other information caused by errors. The primary rationale for the exclusionary rule, according to the modern Supreme Court is one of police deterrence; thus, when police are at fault in improper seizures and searches, the resulting evidence and anything derived from it ("fruit of the poisonous tree") are inadmissible. However, when others (such as court clerks) are responsible for the error, the evidence may still be admissible.

Even though the exclusionary rule did not apply to the states until 1961, California was well ahead of the curve, creating this right in 1955—we'll first review this major case in state history. Next, we'll examine a case pertaining to the good-faith exception, which asks whether errors made by DMV (Department of Motor Vehicles) employees fall within the exception.

CASES-

I. People v. Cahan, 44 Cal.2d 434 (1955)

The following case occurs after the Supreme Court first refused to mandate that states adhere to the exclusionary rule available in federal jurisdictions, and six years before the same court finally did choose to incorporate the exclusionary rule. Pay close attention to the reasoning applied by the California Supreme Court during this pre-Warren Court period. The majority decision was written by one of the California Supreme Court's most renowned decision makers, Justice Traynor.

*****

Traynor, J.

BACKGROUND

Defendant and 15 other persons were charged with conspiring to engage in horse-race bookmaking and related offenses in violation of section 337a of the Penal Code. Six of the defendants pleaded guilty. After a trial without a jury, the court found one defendant not guilty and each of the other defendants guilty as charged. Charles H. Cahan, one of the defendants found guilty, was granted probation for a period of five years on the condition that he spend the first 90 days of his probationary period in the county jail and pay a $2,000 fine. He appeals from the order granting him probation and the order denying his motion for a new trial.

Most of the incriminatory evidence introduced at the trial was obtained by officers of the Los Angeles Police Department in flagrant violation of the United States Constitution (4th and 14th Amendments), the California Constitution (art. I, § 19), and state and federal statutes. Gerald Wooters, an officer attached to the intelligence unit of that department testified that after securing the permission of the chief of police to make microphone installations at two places occupied by defendants, he, Sergeant Keeler, and Officer Phillips one night at about 8:45 entered one "house through the side window of the first floor," and that he "directed the officers to place a listening device under a chest of drawers." Another officer made recordings and transcriptions of the conversations that came over wires from the listening device to receiving equipment installed in a nearby garage. About a month later, at Officer Wooters' direction, a similar device was surreptitiously installed in another house and receiving equipment was also set up in a nearby garage. Such methods of getting evidence have been caustically censured by the United States Supreme Court: "That officers of the law would break and enter a home, secrete such a device, even in a bedroom, and listen to the conversations of the occupants for over a month would be almost incredible if it were not admitted. Few police measures have come to our attention that more flagrantly, deliberately and persistently violate the fundamental principle declared by the Fourth Amendment. ..." Section 653h of the Penal Code does not and could not authorize violations of the Constitution, and the proviso under which the officers purported to act at most prevents their conduct from constituting a violation of that section itself.

The evidence obtained from the microphones was not the only unconstitutionally obtained evidence introduced at the trial over defendants' objection. In addition there was a mass of evidence obtained by numerous forcible entries and seizures without search warrants.

The forcible entries and seizures were candidly admitted by the various officers. For example, Officer Fosnocht identified the evidence that he seized, and testified as to his means of entry: "... and how did you gain entrance to the particular place? I forced entry through the front door and Officer Farquarson through the rear door. You say you forced the front door? ... Yes. And how? I kicked it open with my foot. ..." Officer Schlocker testified that he entered the place where he seized evidence "through a window located I believe it was west of the front door. ... [W]hen you tried to force entry in other words, you tried to knock it [the door] down is that right? We tried to knock it down, yes, sir. What with? A shoe, foot. Kick it? Tried to kick it in, yes. And then you moved over and broke the window to gain entrance, is that right? We did." Officer Scherrer testified that he gained entry into one of the places where he seized evidence by kicking the front door in. He also entered another place, accompanied by Officers Hilton and Horral, by breaking through a window. Officer Harris "just walked up and kicked the door in" to gain entry to the place assigned to him.

Thus, without fear of criminal punishment or other discipline, law enforcement officers, sworn to support the Constitution of the United States and the Constitution of California, frankly admit their deliberate, flagrant acts in violation of both Constitutions and the laws enacted thereunder. It is clearly apparent from their testimony that they casually regard such acts as nothing more than the performance of their ordinary duties for which the city employs and pays them.

DISCUSSION

The Fourth Amendment to the Constitution of the United States provides: "The right of the people to be secure in their persons, houses, papers, and effects, against unreasonable searches and seizures, shall not be violated, and no warrants shall issue but upon probable cause, supported by oath or affirmation, and particularly describing the place to be searched and the persons or things to be seized." Although this amendment, like each of the other provisions of the original Bill of Rights, applies only to the federal government '[t]he security of one's privacy against arbitrary intrusion by the police-which is at the core of the Fourth Amendment-is basic to a free society. It is therefore implicit in 'the concept of ordered liberty' and as such enforceable against the States through the Due Process Clause [of the Fourteenth Amendment.]" (*Wolf v. Colorado*.) An essentially identical guarantee of personal privacy is set forth in article I, section 19 of the California Constitution.

Thus both the United States Constitution and the California Constitution make it emphatically clear that important as efficient law enforcement may be, it is more important that the right of privacy guaranteed by these constitutional provisions be respected.. Since in *no* case shall the right of the people to be secure against unreasonable searches and seizures be violated, the contention that unreasonable searches and seizures are justified by the necessity of bringing criminals to justice cannot be accepted. It was rejected when the constitutional provisions were adopted and the choice was made that all the people, guilty and innocent alike, should be secure from unreasonable police intrusions, even though some criminals should escape. Moreover, the constitutional provisions make no distinction between the guilty and the innocent, and it would be manifestly impossible to protect the rights of the innocent if the police were permitted to justify unreasonable searches and seizures on the ground that they assumed their victims were criminals. Thus, when consideration is directed to the question of the admissibility of evidence obtained in violation of the constitutional provisions, it bears emphasis that the court is not concerned solely with the rights of the defendant before it, however guilty he may appear, but with the constitutional right of all of the people to be secure in their homes, persons, and effects.

The constitutional provisions themselves do not expressly answer the question whether evidence obtained in violation thereof is admissible in criminal actions. Neither Congress nor the Legislature has given an answer, and the courts of the country are divided on the question. The federal courts and those of some of the states exclude such evidence. (*Weeks v. United States*.) In accord with the traditional common-law rule, the courts of a majority of the states admit it and heretofore the courts of this state have admitted it.

The decision of the United States Supreme Court in *Wolf v. Colorado* that the guarantee of the Fourth Amendment applies to the states through the Fourteenth does not require states like California that have heretofore admitted illegally seized evidence to exclude it now. The exclusionary rule is not "an essential ingredient" of the right of privacy guaranteed by the Fourth Amendment, but simply a means of enforcing that right, which the states can accept or reject: "Granting that in practice the exclusion of evidence may be *an* effective way of deterring unreasonable searches, it is not for this Court to condemn as falling below the minimal standards assured by the Due Process Clause a State's reliance upon other methods which *if* consistently enforced *would be* equally effective." The court did not state that the other methods of deterring unreasonable searches and seizures must be "consistently enforced" and be "equally effective." Except in extreme cases it is apparently willing to leave the matter of deterring unreasonable searches and seizures by state officers entirely to the states and is not yet ready to condemn methods other than the exclusion of the evidence as falling below " minimal standards" even though the state makes no effort whatever to enforce them and in practical effect, therefore, has no method of making this basic constitutional guarantee effective. It would appear, therefore, that despite earlier statements of the United States Supreme Court that the Fourth or the Fifth Amendment barred the use of evidence obtained through an illegal search and seizure "the federal exclusionary rule," in the words of Mr. Justice Black, "is not a command of the Fourth Amendment but is a judicially created rule of evidence which Congress might negate." It would seem that it is also a rule that Congress could make binding on the states to deter state invasions of the Fourth Amendment's guarantee, which is now recognized as limiting state as well as federal action.

The rule of the Wolf case that the Fourteenth Amendment does not require the exclusion of evidence obtained by an unreasonable search and seizure was reaffirmed recently in *Irvine v. California*. Thus Wolf remains the law and, as such, is entitled to the respect of this Court's membership. ... Perhaps strict adherence to the tenor of that decision may produce needed converts for its extinction." Justices Frankfurter and Burton, who were among the majority in the Wolf case, would hold that the methods employed in the Irvine case are so repulsive that evidence so obtained must be excluded as a matter of due process of law. Not only was the court closely divided, but Justice Jackson felt it appropriate to declare for the majority: "Now that the Wolf doctrine [the guarantee of the Fourth Amendment is enforceable against the states through the Due Process Clause of the Fourteenth] is known to them, state courts may wish further to reconsider their evidentiary rules. But to upset state convictions even before the states have had adequate opportunity to adopt or reject the [exclusionary] rule would be an unwarranted use of federal power. " Thus, after states that rely on methods other than the exclusionary rule to deter unreasonable searches and seizures have had an opportunity to reconsider their rules in the light of the Wolf doctrine, the way is left open for the United States Supreme Court to conclude that if these other methods are not " consistently enforced" and are therefore not "equally effective" the "minimal standards" of due process have not been met.

Meanwhile, pursuant to the suggestion of the United States Supreme Court, we have reconsidered the rule we have heretofore followed that the unconstitutional methods by which evidence is obtained does not affect its admissibility and have carefully weighed the various arguments that have been advanced for and against the rule. It bears emphasis that in the absence of a holding by the United States Supreme Court that the due process clause requires exclusion of unconstitutionally obtained evidence, whatever rule we adopt, whether it excludes or admits the evidence, will be a judicially declared rule of evidence.

The rule admitting the evidence has been strongly supported by both scholars and judges. Their arguments may be briefly summarized as follows:

The rules of evidence are designed to enable courts to reach the truth and, in criminal cases, to secure a fair trial to those accused of crime. Evidence obtained by an illegal search and seizure is ordinarily just as true and reliable as evidence lawfully obtained. The court needs all reliable evidence material to the issue before it, the guilt or innocence of the accused, and how such evidence is obtained is immaterial to that issue. It should not be excluded unless strong considerations of public policy demand it. There are no such considerations.

Exclusion of the evidence cannot be justified as affording protection or recompense to the defendant or punishment to the officers for the illegal search and seizure. It does not protect the defendant from the search and seizure, since that illegal act has already occurred. If he is innocent or if there is ample evidence to convict him without the illegally obtained evidence, exclusion of the evidence gives him no remedy at all. Thus the only defendants who benefit by the exclusionary rule are those criminals who could not be convicted without the illegally obtained evidence. Allowing such criminals to escape punishment is not appropriate recompense for the invasion of their constitutional rights; it does not punish the officers who violated the constitutional provisions; and it fails to protect society from known criminals who should not be left at large. For his crime the defendant should be punished. For his violation of the constitutional provisions the offending officer should be punished. As the exclusionary rule operates, however, the defendant's crime and the officer's flouting of constitutional guarantees both go unpunished. "The criminal is to go free because the constable has blundered and "Society is deprived of its remedy against one lawbreaker, because he has been pursued by another."

Opponents of the exclusionary rule also point out that it is inconsistent with the rule allowing private litigants to use illegally obtained evidence and that as applied in the federal courts, it is capricious in its operation, either going too far or not far enough. "[S]o many exceptions to [the exclusionary] rule have been granted the judicial blessing as largely to destroy any value it might otherwise have had. Instead of adding to the security of legitimate individual rights, its principal contribution has been to add further technicalities to the law of criminal procedure. A district attorney who is willing to pay the price may easily circumvent its limitations. And the price to be paid is by no means high." Thus, the rule as applied in the federal courts has been held to protect only defendants whose own rights have been invaded by federal officers. If the illegal search and seizure have been conducted by a state officer or a private person not acting in cooperation with federal officers, or if the property seized is not defendant's the rule does not apply.

Finally it has been pointed out that there is no convincing evidence that the exclusionary rule actually tends to prevent unreasonable searches and seizures and that the "disciplinary or educational effect of the court's releasing the defendant for police misbehavior is so indirect as to be no more than a mild deterrent at best."

Despite the persuasive force of the foregoing arguments, we have concluded, as Justice Carter and Justice Schauer have consistently maintained, that evidence obtained in violation of the constitutional guarantees is inadmissible and the cases based thereon are therefore overruled. We have been compelled to reach that conclusion because other remedies have completely failed to secure compliance with the constitutional provisions on the part of police officers with the attendant result that the courts under the old rule have been constantly required to participate in, and in effect condone, the lawless activities of law enforcement officers.

When, as in the present case, the very purpose of an illegal search and seizure is to get evidence to introduce at a trial, the success of the lawless venture depends entirely on the court's lending its aid by allowing the evidence to be introduced. It is no answer to say that a distinction should be drawn between the government acting as law enforcer and the gatherer of evidence and the government acting as judge. "[N]o distinction can be taken between the Government as prosecutor and the Government as judge. If the existing code does not permit district attorneys to have a hand in such dirty business it does not permit the judge to allow such iniquities to succeed. " Out of regard for its own dignity as an agency of justice and custodian of liberty the court should not have a hand in such "dirty business." Courts refuse their aid in civil cases to prevent the consummation of illegal schemes of private litigants; *a fortiori,* they should not extend that aid and thereby permit the consummation of illegal schemes of the state itself. It is morally incongruous for the state to flout constitutional rights and at the same time demand that its citizens observe the law. The end that the state seeks may be a laudable one, but it no more justifies unlawful acts than a laudable end justifies unlawful action by any member of the public. Moreover, any process of law that sanctions the imposition of penalties upon an individual through the use of the fruits of official lawlessness tends to the destruction of the whole system of restraints on the exercise of the public force that are inherent in the "concept of ordered liberty." "Decency, security, and liberty alike demand that government officials shall be subjected to the same rules of conduct that are commands to the citizen. In a government of laws, existence of the government will be imperilled if it fails to observe the law scrupulously. Our Government is the potent, the omnipresent teacher. For good or for ill, it teaches the whole people by its example. Crime is contagious. If the Government becomes a law-breaker, it breeds contempt for law, it invites everyman to become a law unto himself; it invites anarchy. To declare that in the administration of the criminal law the end justifies the means-to declare that the Government may commit crimes in order to secure the conviction of a private criminal-would bring terrible retribution. Against that pernicious doctrine this Court should resolutely set its face."

If the unconstitutional conduct of the law enforcement officers were more flagrant or more closely connected with the conduct of the trial, it is clear that the foregoing principles would compel the reversal of any conviction based thereon. Thus, no matter how guilty a defendant might be or how outrageous his crime, he must not be deprived of a fair trial, and any action, official or otherwise, that would have that effect would not be tolerated. Similarly, he may not be convicted on the basis of evidence obtained by the use of the rack or the screw or other brutal means no matter how reliable the evidence obtained may be. Today one of the foremost public concerns is the police state, and recent history has demonstrated all too clearly how short the step is from lawless although efficient enforcement of the law to the stamping out of human rights. This peril has been recognized and dealt with when its challenge has been obvious; it cannot be forgotten when it strikes further from the courtroom by invading the privacy of homes.

If the unconstitutional guarantees against unreasonable searches and seizures are to have significance they must be enforced, and if courts are to discharge their duty to support the state and federal Constitutions they must be willing to aid in their enforcement If those guarantees were being effectively enforced by other means than excluding evidence obtained by their violation, a different problem would be presented. If such were the case there would be more force to the argument that a particular criminal should not be redressed for a past violation of his rights by excluding the evidence against him. Experience has demonstrated, however, that neither administrative, criminal nor civil remedies are effective in suppressing lawless searches and seizures. The innocent suffer with the gulity, and we cannot close our eyes to the effect the rule we adopt will have on the rights of those not before the court. "Alternatives [to the exclusionary rule] are deceptive. Their very statement conveys the impression that one possibility is as effective as the next. For there is but one alternative to the rule of exclusion. That is no sanction at all." "The difficulty with [other remedies] is in part due to the failure of interested parties to inform of the offense. No matter what an illegal raid turns up, police are unlikely to inform on themselves or each other. If it turns up nothing incriminating, the innocent victim usually does not care to take steps which will air the fact that he has been under suspicion." Moreover, even when it becomes generally known that the police conduct illegal searches and seizures, public opinion is not aroused as it is in the case of other violations of constitutional rights. Illegal searches and seizures lack the obvious brutality of coerced confessions and the third degree and do not so clearly strike at the very basis of our civil liberties as do unfair trials or the lynching of even an admitted murderer. "Freedom of speech, of the press, of religion, easily summon powerful support against encroachment. The prohibition against unreasonable search and seizure is normally invoked by those accused of crime, and criminals have few friends." There is thus all the more necessity for courts to be vigilant in protecting these constitutional rights if they are to be protected at all. [C]ase after case has appeared in our appellate reports describing unlawful searches and seizures against the defendant on trial, and those cases undoubtedly reflect only a small fraction of the violations of the constitutional provisions that have actually occurred. On the other hand, reported cases involving civil actions against police officers are rare, and those involving successful criminal prosecutions against officers are nonexistent. In short, the constitutional provisions are not being enforced.

Granted that the adoption of the exclusionary rule will not prevent all illegal searches and seizures, it will discourage them. Police officers and prosecuting officials are primarily interested in convicting criminals. Given the exclusionary rule and a choice between securing evidence by legal rather than illegal means, officers will be impelled to obey the law themselves since not to do so will jeopardize their objectives. Moreover, the same considerations that justify the privilege against self-incrimination are not irrelevant here. As Wigmore pointed out, that privilege, just as the prohibition against unreasonable searches and seizures, is primarily for the protection of the innocent. "The real objection is that *any system of administration which permits the prosecution to trust habitually to compulsory self-disclosure as a source of proof must itself morally suffer thereby.* The inclination develops to rely mainly upon such evidence, and to be satisfied with an incomplete investigation of the other sources. The exercise of the power to extract answers begets a forgetfulness of the just limitations of that power. The simple and peaceful process of questioning breeds a readiness to resort to bullying and to physical force and torture. If there is a right to an answer, there soon seems to be a right to the expected answer,- that is, to a confession of guilt. Thus the legitimate use grows into the unjust abuse; ultimately, the innocent are jeopardized by the encroachments of a bad system. Such seems to have been the course of experience in those legal systems where the privilege was not recognized." Similarly, a system that permits the prosecution to trust habitually to the use of illegally obtained evidence cannot help but encourage violations of the Constitution at the expense of lawful means of enforcing the law. On the other hand, if courts respect the constitutional provisions by refusing to sanction their violation, they will not only command the respect of law-abiding citizens for themselves adhering to the law, they will also arouse public opinion as a deterrent to lawless enforcement of the law by bringing just criticism to bear on law enforcement officers who allow criminals to escape by pursuing them in lawless ways.

It is contended, however, that the police do not always have a choice of securing evidence by legal means and that in many cases the criminal will escape if illegally obtained evidence cannot be used against him. This contention is not properly directed at the exclusionary rule, but at the constitutional provisions themselves. It was rejected when those provisions were adopted. In such cases had the Constitution been obeyed, the criminal could in no event be convicted. He does not go free because the constable blundered, but because the Constitutions prohibit securing the evidence against him. Their very provisions contemplate that it is preferable that some criminals go free than that the right of privacy of all the people be set at naught. "It is vital, no doubt, that criminals should be detected, and that all relevant evidence should be secured and used. On the other hand, it cannot be said too often that what is involved far transcends the fate of some sordid offender. Nothing less is involved than that which makes for an atmosphere of freedom as against a feeling of fear and repression for society as a whole. " The situation presented differs only in degree from other situations where the choice must be made between securing convictions by illegal means or allowing criminals to go free. Cases undoubtedly arise where a violation of the privilege against self-incrimination, a coerced confession, the testimony of defendant's spouse, a violation of the attorney-client privilege or other privileges is essential to the conviction of the criminal, but the choice has been made that he go unpunished. Arguments against the wisdom of these rights and privileges, just as arguments against the wisdom of the prohibitions against unreasonable searches and seizures, should be addressed to the question whether they should exist at all, but arguments against the wisdom of the constitutional provisions may not be invoked to justify a failure to enforce them while they remain the law of the land.

We are not unmindful of the contention that the federal exclusionary rule has been arbitrary in its application and has introduced needless confusion into the law of criminal procedure. The validity of this contention need not be considered now. Even if it is assumed that it is meritorious, it does not follow that the exclusionary rule should be rejected. In developing a rule of evidence applicable in the state courts, this court is not bound by the decisions that have applied the federal rule, and if it appears that those decisions have developed needless refinements and distinctions, this court need not follow them. Similarly, if the federal cases indicate needless limitations on the right to conduct reasonable searches and seizures or to secure warrants, this court is free to reject them. Under these circumstances the adoption of the exclusionary rule need not introduce confusion into the law of criminal procedure. Instead it opens the door to the development of workable rules governing searches and seizures and the issuance of warrants that will protect both the rights guaranteed by the constitutional provisions and the interest of society in the suppression of crime.

The orders are reversed.

*****

CONCLUSION

From the period between 1955 and 1961, California and a few other states adopted the exclusionary rule. After the decision in *Mapp v. Ohio*, all states were required to exclude illegally obtained evidence from criminal trials.

REVIEW

1.   After a thorough reading of the case, can you identify all the reasons *against* having an exclusionary rule?

2.   What does the court say about its decision to adopt the exclusionary rule in light of the Supreme Court's refusal to apply the rule to the states, in *Wolf v. Colorado*?

3.   What are the major arguments Justice Traynor's opinion makes in favor of adopting the exclusionary rule?

II. People v. Hamilton, 102 Cal.App.4ᵗʰ 1311 (2002)

*****

Reardon, J.

BACKGROUND

On October 6, 2000, approximately 12:40 a.m., Vallejo Police Officer Kevin Bartlett was on patrol when he "ran" a car's license plate number. A DMV source reported that the vehicle registration for that plate had expired in August 2000. A current registration tag on the license plate prompted Bartlett to suspect that the tag might be fraudulent. He stopped the vehicle to investigate.

Officer Bartlett asked the driver-appellant Hurmon Lamech Hamilton-for his driver's license, vehicle registration and proof of insurance. Hamilton provided a valid driver's license but could not produce the vehicle's registration. He told the officer that the vehicle was still registered to another person, but that he owned it.

At Officer Bartlett's request, Hamilton got out of the car. During a search of Hamilton's pants pocket, the officer found a plastic bag containing a white material appearing to be cocaine base, three buds of what appeared to be marijuana, and a small pouch of material that also appeared to be marijuana. Before the car was towed, Officer Bartlett conducted an inventory of the vehicle's contents, finding a loaded .357 magnum handgun in the glove compartment. Hamilton told police that he found the weapon and intended to sell it. During the vehicle search, Officer Bartlett also found a then current registration card for the vehicle. He concluded that the DMV failed to accurately update its vehicle registration records.

Hamilton was charged by information with possession of cocaine base, possession of a firearm by a felon, and possession of less than one ounce of marijuana. The information also alleged an enhancement for having served a prior prison term. Hamilton moved to suppress the evidence obtained against him, arguing that the warrantless search was unjustified. The People countered that Officer Bartlett relied in good faith on the DMV report and thus, an exception to the exclusionary rule applied. The trial court denied the suppression motion.

DISCUSSION

In April 2002, we sought briefing from the parties on the issue of whether the information received about the expired vehicle registration provided a legally sufficient basis for "good faith" reliance by Officer Bartlett. In June 2002, the California Supreme Court held that the so-called good faith exception to the exclusionary rule did not apply where police relied on erroneous information provided by parole authorities or the Department of Corrections which was thought to be accurate at the time of the search. (*People v. Willis.*) Now, Hamilton argues that *Willis* also bars application of the good faith exception to his case.

Thus, the pivotal question is whether the exclusionary rule should apply to a police officer who acts in an objectively reasonable reliance on information provided by the DMV that is later found to be in error. The answer lies in *Willis*. That decision turns on the purpose of the exclusionary rule- to deter misconduct by *law enforcement officials*. Consistent with this purpose, evidence obtained from a search may be suppressed only if it can be said that the police knew or should have known that the search was unconstitutional. When considering whether to apply the good faith exception, we consider the objective reasonableness of both the officer who conducted the search and those who provided information material to the searching officer. We consider whether, in light of the source of the erroneous information, the deterrent effect of exclusion is sufficient to warrant imposition of that sanction. The determination of whether the application of the exclusionary rule is warranted is made on a case-by-case basis.

The United States and California Supreme Courts have ruled that the good faith exception applies when police rely on a statute enacted by legislators, which statute is subsequently determined to be unconstitutional. The officials who enacted the statute are not adjuncts to law enforcement whose conduct could be deterred by application of the exclusionary rule. For the same reason, the good faith exception applies when police rely on information generated by court clerks that is later found to be erroneous. Again, the exclusion of the challenged evidence at trial would not sufficiently deter future errors to warrant imposition of that sanction. Court clerks are not adjuncts of law enforcement and have no stake in the outcome of particular criminal prosecutions. However, if erroneous information from a Department of Corrections parole officer is transmitted to and relied on by police, the parole officer's law enforcement status makes application of the exclusionary rule appropriate in order to deter the Department of Corrections officials from disseminating inaccurate information leading to unreasonable searches. The good faith exception is inapplicable under these circumstances.

Hamilton contends that the DMV is an adjunct of law enforcement sufficient to bar application of the good faith exception to the exclusionary rule. The Attorney General argues that the DMV is not part of law enforcement- that it is merely a bureaucratic agency charged with regulating the statewide use of motor vehicles. Whether a DMV clerk acts as an adjunct to law enforcement is an issue that is as yet unresolved in California. Conflicting answers to this question have arisen around the United States.

By state law, employees of the DMV whose primary duty is law enforcement are considered peace officers. The Legislature accords peace officer status to some DMV employees in order that they might enforce those provisions of the law committed to the department's administration and enforce the law on department premises. Those employees specified by statute are the director and deputy director of the DMV; the deputy director of the department's Investigations and Audits Division; the chief of the Field Investigations branch; and department investigators including rank-and-file, supervisory and management personnel. However, the data entry clerk who-we infer-made the error leading to the detention and search of Hamilton and his vehicle does not appear to be among these enumerated employees. Thus, a DMV clerk is not a peace officer per se.

In our case, Officer Bartlett relied on information received from the DMV. We find his situation similar to that involving information received from court clerks in *Arizona v. Evans.* For the same reasons, we find that the clerks who generated the DMV database are not peace officers, law enforcement officials or adjuncts of law enforcement. They have no stake in the outcome of criminal prosecutions. As such, we are satisfied that United States Supreme Court and California Supreme Court authorities support the conclusion that the good faith exception to the exclusionary rule may apply when a DMV clerk creates an erroneous data base entry subsequently relied on by a police officer who acts objectively in reasonable reliance on the accuracy of the information.

Based on the initial information provided by the DMV and Officer Bartlett's observation of what appeared to be fraudulent registration tags on Hamilton's license plate, we find that the police had reasonable cause to detain Hamilton. When Hamilton could not produce valid registration, the officer's suspicion rose to the level of probable cause to arrest for displaying false registration tags. The search of Hamilton and his vehicle were legally justified as a search incident to arrest, based on the information then known to Officer Bartlett. Although the officer later learned that the vehicle was in fact properly registered, exclusion of the drugs and weapon found during the search falls within the good faith exception to application of the exclusionary rule. Thus, the trial court properly denied Hamilton's motion to suppress.

The judgment is affirmed.

*****

CONCLUSION

The appellant's argument in this case was based on a California case, *People v. Willis*, in which parole authorities and a parole officer made a mistake believing the suspect was still on parole, such that police officers made an illegal administrative search. The good-faith exception was held to be inapplicable since parole officers are adjuncts of law enforcement. In this case, however, the DMV made a mistake in its database, and the court held that *Willis* did not apply, since the person handling the database would not part of the DMV's law enforcement arm.

REVIEW

1.   Does it seem right to you that the major justification of the exclusionary rule is to deter police misconduct and thus if errors made by anyone but law enforcement officers, then the resulting improper searches or seizures should still be upheld in court under a good-faith exception?

2.   What if an agency such as the DMV routinely made thousands of database errors, such that the circumstances in Hamilton were commonplace and searches made pursuant to these errors were frequent. Should the court's analysis in *Arizona v. Evans* still stand? Should there be a point at which the goal should also become to deter other agencies from actions that affect the rights of individuals indirectly, through police enforcement based on their errors? How might this deterrence be accomplished? (By, for example, pressure put on them by law enforcement and the public?)

Section 2: The Defense of Entrapment

OVERVIEW

California employs a test similar to that of the federal government for determining whether police entrapment can be used as a defense for a crime. Entrapment is established if the law enforcement conduct is likely to induce a normally law- abiding person to commit the offense. This in essence boils down to two prongs: first, the government must have induced the conduct; second, the defendant must have not been predisposed toward the behavior.

CASES-

I. People v. Watson, 22 Cal.4th 220 (2000)

The dominant majority of entrapment cases focus on the second prong, whether the prosecution can show that the defendant was predisposed (and was not, thus, a normally law-abiding person.) However, the following California Supreme Court case shows that there still may be controversy over the first prong. In this case, the question is whether the government in fact induced the crime through its sting operation.

*****

Chin, J.

BACKGROUND

One March evening in 1997, Bakersfield police officers conducted a vehicle theft "sting" operation. They staged an arrest of a plainclothes police officer driving a black 1980 Chevrolet Monte Carlo that belonged to the police department. The arresting officers activated the emergency lights and siren of their marked patrol car and stopped the Monte Carlo. The Monte Carlo's driver drove into a parking lot and parked. While a group of spectators watched, a uniformed police officer approached the Monte Carlo, ordered the driver out, patted him down, handcuffed him, placed him in the backseat of the patrol car, and drove away, leaving the Monte Carlo behind. The police left the Monte Carlo unlocked with the keys in the ignition to make it easier to take. They wanted to "give the impression [the driver] was arrested and the vehicle was left there."

A couple of hours later, police arrested defendant after he drove the Monte Carlo from the parking lot. He told the arresting officer that his niece had informed him of the earlier apparent arrest and told him to "come and take" the car. He did just that, intending to use it to "roll," i.e., to drive it.

Defendant was charged with taking a vehicle. At the first trial, the court instructed the jury on entrapment. The jury was unable to reach a verdict, and the court declared a mistrial. At the second trial, the court refused to instruct on entrapment, finding insufficient evidence to support the defense. The jury found defendant guilty. The Court of Appeal reversed the judgment, finding the trial court should have instructed on entrapment. We granted review.

DISCUSSION

The trial court was required to instruct the second jury on the defense of entrapment if, but only if, substantial evidence supported the defense. In California, the test for entrapment focuses on the police conduct and is objective. Entrapment is established if the law enforcement conduct is likely to induce a *normally law- abiding person* to commit the offense. "[S]uch a person would normally resist the temptation to commit a crime presented by the simple opportunity to act unlawfully. Official conduct that does no more than offer that opportunity to the suspect-for example, a decoy program-is therefore permissible; but it is impermissible for the police or their agents to pressure the suspect by overbearing conduct such as badgering, cajoling, importuning, or other affirmative acts likely to induce a normally law-abiding person to commit the crime." (*People v. Baranza.*)

The *Barraza* court described two guiding principles. "First, if the actions of the law enforcement agent would generate in a normally law-abiding person a motive for the crime other than ordinary criminal intent, entrapment will be established." Defendant does not rely on this principle. He does not claim his motive in taking the car was other than ordinary criminal intent. Instead, he relies on the second principle: "Second, affirmative police conduct that would make commission of the crime unusually attractive to a normally law-abiding person will likewise constitute entrapment. Such conduct would include, for example, a guarantee that the act is not illegal or the offense will go undetected, an offer of exorbitant consideration, or any similar enticement.

112

Citing this second principle, the Court of Appeal concluded this case warranted an entrapment instruction because the jury might have found that "the police made taking the car unusually attractive" by sending the message, " 'You can take this car and get away with it.' " Such a message, the Court of Appeal concluded, might constitute "any similar enticement" under *Barraza*. We disagree. The *Barraza* language must be considered in its context. *Barraza* involved communications directly between the law enforcement agent and the defendant. Normally, police conduct must be directed at a specific person or persons to constitute entrapment. The police must "pressure the suspect by overbearing conduct ...." Except perhaps in extreme circumstances, the second *Barraza* principle is limited to instances of individual, personal enticement, excluding communications made to the world at large. Merely providing people in general an opportunity to commit a crime is not an improper enticement or otherwise entrapment. "[T]he rule is clear that 'ruses, stings, and decoys are permissible stratagems in the enforcement of criminal law, and they become invalid only when badgering or importuning takes place to an extent and degree that is likely to induce an otherwise law-abiding person to commit a crime.'"

The sting operation in this case presents no evidence of entrapment, both because the police did not specifically intend it as a communication to defendant personally, and because it did not actually *guarantee* anything, but merely conveyed the idea detection was unlikely. The police did nothing more than present to the general community a tempting opportunity to take the Monte Carlo. Some persons, obviously including defendant, might have found the temptation hard to resist. But a person who steals when given the opportunity is an opportunistic thief, not a normally law-abiding person. Specifically, normally law-abiding persons do not take a car not belonging to them merely because it is unlocked with the keys in the ignition and it appears they will not be caught. Defendant presented no evidence of any personal contact whatever between police and himself; certainly he could not show that the police cajoled him, gave him any enticement or guarantee, or even knew or cared who he was.

Defendant argues the jury might have found that the police used his niece as an unwitting agent to entrap him. *However, no more evidence of contact between the police and the niece existed than evidence of contact between the police and defendant.*

Justice Mosk argues that "next we may anticipate arranging for a homeowner to leave his front door open all night to attract a burglar. Or a bank to leave a signed check on the counter to attract a forger. Or leaving a loaded gun on a park bench to attract a potential robber." (Conc. opn., *post*, at p. 225.) A big difference exists, however, between the police risking their own property in tightly controlled circumstances and asking the public to do the same (or, in the loaded gun hypothetical, to invite violence) in uncontrolled circumstances. Moreover, the police might reasonably believe that sting operations like this *deter*, not encourage, crime. For example, once word of this case circulated in the community, future would-be car thieves might hesitate before taking advantage of what appears to be an easy target.

The trial court correctly refused to instruct the second jury on entrapment. Accordingly, we reverse the judgment of the Court of Appeal and remand the matter for further proceedings consistent with our opinion.

Mosk, J. (Concurring)

I concur in the judgment.

I concede that the result that the majority opinion reaches is sound under the law.

But I cannot resist expressing my reservations about the morality of the conduct by the police.

It is a primary function of a law enforcement agency not only to investigate the commission of crimes but also to prevent their commission in the first place, certainly not to encourage them. Members of the public are persuaded to lock their motor vehicles and to remove the keys therefrom. The police acted to the contrary here and thus deliberately encouraged commission of a crime. The defendant, so motivated, accommodated them.

If leaving the keys in an open motor vehicle is sound law enforcement, then next we may anticipate arranging for a homeowner to leave his front door open all night to attract a burglar. Or a bank to leave a signed check on the counter to attract a forger. Or leaving a loaded gun on a park bench to attract a potential robber. Police may thus apprehend more criminals. But there will be more crimes.

In a strange rebuttal, the majority opinion refers to the police "risking their own property." The fact, of course, is that police possess and use *public property* and must act with that in mind.

My preference is for law enforcement agencies to take steps to make the commission of crimes impossible, or at least more difficult, rather than simpler. Admittedly there are potential criminals in our midst, and weak-willed persons who will take advantage of criminal opportunity. I would prefer discouraging them rather than devising techniques to make their task easier.

*****

CONCLUSION

California has laid out a fairly narrow definition of government-induced conduct. The state's Supreme Court holds that the government has to specifically encourage a person (or perhaps a few people) in order for an entrapment defense to have a shot. This is different from some other states (that use the two-pronged subjective test) but still allow the entrapment defense in instances where police lay out attractive decoys (such as a drunk in an alley with a ten-dollar bill sticking out of his pocket) but do not have any particular target in mind (and so any person happening down the alley who takes the money may suffice).

REVIEW

1. What is the reasoning in the majority's opinion? Can you find fault with it?

2. What was the point of Mosk's concurring opinion if he believes the majority opinion was sound legal reasoning?

CHAPTER ELEVEN

Constitutional Violations: Other Remedies Against Government Misconduct

The exclusionary rule assists defendants who have been victims of illegal searches or seizures, in their criminal trials, and the entrapment defense may in some instances earn acquittals for defendants. Other remedies exist, however, both in addition to these, and at times in combination. A major area of recent litigation involves racial profiling by police departments. The Fourth Amendment often is not beneficial to profiling victims, because the Supreme Court has held that pretext stops and subsequent searches do not violate the Fourth Amendment (*Whren v. United States,* 517 U.S. 806 (1996)). Even though profiling victims may not be able to suppress any evidence against them, they (and profiling victims who were not found with any illegal contraband) still have an arsenal of tools in terms of suing law enforcement.

Take, for example, the ACLU of Northern California's recent suit against the California Highway Patrol, alleging that the CHP was profiling black and Latino motorists on Interstate 5 throughout Northern California. This was a class-action lawsuit asking for both money damages and injunctive relief which would prevent the CHP from further such conduct. Among the various causes of action (not involving the Fourth Amendment) alleged by the ACLU were the following:

- Racial discrimination in federally funded programs, under Title VI of the Civil Rights Act of 1964.
- Section 1983 violation of 14th Amendment's fundamental rights to liberty.
- Section 1983 violation of Commerce Clause right to interstate travel.
- Section 1983 violation of Equal Protection Clause.
- Violation of Sections 1985 and 1986: conspiracy to violate civil rights.
- Violation of Article I, section 7(a) of the California Constitution (deprivation of due process and equal protection of laws).
- Violation of California Civil Code section 52.1(b) (interference with exercise and enjoyment of rights afforded by U.S. and California Constitutions).
- Tort claim (intentional infliction of emotional distress).
- Tort claim (negligent infliction of emotional distress).
- Tort claim (false imprisonment).

Additionally, since illegal searches were claimed pursuant to pretextual stops, the ACLU alleged violations of the 4th Amendment. The stops themselves could not be attacked under the 4th as long as there was a technically valid reasons for the stops

[For a full description of this lawsuit, see www.aclunc.org/discrimination/dwb-complaint.html. Eventually a settlement was reached by which the CHP agreed to a number of reforms, and the lawsuit did not go forward.]

Plaintiffs who sue the government, as seen in the above example, attempt to identify every possible legal theory by which the lawsuit may result in civil remedies such as damages and injunctions (forcing the police to stop behaving a certain way). Additionally, in egregious circumstances, victims may be able to convince prosecutors to criminally charge police officers under various state and federal statutes. Victims may also file complaints against the police to the department (internal review) and any civilian review mechanisms (external review).

In the following three sections we'll look at a California code that protects individuals from constitutional violations by both the government and private actors; next we'll examine a tort claim arguing that police failed to protect a domestic violence victim; and finally, we'll address a recent controversial phenomenon in California: police who file defamation suits against those who file complaints against the officers.

Section 1: Civil Actions

OVERVIEW

For violations of the U.S. Constitution, Section 1983 lawsuits are the primary tool victims of police misconduct rely on when suing for damages and injunctive relief. Section 1983 applies to those acting under color of state law (such as police officers on-duty or off-duty but acting as police). However, states usually have other options under state law. A primary example from California is Civil Code section 52.1, which provides remedies for individuals who Constitutional rights are interfered with by others who may or may not be acting under color of state law. The rights must be interfered with "by threats, intimidation, or coercion." Thus this statute applies only to the more egregious forms of police behavior, although "intimidation" may be interpreted broadly. The statute allows both the government (section a) and private individuals (section b) to sue those who violate their rights. The primary purpose of the statute was to remedy hate crimes, but in application, government misconduct may come within the scope of the statute. For example, in *Rose v. City of Los Angeles*, 814 F.Supp.878 (1993) the mother of a man killed by police officers alleged that they used excessive force and brought action not only under Section 1983, but also under Civil Code 52.1, for the wrongful death of her son.

California Civil Code 52.1. Civil actions for protection of rights; damages, injunctive and other equitable relief; violations of orders

(a) If a person or persons, whether or not acting under color of law, interferes by threats, intimidation, or coercion, or attempts to interfere by threats, intimidation, or coercion, with the exercise or enjoyment by any individual or individuals of rights secured by the Constitution or laws of the United States, or of the rights secured by the Constitution or laws of this state, the Attorney General, or any district attorney or city attorney may bring a civil action for injunctive and other appropriate equitable relief in the name of the people of the State of California, in order to protect the peaceable exercise or enjoyment of the right or rights secured. An action brought by the Attorney General, any district attorney, or any city attorney may also seek a civil penalty of twenty-five thousand dollars ($25,000). If this civil penalty is requested, it shall be assessed individually against each person who is determined to have violated this section and the penalty shall be awarded to each individual whose rights under this section are determined to have been violated.

(b) Any individual whose exercise or enjoyment of rights secured by the Constitution or laws of the United States, or of rights secured by the Constitution or laws of this state, has been interfered with, or attempted to be interfered with, as described in subdivision (a), may institute and prosecute in his or her own name and on his or her own behalf a civil action for damages, including, but not limited to, damages, injunctive relief, and other appropriate equitable relief to protect the peaceable exercise or enjoyment of the right or rights secured.

Section 2: Failure to Protect by Law Enforcement

OVERVIEW

The general rule is that there is no duty on the part of government actors to protect members of the public from harm. This applies to police officers in execution of their duties. However, California does allow for the possibility of a successful tort claim against the police if the victim can show a "special relationship" with the police that gave rise to a duty to protect. In the following case we'll see how the court analyzes the question of whether such a relationship exists in an instance of domestic violence. In other states, domestic violence victims have also been successful at times in Section 1983 suits by arguing that police violate their equal protection rights by failing to help female victims of spousal abuse. Generally, however, it is an uphill battle for individuals arguing that the police failed to protect them.

CASES-

I. Benavidez v. San Jose Police Department, 71 Cal.App.4th 853 (1999)

In this case a domestic violence victim accuses police of failing to protect her. The defense (the police officer, chief, department, and city) moved for the dismissal of all causes of action prior to trial (called "summary judgment") and the trial court granted their motion. The plaintiff-victim now challenges the dismissal of these causes, but only does so based on two theories: the tort claims for negligently causing her harm and for negligently inflicting upon her emotional distress. Likely, this means her attorney decided they did not have reasonable grounds to appeal the dismissal of the other causes of action.

*****

Cottle, P.J.

BACKGROUND

In 1993, plaintiff and her son Joey were living with plaintiff's boyfriend, Richard Cortez. Cortez verbally abused plaintiff and, on occasion, physically abused her as well. In August 1993, plaintiff had to call the Police because Cortez had beaten her up. She described the August 1993 incident as the only other incident "of equally serious physical abuse" as the incidents that are the subject of this lawsuit.

On the evening of December 11, 1993, plaintiff and Cortez went to a company party where Cortez had several drinks. When they arrived home, plaintiff and Cortez began arguing about his drinking and about her radio, and Cortez attacked her. He punched plaintiff, kicked her, and then threw her down the stairs. He took her car keys and was heading out the door when plaintiff went running after him. She told him he could not take her car. He punched her in the eye and left. After he was gone, Benavidez called a women's shelter. The shelter asked her if she had transportation. She then phoned for a taxi, picked up her son at the babysitter's, and went to a motel. She did not call the police that night because she was embarrassed.

Plaintiff returned home about 10:30 or 11:00 a.m. the next morning after talking to Cortez on the phone. He told her he was moving out, and she told him to go ahead but to leave the house unlocked and to leave her car. When she arrived, however, the house was locked and her car was not there. As plaintiff began breaking into her house, Cortez arrived. He immediately started attacking her, and he threw two pots through her front windows. Plaintiff told Joey to call 911, and when he did, Cortez fled, again in plaintiff's car. Joey's call was made at 11:39 a.m.

Officer Michael Lloyd and Sergeant Michael Ross arrived at plaintiff's house at 11:42 a.m. When Ross arrived, he told Joey to put down a stick he was holding and to "stop acting macho." Plaintiff was upset and kept changing the subject, and Lloyd had a hard time trying to get her to sit down and tell him what had happened. Plaintiff was holding her stomach and had to go to the bathroom because she was nauseous. She told the police that Cortez had beaten her up and taken her car, and that he might be at his mother's house. She gave them that address and a physical description of Cortez, which the police broadcast to other officers. Lloyd put out an "A[ll] P[oints] B[ulletin]" for Cortez for felony battery and car theft.

During the interview Lloyd asked plaintiff if she wanted an ambulance or if she wanted to go to the hospital. Each time she told him no. The police did not talk to plaintiff about staying in the apartment. Around 12:10 p.m. both officers left. In her deposition, plaintiff explained that she understood that Ross was "just leav[ing because] it was over" and that Lloyd was heading to Cortez's mother's house to see if he could find her car and apprehend Cortez. When she asked them what she should do if Cortez returned, they told her to call 911.

Within minutes of the police leaving, Cortez called. Joey picked up the phone, and Cortez began threatening him. Joey's mother told him to hang up. As soon as he did, the phone started ringing again, but plaintiff did not pick it up. This lasted for about 10 minutes.

Lloyd arrived at Cortez's mother's house at 12:18 p.m. Thus, the trip took him about eight minutes. He drove around the neighborhood looking for plaintiff's car. Not finding it, he decided to return to plaintiff's house to get additional information from her.

As Officer Lloyd was on his way back, Cortez reappeared at plaintiff's house. Plaintiff heard him at the screen door trying to break in, and she called 911. While she was on the phone with the 911 operator, Cortez moved over to the broken window, which he was attempting to enter. Plaintiff apparently dropped the phone at that point and ran up to the window, to keep him from coming in. From outside, Cortez reached in and grabbed plaintiff. He pulled a glass shard from the broken window and used it to stab her in the head and neck. Meanwhile, Lloyd and other officers arrived. They subdued Cortez by using Mace and a baton.

118

A transcript of the 911 call, time stamped 12:35 p.m., records plaintiff asking for help, then yelling at Cortez to go, warning him that police were on the way; it then records screams, then the voices of Officer Lloyd and other officers telling Cortez to get down on the ground. The transcript ends with plaintiff requesting an ambulance.

The City of San Jose Police Duty Manual and the Police Chiefs' Domestic Violence Protocol for Law Enforcement provided in 1993 that "Officers shall assist victims of domestic violence in the following manner: ... [¶] Assist in making arrangements to transport the victim to an alternate shelter if the victim expresses a concern for safety or [if] the officer determines a need exists."

In March 1995, plaintiff and her son Joey filed suit against the City/Police defendants. On February 20, 1997, defendants moved for summary judgment. In opposition to the motion, plaintiff submitted a declaration in which she stated, inter alia, (1) "When Officer Lloyd and Sergeant Ross first arrived on the scene on December 12, 1993, Officer Lloyd announced, 'Don't worry, we're here!' or very similar words to that effect. I understood this as a statement that the officers had taken control of the scene and that they would protect me and my son Joey"; and (2) "During the interview by Officer Lloyd and Sergeant Ross on the morning of December 12, 1993, I *did* ask whether I could be taken to a shelter. The officers did not say 'yes' or 'no'; in fact, they did not respond to my inquiry in any manner." She also submitted a declaration from a police procedures expert who opined that a special relationship was created when the officers responded to plaintiff's 911 call, and the deposition testimony of a neighbor who felt that the police should not have left plaintiff without protection.

The trial court granted defendant's motion. In its written order, the court explained that the second, sixth and seventh causes of action were insufficient irrespective of the inconsistencies between the deposition testimony and declaration of plaintiff Adela Benavidez. "As to the first and third causes of action, Ms. Benavide[z]' deposition testimony establishes that no special relationship was created between plaintiffs and defendant officers as a matter of law. To the extent the deposition testimony is contradicted by Ms. Benavide[z]' declaration in opposition to the instant motion, the Court must defer to the deposition testimony.

DISCUSSION

Plaintiffs' first and third causes of action for negligence are premised upon the police department's failure to protect them from the final attack by Cortez. In granting summary judgment for the City/Police defendants, the trial court found that, as a matter of law, the police did not have a duty to plaintiffs under the circumstances of this case.

The existence of a duty is a question of law. [This means that a jury cannot decide whether the duty exists—courts must.] As a general rule, a person who has not created a peril has no duty to come to the aid of another "no matter how great the danger in which the other is placed, or how easily he could be rescued, unless there is some relationship between them which gives rise to a duty to act. [Citations.]" This rule applies to police officers as well as to other citizens: The police owe duties of care only to the public at large and, except where they enter into a "special relationship," have no duty to offer affirmative assistance to anyone in particular. (*Williams v. State of California*).

Plaintiff contends she produced evidence that a "special relationship" was created between her, her son, and the officers, and that therefore the trial court erred in granting summary judgment on the negligence causes of action. The evidence of a special relationship was set forth, she asserts, (1) in her declaration in opposition to the summary judgment motion, (2) in her police procedures expert's declaration, and (3) in her neighbor's deposition. We shall examine plaintiff's declaration first and then the two remaining items of evidence.

(1) Plaintiff's Declaration

As noted earlier, plaintiff made the following statements in her declaration in opposition to summary judgment, which she contends establish that a special relationship was created: (1) "When Officer Lloyd and Sergeant Ross first arrived on the scene on December 12, 1993, Officer Lloyd announced, 'Don't worry, we're here!' or very similar words to that effect. I understood this as a statement that the officers had taken control of the scene and that they would protect me and my son Joey"; and (2) "During the interview by Officer Lloyd and Sergeant Ross on the morning of December 12, 1993, I *did* ask whether I could be taken to a shelter. The officers did not say 'yes' or 'no'; in fact, they did not respond to my inquiry in any manner."

In analyzing these statements, we are constrained by the well settled rule that "[a] party cannot create an issue of fact by a declaration which contradicts his prior [discovery responses]. [Citation.] In determining whether any triable issue of material fact exists, the trial court may, in its discretion, give great weight to admissions made in deposition and disregard contradictory and self-serving affidavits of the party."

This is because, as the California Supreme Court explained in *D'Amico v. Board of Medical Examiners*, " 'Where ... there is a clear and unequivocal admission by the plaintiff ... in his deposition ... [the trial court is] forced to conclude there is no substantial evidence of the existence of a triable issue of fact [notwithstanding a contradictory declaration in opposition to summary judgment].' ... [¶] ... [A]dmissions against interest have a very high credibility value. This is especially true when, as in this case, the admission is obtained not in the normal course of human activities and affairs but in the context of an established pretrial procedure whose purpose is to elicit facts. Accordingly, when such an admission becomes relevant to the determination, on motion for summary judgment, of whether or not there exist triable issues of fact (as opposed to legal issues) between the parties, it is entitled to and should receive a kind of deference not normally accorded evidentiary allegations in affidavits."

With these rules in mind, we examine the two statements plaintiff made in her declaration. Her statement that she "*did* ask whether [she] could be taken to a shelter" directly contradicts her repeated testimony at her deposition that she did not "tell the police officers that [she] wanted to leave the apartment ...." Plaintiff relies heavily on this statement in her brief on appeal. She contends that her request "trigger[ed] a duty of assistance under the internal police department regulations, which the officers failed to fulfill." The statement, however, flies in the face of her unequivocal testimony during her deposition, during which she admitted that she *did* not tell the officers she wanted to leave: "Q. Did you tell them that you wanted to leave the apartment? [¶] A. No, I was throwing up most of the time. I could hardly talk.... [¶] Q. And you did not tell the police officers that you wanted to leave the apartment; is that correct? [¶] A. No. [¶] Q. Pardon me? ¶] A. No. [¶] Q. No, meaning? [¶] A. *I didn't say anything*." (Italics added.) Plaintiff's statement that she told the officers she wanted to go to a shelter and that they ignored her directly and unequivocally contradicts her testimony that she did not "say anything" and that she did not tell them she wanted to leave her apartment. Under the case law, her latter statement must be disregarded.

Similarly, plaintiff's statement in her declaration that the officers told her " 'Don't worry, we're here!' " which led her to believe that they would remain to "protect [her] and [her] son" is belied by her deposition testimony. There she made it clear that she knew that both officers were leaving her and were not remaining to protect her and her son. Ross left, she explained, because the incident "was over"; Lloyd left to see if Cortez was at his mother's house and "to look for [her] car." Knowing that both of the officers were leaving and would no longer be there to protect her, she asked them what she should do if Cortez returned. She was told to call 911. Any reliance on the officer's statement, "Don't worry, we're here!" surely could only apply when the officers were "here" (i.e., at plaintiff's house), not when they had left the scene to take on other police assignments (Ross) or to go to Cortez's mother's house (Lloyd) some seven or eight minutes away from plaintiff's apartment.

Plaintiff relies upon two cases which held that declarations that contradict earlier discovery responses may sometimes be considered. However, both cases are clearly distinguishable. *Price v. Wells Fargo Bank*, which cited with approval the *D'Amico* rule, involved admissions which were "circumstantial," "tacit ... or fragmentary and equivocal concessions." Here, in contrast, the admissions in the earlier deposition were not equivocal-they directly and unequivocally contradicted the later statements. *Nederer v. Ferreira* involved a plaintiff's misunderstanding of a legal term of art (an "assignment"). Notwithstanding that the plaintiff thought she did not have an assignment, "it is clear defendant treated the note as assigned to plaintiff and accordingly made payments on the note, to her, over a period of time. He presented no evidence he ever challenged the genuineness of the assignment or plaintiff's right to receive payments thereunder." Thus, the contradiction between plaintiff's deposition and later declaration was explained; she now understood that the payments had been made because the note was assigned to her.

The contradiction in the instant case cannot be explained based on plaintiff's lack of understanding of a legal term of art. Either she did not say anything or she asked to go to a shelter; either she thought the officers were staying to protect her or she thought they were leaving. The responses are contradictory and mutually exclusive. Under these circumstances, the trial court did not abuse its discretion in ruling that the contradictory statements in plaintiff's declaration must be disregarded, and therefore that those statements failed to raise a triable issue of fact.

(2) *Plaintiff's Neighbor's Deposition Testimony and Her Police Procedures Expert's Declaration*

Plaintiff also contends that a special relationship was created when the officers engaged in affirmative acts that increased the risk to plaintiff and her son. Specifically, she argues that the officers created a peril for her and Joey by using them as "bait" to lure Cortez back to the apartment. In support of this theory, she introduced the declaration of a police procedures expert and the deposition testimony of her neighbor.

It is true that under certain circumstances, a special relationship may be created when police engage in affirmative acts that increase the risk of harm to others. In *Mann v. State of California*, a highway patrol officer saw two stranded cars in a speed-change lane of a freeway and pulled up behind them. He stood in the lane and did not instruct anyone to get back into his or her car. Later a tow truck arrived, and the officer left without telling anyone, and without waiting for the tow truck to assume the protective rearward position with a flashing light. Furthermore, the officer did not put any flares on the freeway. Shortly after he left, another car driven by a partially blind driver sideswiped one of the stalled cars and struck the plaintiff. The Court of Appeal reversed the trial judge's direct verdict for the state, noting that, "While no special relationship may exist between members of the California Highway Patrol and the motoring public generally, or between the Patrol and stranded motorists generally, once a state traffic officer has chosen to investigate the plight of specific persons on a freeway and informed himself of the foreseeable danger to them from passing traffic, a special relationship requiring him to protect them by readily available means arises and liability may attach if the officer's limited duty to protect these people under these special circumstances is not performed."

121

Plaintiff contends that her situation is comparable to the situation in *Mann*. She asserts that the police informed her not to worry because they were there, and then they left leaving her and Joey as "bait" to lure Cortez back to the apartment. To support this theory, she attached in her opposition to defendant's motion for summary judgment the deposition testimony of her neighbor, Jeffrey Scott, and the declaration of Frank Saunders, a police procedures expert.

Plaintiff's neighbor Jeffrey Scott was asked the following in his deposition: "Q. What about this incident made you think that they were using Mrs. Benavidez as bait? [¶] A. Well, they didn't know where this guy was. They looked around for him, they asked me if I had seen him. And I felt like they could have taken her and the boy out of the house, and he still would have come back. [¶] By her and the boy being there, he came back and stayed, so I felt like they used him- or they used these people as bait for this guy to come back, because more than likely he was watching-because it's very easy to do-he was watching when they came back and when they left the first time." He also stated that he had seen a lot of domestic violence in his neighborhood and that he had observed that the perpetrator often leaves and then comes back.

Plaintiff also submitted the declaration of Frank Saunders, a retired field training police officer who has testified as an expert in police procedures in over 300 cases. Saunders concluded that defendants were "grossly negligent and [their conduct] fell well below the reasonable standard of care for police officers in the San Jose community ...." The officers "could and should have" taken plaintiffs to an emergency room or alternatively to a shelter to remove them from the zone of danger. He believed the officers "negligently increased the peril" to plaintiff and her son by stating "Don't worry, we're here!" which "suggested [to plaintiffs] there was no imminent threat ...." Furthermore, it appeared to Saunders, based on neighbor Scott's deposition, that the officers left the plaintiffs as "bait" to lure Cortez back to the apartment. Saunders opined that "a 'special relationship' was clearly established between plaintiffs ... from and after the time Officer Lloyd and Sergeant Ross responded to plaintiffs' original 911 call for emergency assistance."

Although defendants interposed evidentiary objections to Saunders's declaration, the record does not show that the trial court ever formally ruled on any of the objections. Accordingly, all the evidence "submitted was available for the trial court's consideration and is available for ours." Nevertheless, "it is presumed on appeal [from a summary judgment] that a judge has not relied on irrelevant or incompetent evidence."

Here some of Saunders's legal conclusions are based on incompetent evidence: (1) plaintiff's declaration that contradicts her earlier deposition testimony and (2) the speculations of a neighbor who had opinions on how the police could have performed their job better. Furthermore, the ultimate issue-whether the police owed a duty to plaintiffs-is a question of law for the trial court. Courts must be cautious where an expert offers legal conclusions as to ultimate facts in the guise of an expert opinion.

In *Martinez*, a mother and daughter brought a wrongful death action against the sheriff's office for shooting and killing the decedent, who deputies believed had been brandishing a knife in public. The family of the decedent submitted a declaration of the same Frank Saunders in their opposition to the county's motion for summary judgment. In that case, Saunders opined that the officers were " 'totally premature' " in shooting decedent, that the officers' conduct " 'fell to a level of gross negligence ...,' " and that the county's failure to train the officers " 'rises to a level of deliberate indifference to the misuse of deadly force ....' " In disregarding Saunders's declaration and upholding summary judgment, the court stated "[C]ourts have been highly critical ... when an expert offers legal conclusions as to ultimate facts in the guise of an expert opinion. [Citations.] Saunders's declaration falls into the latter category by inappropriately drawing legal conclusions concerning such matters as the objective reasonableness of the deputies' conduct and the county defendants' 'deliberate indifference' to misuse of force. [Citation.] To the extent it does so, we reject that declaration."

In the instant case, the same result is called for. To the extent Saunders's declaration draws legal conclusions such as whether a special relationship was created when the officers replied to the 911 call, whether the officers increased the risk to plaintiffs, and whether the officers used plaintiffs as "bait," we reject the declaration. Thus, unlike the situation in *Mann v. State of California*, there was no competent evidence presented that the affirmative acts of Officers Lloyd and Ross increased the risk of harm to plaintiff or Joey.

[The court goes on to reject plaintiff's further claim that the defendants owed an independent duty of care toward Joey.]

As we have said earlier, without a special relationship, the police owed no duty to plaintiffs, and without a duty, no negligence cause of action can be stated. The trial court did not err in granting summary judgment.

The judgment is affirmed.

*****

CONCLUSION

The court held that although in some instances a special relationship may be formed between police and an individual resulting in a duty for the police to protect her, the circumstances in this case did not give rise to this duty. Additionally, when police through their actions increase peril, there may be a duty to protect; again, in these circumstances there was insufficient evidence that the police created this peril.

REVIEW

1.   What was the plaintiff's evidence for a special relationship? Do you side with the court's analysis in determining that there was no special relationship?

2.   What was the plaintiff's evidence for the claim that the police increased her peril? Why as this rejected as well?

3.   Can you construct a hypothetical domestic violence scenario by which police would have a legal duty to protect a victim?

Section 3: Administrative Remedies

OVERVIEW

People who feel that the police have engaged in misconduct can also file complaints against officers through administrative mechanisms, including internal affairs or external review boards. In California it is a misdemeanor, however, to file false complaints against the police. Thus, an individual opens herself up to potential criminal liability when filing such a complaint. Moreover, officers have been increasingly filing defamation suits against people who file complaints against them. In response, attorneys have been relying on a state law which is designed to protect citizens from defamation suits in response to "public participation" in order to attempt to have these suits rapidly dismissed. The following excerpts include this state law, and a press release by the ACLU of Northern California pertaining to the use of this law.

Code of Civil Procedure section 425.16. Actions arising from exercise of free speech or right of petition; legislative findings; motion to strike; stay of discovery; fees, costs; exception; report to legislature

(a) The Legislature finds and declares that there has been a disturbing increase in lawsuits brought primarily to chill the valid exercise of the constitutional rights of freedom of speech and petition for the redress of grievances. The Legislature finds and declares that it is in the public interest to encourage continued participation in matters of public significance, and that this participation should not be chilled through abuse of the judicial process. To this end, this section shall be construed broadly.

(b)(1) A cause of action against a person arising from any act of that person in furtherance of the person's right of petition or free speech under the United States or California Constitution in connection with a public issue shall be subject to a special motion to strike, unless the court determines that the plaintiff has established that there is a probability that the plaintiff will prevail on the claim.

Attorneys Move to Block Police Retaliation Against Citizen Complaints -- Motion Filed to Dismiss Police Defamation Suit

FOR IMMEDIATE RELEASE
November 12, 1998

Seeking to stop the growing number of defamation suits filed by California law enforcement officers against citizens who file complaints against them, attorneys representing police accountability groups and free speech activists filed a motion today (November 12, 1998) in San Francisco Superior Court to dismiss SFPD Officer Joseph McCloskey's defamation suit against Betty Evans.

Evans' attorneys filed the motion under a special state law (Code of Civil Procedure, Section 425.16) enacted in 1992 to protect Californians from defamation and other Strategic Lawsuits Against Public Participation (SLAPP's) by allowing the lawsuits to be quickly dismissed if they are based on citizen's exercise of their free speech rights.

On September 8, 1997, Betty Evans heard a commotion outside her apartment door in San Francisco. Through the peephole she saw Officer McCloskey kicking a handcuffed suspect on the floor. She opened her door and yelled at the officer, "Don't kick him," and he stopped. Concerned for the suspect's safety, she immediately called 911 to report the incident.

The Office of Citizen Complaints (OCC) investigated the incident, using Betty Evans as a witness, and sustained a finding of excessive force against Officer McCloskey. Officer McCloskey then sued Evans for $25,000 damages based solely on her testimony to the OCC (McCloskey v. Evans).

"Ms. Evans' actions exemplify what is vital for our democracy to work -- that citizens participate in the process of government and speak out when they see government misconduct. To be the target of a defamation action for her conduct is not just a cruel irony, but an affront to our democratic principles of self government," stated ACLU attorney Alan Schlosser.

The growing use of such defamation suits and other SLAPP's is a cause of great concern for the attorneys representing the defendant. "Police officers are the only public employees in the state who are allowed to sue people who file official complaints against them," stated Mark Goldowitz, an attorney with the California Anti-SLAPP Project working on the case.

"The Legislature has refused to repeal this law which is being used by police officers to frighten and intimidate people from pursuing valid complaints. It is up to the courts to find it unconstitutional," stated Matthew Kumin, the private attorney who was asked by Bay Area PoliceWatch to represent Evans. "Given the unique powers delegated to police in a free society -- the power to use force, to take lives and to deprive us of our freedom-- it is particularly important that the First Amendment right to petition our government about grievances involving police officers not be abridged in any way."

Mary Dunlap, Director of the San Francisco OCC, in a declaration filed in support of Evans noted, "It has been the experience of the OCC that complainants frequently express fear of retaliation. The mere threat of being sued for defamation by an accused officer, let alone an actual lawsuit, will have the effect of chilling citizens from making legitimate complaints and will undermine the OCC's ability to investigate and help resolve potential police misconduct."

Van Jones of Bay Area PoliceWatch concurred, "Citizens such as Betty Evans, with nothing to gain personally from bringing their allegations to the attention of the appropriate officials could be scared off by the threat of a SLAPP suit and decide not to use the official process to investigate complaints."

Evans' attorneys are asking the court to declare unconstitutional the state law (Civil Code Section 47.5) which allows law enforcement officers (and only law enforcement officers among public employees) to file defamation suits against people who make citizen complaints against them. The motion argues that the filing of official complaints of police misconduct is protected by the First Amendment right to petition the government for redress of grievances. The motion also argues that the

125

special police defamation law violates free speech by targeting only speech critical of police officers.

Finally, the attorneys argue that, especially since the OCC sustained Ms. Evans' allegations, Officer McCloskey cannot possibly prevail even under the special police defamation law that requires a citizen's complaint to be false, "filled with the knowledge it was false, and made with spite, hatred or ill will." (Evans had no prior connection to either McCloskey or the person she reported he kicked.)

If the lawsuit is found to be a SLAPP and dismissed, the plaintiff --in this case, Officer McCloskey -- is required to pay the attorneys fees and costs of the parties they sued.

ACLU-NC managing attorney Alan Schlosser added, "This case should send a message to California police officers. If you bring retaliatory lawsuits against people who file legitimate police misconduct complaints, you can be held personally responsible for their attorneys fees and costs. The ACLU will not tolerate police attempts to bully and intimidate citizens who make police misconduct complaints. The California anti-SLAPP law was designed for exactly this purpose and we intend to use it wherever necessary."

CHAPTER TWELVE

Starting Court Proceedings

Once the defendant has been arrested, the case gets turned over from the police to the prosecutor or district attorney's office. This is an important intermediate area between enforcement and trial. Within 48 hours there must be a probable cause declaration, meaning a judge or magistrate must rule that there is enough evidence to hold the suspect. The prosecutor must decide, in his or her discretion, whether to charge the suspect with a crime. The suspect must be informed of the charges against them and informed of key constitutional rights such as the right to counsel. Bail will be set in many cases (and at times suspects will be held without bail or released on their own recognizance). Attorneys must be appointed for indigents (those who cannot afford their own representation).

Section 1: The Decision to Charge

OVERVIEW

Prosecutors generally enjoy great leeway in deciding when to charge suspects. For example, during Terrence Hallinan's tenure as District Attorney of San Francisco, misdemeanor drug cases were de-emphasized and even many felony drug charges were not prosecuted. Some of this was due to his liberal leaning and some due to the office's concern that police violated procedures in many drug cases. Whatever the reason, it stood out that the prosecutor behaved with much discretion in those cases. Two regulations are important in this area. Government Code section 26501 builds in prosecutorial discretion to the office's duties by ordering that prosecutors should institute proceedings for those who are "reasonably suspected" with public offenses. The term "reasonable" allows much latitude. Second, the State Bar of California's Rules of Professional Conduct orders that prosecutors should not institute proceedings when they know the charges aren't backed by probable cause.

> **Government Code Section 26501. Criminal proceedings; attendance before magistrates and grand jury**
>
> The district attorney shall institute proceedings before magistrates for the arrest of persons charged with or reasonably suspected of public offenses when he has information that such offenses have been committed. For that purpose, when not engaged in criminal proceedings in the superior court or in civil cases on behalf of the people, he shall attend upon the magistrates in cases of arrest when required by them and shall attend before and give advice to the grand jury whenever cases are presented to it for its consideration.

California Rules of Professional Conduct Rule 5-110. Performing the Duty of Member in Government Service

A member in government service shall not institute or cause to be instituted criminal charges when the member knows or should know that the charges are not supported by probable cause. If, after the institution of criminal charges, the member in government service having responsibility for prosecuting the charges becomes aware that those charges are not supported by probable cause, the member shall promptly so advise the court in which the criminal matter is pending.

Section 2: Probable Cause to Detain Suspects

OVERVIEW

Pursuant to the Supreme Court's ruling in *County of Riverside v. McLaughlin*, 500 U.S. 44 (1991), once arrested, a defendant must be brought before a magistrate or judge within 48 hours for a probable cause declaration. This is the rule under California law—see Penal Code section 825, below. Sundays and Holidays are excluded. However, even if this timeline is met, any unnecessary delays are illegal—these include any delays outside the following: time to complete the arrest, to book the suspect, to transport the suspect to court, for the district attorney to evaluate the evidence, and to prepare a pleading. See *People v. Powell*, 67 Cal.2d 32 (1967). Additionally, there is an exception to the general 48-hour rule in California for emergencies, such as the riots following the Rodney King verdict in Los Angeles. This exception is codified in Government Code 68115(d), below, and allows for an extension of the time period when meeting the deadline is unfeasible due to "public calamities." Emergency dates are considered to be holidays for the purpose of calculating the 48 hours.

Penal Code Section 825. Appearance before magistrate; unnecessary delay; maximum time; right of attorney to visit prisoner; refusal to permit visit; offense; forfeiture

(a)(1) Except as provided in paragraph (2), the defendant shall in all cases be taken before the magistrate without unnecessary delay, and, in any event, within 48 hours after his or her arrest, excluding Sundays and holidays.

(2) When the 48 hours prescribed by paragraph (1) expire at a time when the court in which the magistrate is sitting is not in session, that time shall be extended to include the duration of the next court session on the judicial day immediately following. If the 48-hour period expires at a time when the court in which the magistrate is sitting is in session, the arraignment may take place at any time during that session. However, when the defendant's arrest occurs on a Wednesday after the conclusion of the day's court session, and if the Wednesday is not a court holiday, the defendant shall be taken before the magistrate not later than the following Friday, if the Friday is not a court holiday.

(b) After the arrest, any attorney at law entitled to practice in the courts of record of California, may, at the request of the prisoner or any relative of the prisoner, visit the prisoner. Any officer having charge of the prisoner who willfully refuses or neglects to allow that attorney to visit a prisoner is guilty of a misdemeanor. Any officer having a prisoner in charge, who refuses to allow the attorney to visit the prisoner when proper application is made, shall forfeit and pay to the party aggrieved the sum of five hundred dollars ($500), to be recovered by action in any court of competent jurisdiction.

Government Code Section 68115. Public calamities, destruction of court building, influx of criminal cases; orderly operation of court; alternate judicial processes

When war, insurrection, pestilence, or other public calamity, or the danger thereof, or the destruction of or danger to the building appointed for holding the court, renders it necessary, or when a large influx of criminal cases resulting from a large number of arrests within a short period of time threatens the orderly operation of a superior court location or locations within a county, the presiding judge may request and the Chair of the Judicial Council may, notwithstanding any other provision of law, by order authorize the court to do one or more of the following:

(d) Declare that a date on which an emergency condition, as described in this section, prevented the court from conducting proceedings governed by Section 825 of the Penal Code [and other codes] be deemed a holiday for purposes of computing time under those statutes. This subdivision shall apply to the fewest days necessary under the circumstances of the emergency, as determined by the Chair of the Judicial Council.

Section 3: First Appearance

OVERVIEW

At first appearance, several things are necessary. Suspects are informed of their charges and rights to remain silent, to have counsel, and to be tried by jury. Bail is set or suspects are detained without bail (for serious crimes) or on the other end, perhaps released on their own recognizance (for minor offenses). During this time attorneys are also appointed for indigent (poor) defendants. Attorneys who represent clients must provide "effective assistance"; else, there are potential grounds for reversal of any resulting conviction.

Bail in California is covered by Article I, section 12 of the California Constitution (see Appendix). The requirement is that individuals shall be released on bail with some exceptions: capital crimes; felony acts of violence where release bears substantial likelihood of great bodily harm to others; felony offenses where there is evidence the person has threatened great bodily harm and there is substantial likelihood the person will make good on the threat if released. For all other offenses bail is available as a matter of right, under Penal Code section 1271, below.

Penal Code Section 1271. Before conviction; bail as of right

IN WHAT CASES DEFENDANT MAY BE ADMITTED TO BAIL BEFORE CONVICTION. If the charge is for any other offense, he may be admitted to bail before conviction, as a matter of right.

The right to counsel in California, as within the federal system, attaches at each "critical stage" in the process. This includes the following: interrogation, first appearance, when pleading guilty, when indicted but not in custody, at a compulsory police lineups, at a preliminary hearing, at an arraignment, during pleading and plea bargaining, throughout trial, at sentencing, and during a first-appeal.

An important difference between federal and California law pertains to the question of when the right to appointed counsel for indigents is necessary. In *Scott v. Illinois*, 440 U.S. 367 (1979) the Supreme Court said such a right is not necessary when imprisonment is not involved. In California, however, courts have interpreted the state constitution (see Appendix, Article I section 15) as requiring appointed counsel in all misdemeanor cases, regardless of whether imprisonment is authorized or likely. See, e.g., *In Re Kevin G.*, 40 Cal.3d 644 (1985). Infractions generally do not give rise to this right. Indigents must be screened to make sure they indeed cannot afford their own counselor. The following statutes, below, pertain to these rights. Penal Code section 858 mandates that defendants during their first appearance must be informed of their rights to counsel. Penal Code section 987 pertains to the right to counsel, generally, and the proof requirements for indigents. Penal Code section 987.2(i) requires counsel for misdemeanor defendants when such counsel is necessary for an "adequate and effective" defense.

Penal Code Section 858. Informing defendant of charge and right to counsel; minors; members of armed forces

When the defendant is brought before the magistrate upon an arrest, either with or without warrant, on a charge of having committed a public offense, the magistrate must immediately inform him of the charge against him, and of his right to the aid of counsel in every stage of the proceedings. If it appears that the defendant may be a minor, the magistrate shall ascertain whether such is the case, and if the magistrate concludes that it is probable that the defendant is a minor, and unless the defendant is a member of the armed forces of the United States and the offense charged is a misdemeanor, he shall immediately either notify the parent or guardian of the minor, by telephone, telegram, or messenger, of the arrest, or appoint counsel to represent the minor.

987. Right to counsel; assignment and duties of counsel; financial statement; cocounsel

(a) In a noncapital case, if the defendant appears for arraignment without counsel, he or she shall be informed by the court that it is his or her right to have counsel before being arraigned, and shall be asked if he or she desires the assistance of counsel. If he or she desires and is unable to employ counsel the court shall assign counsel to defend him or her.

(b) In a capital case, if the defendant appears for arraignment without counsel, the court shall inform him or her that he or she shall be represented by counsel at all stages of the preliminary and trial proceedings and that the representation is at his or her expense if he or she is able to employ counsel or at public expense if he or she is unable to employ counsel, inquire of him or her whether he or she is able to employ counsel and, if so, whether he or she desires to employ counsel of his or her choice or to have counsel assigned, and allow him or her a reasonable time to send for his or her chosen or assigned counsel. If the defendant is unable to employ counsel, the court shall assign counsel to defend him or her. If the defendant is able to employ counsel and either refuses to employ counsel or appears without counsel after having had a reasonable time to employ counsel, the court shall assign counsel.

(c) In order to assist the court in determining whether a defendant is able to employ counsel in any case, the court may require a defendant to file a financial statement or other financial information under penalty of perjury with the court or, in its discretion, order a defendant to appear before a county officer designated by the court to make an inquiry into the ability of the defendant to employ his or her own counsel. If a county officer is designated, the county officer shall provide to the court a written recommendation and the reason or reasons in support of the recommendation. The determination by the court shall be made on the record. Except as provided in Section 214, the financial statement or other financial information obtained from the defendant shall be confidential and privileged and shall not be admissible in evidence in any criminal proceeding except the prosecution of an alleged offense of perjury based upon false material contained in the financial statement. The financial statement shall be made available to the prosecution only for purposes of investigation of an alleged offense of perjury based upon false material contained in the financial statement at the conclusion of the proceedings for which the financial statement was required to be submitted. The financial statement and other financial information obtained from the defendant shall not be confidential and privileged in a proceeding under Section 937.8

(d) In a capital case, the court may appoint an additional attorney as a cocounsel upon a written request of the first attorney appointed. The request shall be supported by an affidavit of the first attorney setting forth in detail the reasons why a second attorney should be appointed. Any affidavit filed with the court shall be confidential and privileged. The court shall appoint a second attorney when it is convinced by the reasons stated in the affidavit that the appointment is necessary to provide the defendant with effective representation. If the request is denied, the court shall state on the record its reasons for denial of the request.

987.2. Assigned counsel; compensation; public defenders; multiple county representation; recovery of costs

(i) Counsel shall be appointed to represent, in a misdemeanor case, a person who desires but is unable to employ counsel, when it appears that the appointment is necessary to provide an adequate and effective defense for the defendant.

In addition to the right to counsel in general, defendants have the right to effective assistance of counsel. The Supreme Court standard is set forth in *Strickland v. Washington*, 466 U.S. 668 (1984). To gain a reversal based on an ineffective assistance of counsel argument, defendants must show first that their representation did not meet an objective standard of reasonableness, and second, that the poor representation affected the outcome (i.e., resulted in a guilty verdict when effective representation could have achieved an acquittal). The California courts generally follow *People v. Pope*, 23 Cal.3d 412 (1979), which predated *Strickland* but is similar in substance. In this case the defendant's counsel made little effort to confront the defendant's alleged co-felons, and did not introduce any evidence of defendant's abnormally low intelligence. The California Supreme Court refused to reverse the conviction, holding that the defendant bears the burden of proof on such a claim and must show the attorney failed to act "in a manner to be expected of a reasonably competent attorney acting as a diligent advocate, and that counsel's acts or omissions resulted in the withdrawal of a potentially meritorious defense." (*Pope*, p. 412). Additionally, defense must prepare a record showing why their counsel acted as he or she did, and must have on this record a request for an explanation by the defendant of his counsel of why the counsel took certain actions or failed to act in a certain way. (*Pope*, p. 413). Needless to say, the standards under Strickland and Pope make it very difficult for defendants to achieve reversals by arguing that their attorneys failed to represent them effectively.

CHAPTER THIRTEEN

Pretrial, Trial, and Conviction

A preliminary hearing or grand jury indictment is necessary to bind a defendant over for trial. The defendant is arraigned and usually during the arraignment enters a plea. Before the trial, defense attorneys may make certain key motions, such as a motion to suppress evidence or to move the trial to a new county. If a guilty plea or a plea of no context is not entered and the charges against the defendant are not dismissed for any reason, the case will go to trial, which follows a set sequence of events, ranging from opening arguments to jury deliberations, verdict, sentencing, and ensuing appeals.

Section 1: Testing the Government's Case

OVERVIEW

Although grand jury indictments are mandated in the federal system, states have the choice as to which approach to use to establish that there is sufficient evidence against a defendant to proceed to trial. In California, Proposition 115, passed by the voters and effective in mid-1990, prosecutors can bypass preliminary hearings by having a grand jury return an indictment against a criminal suspect. This is codified in the California Constitution, Article I, section 14 (see Appendix). Grand jury hearings, unlike most preliminary hearings, are closed to the public (but not necessarily entirely secret), and the defendant in grand jury hearings does not have the right to present evidence or cross-examine witnesses.

Grand juries are not used too often for criminal cases in California. Special types of cases may be more likely to be routed through a grand jury. For example, when Terrence Hallinan, the District Attorney of San Francisco, was trying to decide in 2003 which upper-level police administrators may be guilty of obstruction of justice charges pertaining to an investigation of three rank-and-file officers accused of assault (known as the "Fajita-gate scandal" since the alleged assault supposedly originated with one of the officers demanding leftover Fajitas from the victim after closing-time at the bars), he asked a grand jury to determine what charges applied for which officers. He probably did this to attempt to characterize any prosecution of the administrators as reflecting fairness and impartiality rather than the animosity between his office and the police administration. Generally, however, preliminary hearings are the standard for binding defendants over for trial.

Grand juries in California consist of 23 members in counties of more than four million persons, 11 members in counties with 20,000 or fewer persons if approved by the county's board of supervisors, and 19 members in the remaining counties (Penal Code section 888.2). Each county must have at least one grand jury per year. (See California Constitution, Article I, section 23, in Appendix.)

Penal Code section 738, below, mandates preliminary hearings (also called "preliminary examinations" in California). As mentioned above, the state constitution waives them when grand jury indictments are returned. Individual defendants can also waive their right to a preliminary hearing, pursuant to Penal Code section 860(3). Preliminary hearings are necessary for felony cases, but not for misdemeanors or infractions (Penal Code section 682(3)). Preliminary hearings are like mini-trials that make sure the case is not too weak to proceed to regular trial. According to Penal Code section 861, preliminary examinations should be held in one session; there are exceptions, in section 861.5, for good cause or for special needs involving child witnesses. Preliminary hearings are decided by judges, not juries. Once the judge rules that the evidence is sufficient (based on probable cause, not "beyond reasonable doubt") the path has been cleared for the case to go to full trial.

Penal Code Section 738. Offenses triable in superior court; preliminary examination; order holding to answer; commencement by complaint.

Before an information is filed there must be a preliminary examination of the case against the defendant and an order holding him to answer made under Section 872. The proceeding for a preliminary examination must be commenced by written complaint, as provided elsewhere in this code.

Section 2: Pretrial Motions

OVERVIEW

Before trial, defense attorneys may make crucial motions to the judge, including among others, to dismiss due to double jeopardy, for a speedy trial, to change venue, or to suppress evidence. If motions are not made at the appropriate time, it is conceivable that they may be "lost on appeal," meaning that the defendant cannot make the argument after the trial has concluded and the verdict has been returned.

The guarantee against double jeopardy is based on the U.S. Constitution's Fifth Amendment, and in the California Constitution, Article I, section 15 (see Appendix). Generally, double jeopardy prevents second prosecutions for the same offense after acquittal or conviction; multiple punishments for the same offense; and multiple prosecutions for the same criminal act under different statutes that contain the same material elements. California codifies several aspects of the guarantee against double jeopardy in various penal code sections. Examples below are section 687 (multiple prosecutions for same offense within California) and 656 (prosecution in California for offense in another state, government, or country, which resulted in conviction or acquittal). Note, these provisions do not disallow the federal government, for example, to try someone who was convicted on state charges, for a federal offense; nor do they prevent a retrial within the state for an offense which was tried but resulted in a mistrial.

Penal Code Section 687. Double jeopardy

SECOND PROSECUTION FOR THE SAME OFFENSE PROHIBITED. No person can be subjected to a second prosecution for

134

a public offense for which he has once been prosecuted and convicted or acquitted.

Penal Code Section 656. Offenses also punishable by foreign law; double jeopardy

FOREIGN CONVICTION OR ACQUITTAL. Whenever on the trial of an accused person it appears that upon a criminal prosecution under the laws of another State, Government, or country, founded upon the act or omission in respect to which he is on trial, he has been acquitted or convicted, it is a sufficient defense.

Defendants have the right to a speedy trial, under the Sixth Amendment to the U.S. Constitution, and California Constitution, Article I, section 15 (see Appendix). In California, this right begins when the criminal complaint is filed. For felony cases, the Supreme Court has held that prejudice to the defendant results if the trial is delayed for eight months or more. *Doggett v. United States*, 505 U.S. 647 (1992). For misdemeanor cases, the California Supreme Court has held that prejudice occurred when the delay was more than a year. See *Serna v. Superior Court*, 40 Cal.3d 239 (1985). Various penal code provisions lay out different time periods for the various stages of a criminal prosecution. Remember, a defendant may waive the right to speedy trial (usually so defense attorneys may mount an effective defense). Pretrial motions for a speedy trial ensure this right. Such motions are usually made when the defense believes the prosecution will be less successful if hurried.

Attorneys may at times wish to change the location of the trial (when they believe a fair trial cannot be obtained in the jurisdiction in which the charges were filed). For example, in the famous Scott Peterson case ongoing at the time of the writing of this text, defense attorneys had the trial removed from Stanislaus County to San Mateo County, where they felt Peterson could have jurors more removed and partial. The court may also change the venue if it feels a jury cannot be successfully impaneled in the original county. See Penal Code section 1033 below, for these statutory provisions. Under certain conditions trials might be returned to the original jurisdiction. See Penal Code section 1033.1, below.

Penal Code Section 1033. Superior courts; fair and impartial trial impossible in county; proceedings before trial; exhaustion of jury panels

In a criminal action pending in the superior court, the court shall order a change of venue:

(a) On motion of the defendant, to another county when it appears that there is a reasonable likelihood that a fair and impartial trial cannot be had in the county. When a change of venue is ordered by the superior court, it shall be for the trial itself. All proceedings before trial shall occur in the county of original venue, except when it is evident that a particular proceeding must be heard by the judge who is to preside over the trial.

(b) On its own motion or on motion of any party, to an adjoining county when it appears as a result of the exhaustion of all of the jury panels called that it will be impossible to secure a jury to try the cause in the county.

Penal Code Section 1033.1. Reversal of judgment; return of case to original place of trial

In any criminal action or proceeding in which the place of trial has been changed for any of the reasons set forth in Section 1033, the court, upon its own motion or upon the motion of any party, may return the action or proceeding to the original place of trial if both of the following conditions apply:

(a) The action or proceeding is pending before the court after reversal of the original judgment by the appellate court.

(b) The court finds that the conditions which originally required the order to change venue no longer apply. Prior to making such a finding, the court shall conduct a hearing, upon notice to all parties. At the hearing, the burden shall be on the prosecution to establish that the conditions which originally required the order to change venue no longer apply, unless the defendant and his or her attorney consent to the return of the action or proceeding to the original place of trial.

One of the most important motions defense attorneys make is to suppress evidence the prosecutor has that they believe has been obtained in violation of the rules of procedure. In California this is known as a 1538.5 motion, referring to the section of the Penal Code by which such as motion is made.

Penal Code Section 1538.5. Motion to return property or suppress evidence

(a)(1) A defendant may move for the return of property or to suppress as evidence any tangible or intangible thing obtained as a result of a search or seizure on either of the following grounds:

(A) The search or seizure without a warrant was unreasonable.

(B) The search or seizure with a warrant was unreasonable because any of the following apply:

(i) The warrant is insufficient on its face.

(ii) The property or evidence obtained is not that described in the warrant.

(iii) There was not probable cause for the issuance of the warrant.

(iv) The method of execution of the warrant violated federal or state constitutional standards.

(v) There was any other violation of federal or state constitutional standards.

Section 3: Conviction by Jury Trial

OVERVIEW

The right to a jury trial is afforded by the U.S. Constitution. Additionally, in the California Constitution, Article I, section 16, trial by jury in criminal cases is guaranteed, and such a jury shall consist of 12 members for felony cases, and 12 for misdemeanor cases or fewer if agreed upon by the parties. According to case law, for felony cases defendants can also agree to fewer jurors, by waiving this right to a 12-person jury. *People v. Trejo*, 217 Cal.App.3d 1026 (1990). A defendant can waive his or her right to juries in general, opting for a bench trial over which a judge reigns.

The right to a public trial is embedded in the Sixth Amendment to the U.S. Constitution, and Article I, section 15, of the California Constitution (see Appendix). Under Proposition 115, effective in California in mid-1990, defendants can waive their right to a public trial. However, the defendant cannot necessarily gain a private trial, because in the California Constitution, Article I, section 29, the people have a right to a public trial, meaning that the defendant cannot demand the public or press should be excluded. Attorneys have some obligations pertaining to trial publicity. Rule 5-120 of the state bar association's Rules of Professional Conduct disallows attorneys to make a statement outside of the courtroom that will reasonably become circulated in the public and that the attorney knows may have a "substantial likelihood" of materially prejudicing the proceeding. California is a state that permits the broadcasting (by, for example, television) of trial coverage, subject to some limitations, as laid out in California Rules of Court, Rule 980.

Jury selection prior to trial is straightforward in many cases and complex and drawn out in some cases (usually involving serious charges). Panels are selected after randomly drawing from the population of eligible jurors. Voir dire consists of narrowing a panel down to an actual jury, which normally consists of 12 members and 6 alternates. Judges question jurors initially; attorneys then examine potential jurors and eliminate them through challenges. Challenges may be "for-cause", meaning there is a specific reason for which the attorney believes the juror cannot be unbiased, or peremptory. Peremptory challenges can be made for virtually any unstated reason, although the Supreme Court has prohibited the use of race when making such challenges in *Batson v. Kentucky*, 476 U.S. 79 (1986), *Powers v. Ohio*, 499 U.S. 400 (1991), and *Georgia v. McCollum*, 505 U.S. 42 (1992).

In California, case law has expanded race to several other "cognizable groups" under the theory that using peremptory challenges to rid the jury of members of these groups means that defendants will be denied a jury that represents a fair cross-section of the community. The following are examples of groups deemed to be "cognizable" by California courts: racial minorities, females, Spanish-surnamed individuals, men, and homosexuals. Example of groups not deemed to be "cognizable" include youths, battered women, blue-collar workers, and ex-felons. Attorneys challenge members of groups to attempt to better their chances at success. For example, prosecutors in a case involving a charge that defendant battered his spouse used

137

peremptory challenges to remove males as potential jurors. The court held that men are a cognizable group and cannot be removed with peremptory challenges. *People v. Cervantes*, 233 Cal.App.3d 323 (1991).

The following are some of the most important (of many) statutes pertaining to jury selection. Sections 191 and 918 pertain to general issues of jury selection and sections 223 and 225 relate to examinations of jurors through voir dire.

Penal Code Section 191. State policy; random selection; opportunity and obligation to serve

The Legislature recognizes that trial by jury is a cherished constitutional right, and that jury service is an obligation of citizenship.

It is the policy of the State of California that all persons selected for jury service shall be selected at random from the population of the area served by the court; that all qualified persons have an equal opportunity, in accordance with this chapter, to be considered for jury service in the state and an obligation to serve as jurors when summoned for that purpose; and that it is the responsibility of jury commissioners to manage all jury systems in an efficient, equitable, and cost-effective manner, in accordance with this chapter.

Penal Code Section 198. Master and qualified juror lists; random selection; use of lists

(a) Random selection shall be utilized in creating master and qualified juror lists, commencing with selection from source lists, and continuing through selection of prospective jurors for voir dire.

(b) The jury commissioner shall, at least once in each 12-month period, randomly select names of prospective trial jurors from the source list or lists, to create a master list.

(c) The master jury list shall be used by the jury commissioner, as provided by statute and state and local court rules, for the purpose of (1) mailing juror questionnaires and subsequent creation of a qualified juror list, and (2) summoning prospective jurors to respond or appear for qualification and service.

Penal Code Section 223. Criminal cases; voir dire examination by court and counsel

In a criminal case, the court shall conduct an initial examination of prospective jurors. The court may submit to the prospective jurors additional questions requested by the parties as it deems proper. Upon completion of the court's initial examination, counsel for each party shall have the right to examine, by oral and direct questioning, any or all of the prospective jurors. The court may, in the exercise of its discretion, limit the oral and direct questioning of prospective jurors by counsel. The court may specify the maximum amount of time that counsel for each party may question an individual juror, or may specify an aggregate amount of time for each party, which can then be allocated among the prospective jurors by counsel. Voir dire of any prospective jurors shall, where practicable, occur in the presence of the other jurors in all criminal cases, including death penalty cases. Examination of prospective jurors shall be conducted only in aid of the exercise of challenges for cause.

The trial court's exercise of its discretion in the manner in which voir dire is conducted, including any limitation on the time which will be allowed for direct questioning of prospective jurors by counsel and any determination that a question is not in aid of the exercise of challenges for cause, shall not cause any conviction to be reversed unless the exercise of that discretion has resulted in a miscarriage of justice, as specified in Section 13 of Article VI of the California Constitution
.

Penal Code Section 225. Challenges; definition; classes and types

A challenge is an objection made to the trial jurors that may be taken by any party to the action, and is of the following classes and types:

(a) A challenge to the trial jury panel for cause.

(1) A challenge to the panel may only be taken before a trial jury is sworn. The challenge shall be reduced to writing, and shall plainly and distinctly state the facts constituting the ground of challenge.

(2) Reasonable notice of the challenge to the jury panel shall be given to all parties and to the jury commissioner, by service of a copy thereof.

(3) The jury commissioner shall be permitted the services of legal counsel in connection with challenges to the jury panel.
(b) A challenge to a prospective juror by either:

(1) A challenge for cause, for one of the following reasons:

(A) General disqualification--that the juror is disqualified from serving in the action on trial.

(B) Implied bias--as, when the existence of the facts as ascertained, in judgment of law disqualifies the juror.

(C) Actual bias--the existence of a state of mind on the part of the juror in reference to the case, or to any of the parties, which will prevent the juror from acting with entire impartiality, and without prejudice to the substantial rights of any party.

(2) A peremptory challenge to a prospective juror.

Section 4: The Stages and Rules of Jury Trials

OVERVIEW

The stages of a criminal trial are fairly straightforward. Opening statements are made first, by prosecutors and defense. Each side then presents its case-in-chief. For the prosecution this is mandatory (else it has no evidence!), but for defense this is optional (for at times, the prosecution clearly fails to present sufficient evidence). Then each side makes closing arguments (prosecution first, then defense, then the option of a rebuttal by the prosecution). The judge reads instructions to the jury, which deliberates until it reaches a verdict (or cannot reach a verdict, in which a mistrial is declared).

One area that requires some discussion is the issue of jury unanimity. There is no federal law requiring unanimous jury decisions for criminal trials. The Supreme Court has prohibited anything but unanimous verdicts for six person juries, but allowed 10-2 verdicts for 12-person juries. In California, however, Article I, section 16 of the constitution requires a unanimous verdict. This does not mean, though, that jurors must unanimously agree on the theory by which defendant is guilty of a specific offense; they must simply agree that the defendant is guilty of that offense. But the situation may be more complicated in some cases. What if a defendant is guilty of diverting funds, but the prosecution offers four different acts by which he might have done so? In each of the avenues, the defendant offers a separate defense. The jury unanimously agrees that he is guilty of diverting funds—but what if some jurors believe he did it through one act and others believe he did it by another approach. This is separate from the "different theory" approach because it involves different acts altogether. When this happens, a California court has held that the jury must receive instructions that they must agree unanimously beyond a reasonable doubt that the defendant committed the same specific act. See *People v. Thompson*, 36 Cal.App.4th 843 (1995).

Section 5: Conviction by Guilty Plea

Most cases are settled prior to trial by guilty pleas, and most of these are negotiated through plea bargaining. Plea bargaining may involve pleading guilty to lesser charges, reducing the overall number of charges, and negotiating a lesser sentence. Two penal code provisions lay out the parameters of and limit the use of plea bargaining in California. The first, Penal Code section 1192.5, provides the general rules for plea bargaining, and excludes the following: various types of rape, sodomy, lewd acts on children or dependent adults, oral copulation by force, and anal or genital penetration with foreign objects. The second, Penal Code 1192.7, codifying the 1982 Victim's Bill of Rights, prohibits plea bargaining with a number of serious felonies (see below), felonies using firearms, and driving under the influence. However, these prohibitions are significantly limited. First, section 1192.7(a) lists some exceptions: insufficient evidence for the prosecution, inability for prosecutor to obtain testimony of a material witness, and where the plea bargaining would not substantially change the sentence. Furthermore, the section only applies to plea bargaining of felonies in superior courts after the defendant has been bound over. Plea bargaining is still rampant in California.

Penal Code Section 1192.5. Plea of guilty or nolo contendere; specification of punishment and exercise of powers; procedure on approval; withdrawal

Upon a plea of guilty or nolo contendere to an accusatory pleading charging a felony, other than a violation of [various sexual offense statutes] by force, violence, duress, menace or threat of great bodily harm, the plea may specify the punishment to the same extent as it may be specified by the jury on a plea of not guilty or fixed by the court on a plea of guilty, nolo contendere, or not guilty, and may specify the exercise by the court thereafter of other powers legally available to it.

Where the plea is accepted by the prosecuting attorney in open court and is approved by the court, the defendant, except as otherwise provided in this section, cannot be sentenced on the plea to a punishment more severe than that specified in the plea and the court may not proceed as to the plea other than as specified in the plea.

If the court approves of the plea, it shall inform the defendant prior to the making of the plea that (1) its approval is not binding, (2) it may, at the time set for the hearing on the application for probation or pronouncement of judgment, withdraw its approval in the light of further consideration of the matter, and (3) in that case, the defendant shall be permitted to withdraw his or her plea if he or she desires to do so. The court shall also cause an inquiry to be made of the defendant to satisfy itself that the plea is freely and voluntarily made, and that there is a factual basis for the plea.

If the plea is not accepted by the prosecuting attorney and approved by the court, the plea shall be deemed withdrawn and the defendant may then enter the plea or pleas as would otherwise have been available.

If the plea is withdrawn or deemed withdrawn, it may not be received in evidence in any criminal, civil, or special action or proceeding of any nature, including proceedings before agencies, commissions, boards, and tribunals.

Penal Code Section 1192.7. Plea bargaining; limitation; definitions; amendment of section

(a) Plea bargaining in any case in which the indictment or information charges any serious felony, any felony in which it is alleged that a firearm was personally used by the defendant, or any offense of driving while under the influence of alcohol, drugs, narcotics, or any other intoxicating substance, or any combination thereof, is prohibited, unless there is insufficient evidence to prove the people's case, or testimony of a material witness cannot be obtained, or a reduction or dismissal would not result in a substantial change in sentence.

(b) As used in this section "plea bargaining" means any bargaining, negotiation, or discussion between a criminal defendant, or his or her counsel, and a prosecuting attorney or judge, whereby the defendant agrees to plead guilty or nolo contendere, in exchange for any promises, commitments, concessions, assurances, or consideration by the prosecuting attorney or judge relating to any charge against the defendant or to the sentencing of the defendant.

(c) As used in this section, "serious felony" means any of the following: (1) Murder or voluntary manslaughter; (2) mayhem; (3) rape; (4) sodomy by force, violence, duress, menace, threat of great bodily injury, or fear of immediate and unlawful bodily injury on the victim or another person; (5) oral copulation by force, violence, duress, menace, threat of great bodily injury, or fear of immediate and unlawful bodily injury on the victim or another person; (6) lewd or lascivious act on a child under the age of 14 years; (7) any felony punishable by death or imprisonment in the state prison for life; (8) any felony in which the defendant personally inflicts great bodily injury on any person, other than an accomplice, or any felony in which the defendant personally uses a firearm; (9) attempted murder; (10) assault with intent to commit rape or robbery; (11) assault with a deadly weapon or instrument on a peace officer; (12) assault by a life prisoner on a noninmate; (13) assault with a deadly weapon by an inmate; (14) arson; (15) exploding a destructive device or any explosive with intent to injure; (16) exploding a destructive device or any explosive causing bodily injury, great bodily injury, or mayhem; (17) exploding a destructive device or any explosive with intent to murder; (18) any burglary of the first degree; (19) robbery or bank robbery; (20) kidnapping; (21) holding of a hostage by a person confined in a state prison; (22) attempt to commit a felony punishable by death or imprisonment in the state prison for life; (23) any felony in which the defendant personally used a dangerous or deadly weapon; (24) selling, furnishing, administering, giving, or offering to sell, furnish, administer, or give to a minor any heroin, cocaine, phencyclidine (PCP), or any methamphetamine-related drug, or any of the precursors of methamphetamines; (25) any violation of subdivision (a) of Section 289 where the act is accomplished against the victim's will by force, violence, duress, menace, or fear of immediate and unlawful bodily injury on the victim or another person; (26) grand theft involving a firearm; (27) carjacking; (28) any felony offense, which would also constitute a felony violation of Section 186.22; (29) assault with the intent to commit mayhem, rape, sodomy, or oral copulation; (30) throwing acid or flammable substances; (31) assault with a deadly weapon, firearm, machinegun, assault weapon, or semiautomatic firearm or assault on a peace officer or firefighter; (32) assault with a deadly weapon against a public transit employee, custodial officer, or school employee; (33) discharge of a firearm at an inhabited dwelling, vehicle, or aircraft; (34) commission of rape or sexual penetration in concert with another person; (35) continuous sexual abuse of a child; (36) shooting from a vehicle; (37) intimidation of victims or witnesses; (38) criminal threats; (39) any attempt to commit a crime listed in this subdivision other than an assault; (40) any violation of Section 12022.53; (41) a violation of subdivision (b) or (c) of Section 11418; and (42) any conspiracy to commit an offense described in this subdivision.

CHAPTER FOURTEEN

After Conviction

In this chapter we'll discuss sentencing in California. In the first section we'll review some of the most important sentencing statutes in California, including the statute codifying the state's move to determinate sentencing in 1977. We'll also look at the state's approach to sentencing people to death. In the second section we'll examine California's famous Three Strikes law and discuss a recent Supreme Court Case that has upheld it.

Section 1: California's Sentencing Approach

OVERVIEW

According to the California Rules of Court, sentencing entails a number of objectives, including protecting society, punishing the defendant, deterring others from misconduct, and so forth. Note the wide range of objectives listed in Rule 4.410, below:

California Rules of Court Rule 4.410. General objectives in sentencing

(a) General objectives of sentencing include:

(1) Protecting society.

(2) Punishing the defendant.

(3) Encouraging the defendant to lead a law abiding life in the future and deterring him or her from future offenses.

(4) Deterring others from criminal conduct by demonstrating its consequences.

(5) Preventing the defendant from committing new crimes by isolating him or her for the period of incarceration.

(6) Securing restitution for the victims of crime.

(7) Achieving uniformity in sentencing.

(b) Because in some instances these objectives may suggest inconsistent dispositions, the sentencing judge must consider which objectives are of primary importance in the particular case. The sentencing judge should be guided by statutory statements of policy, the criteria in these rules, and the facts and circumstances of the case.

Section (b) of Rule 4.410 notes that judges must at times choose among these objectives when deciding upon a sentence, since the different objectives may imply different types of sentences. In reality, we'll see that California has moved to a "determinate sentencing" approach, in which judges generally do not exercise much discretion in sentencing, and the primary objective tends to be punishment. Still, there is variation both within and across jurisdictions, and judges have some leeway outside of the determinate sentencing regime in which to inject philosophical views. Before we reach the determinate sentencing statute, let's review some of the particulars about the process of sentencing (mostly looking at felonies). Penal Code section 1191 lays out the timeline for sentencing hearings following conviction or guilty pleas (usually 20 days); section 1193 deals with the necessity that the defendant be at the sentencing hearing (usually required for felons but not so for misdemeanants); section 1191.1 allows victims to be present and have voice at sentencing hearings; California Rules of Court rule 4.433 discusses the matters which must be dealt with by the judge during the sentencing hearing.

Penal Code Section 1191. Appointment of time for pronouncing judgment; reference to probation officer or placement in diagnostic facility; extension of time

In a felony case, after a plea, finding, or verdict of guilty, or after a finding or verdict against the defendant on a plea of a former conviction or acquittal, or once in jeopardy, the court shall appoint a time for pronouncing judgment, which shall be within 20 judicial days after the verdict, finding, or plea of guilty, during which time the court shall refer the case to the probation officer for a report if eligible for probation. However, the court may extend the time not more than 10 days for the purpose of hearing or determining any motion for a new trial, or in arrest of judgment, and may further extend the time until the probation officer's report is received and until any proceedings for granting or denying probation have been disposed of. If, in the opinion of the court, there is a reasonable ground for believing a defendant insane, the court may extend the time for pronouncing sentence until the question of insanity has been heard and determined, as provided in this code. If the court orders the defendant placed in a diagnostic facility, the time otherwise allowed by this section for pronouncing judgment is extended by a period equal to (1) the number of days which elapse between the date of the order and the date on which notice is received from the Director of Corrections advising whether or not the Department of Corrections will receive the defendant in the facility, and (2) if the director notifies the court that it will receive the defendant, the time which elapses until his or her return to the court from the facility.

Penal Code Section 1193. Pronouncement of judgment; felony cases; presence or absence of defendant; death sentence after affirmance on appeal; appointment of day for execution; certified copies to warden and governor; representation of pro se defendants at in absentia sentencing; misdemeanor cases

Judgment upon persons convicted of commission of crime shall be pronounced as follows:

(a) If the conviction is for a felony, the defendant shall be personally present when judgment is pronounced against him or her, unless the defendant, in open court and on the record, or in a notarized writing, requests that judgment be pronounced against him or her in his or her absence, and that he or she be represented by an attorney when judgment is pronounced, and the court approves his or her absence during the pronouncement of judgment, or unless, after the exercise of reasonable diligence to procure the presence of the defendant, the court shall find that it will be in the interest of justice that judgment be pronounced in his or her absence; provided, that when any judgment imposing the death penalty has been affirmed by the appellate court, sentence may be reimposed upon the defendant in his or her absence by the court from which the appeal was taken, and in the following manner: upon receipt by the superior court from which the appeal is taken of the certificate of the appellate court affirming the judgment, the judge of the superior court shall forthwith make and cause to be entered an order pronouncing sentence against the defendant, and a warrant signed by the judge, and attested by the clerk under the seal of the court, shall be drawn, and it shall state the conviction and judgment and appoint a day upon which the judgment shall be executed, which shall not be less than 60 days nor more than 90 days from the time of making the order; and that, within five days thereafter, a certified copy of the order, attested by the clerk under the seal of the court, and attached to the warrant, shall, for the purpose of execution, be transmitted by registered mail to the warden of the state prison having the custody of the defendant and certified copies thereof shall be transmitted by registered mail to the Governor; and provided further, that when any judgment imposing the death penalty has been affirmed and sentence has been reimposed as above provided there shall be no appeal from the order fixing the time for and directing the execution of the judgment as herein provided. If a pro se defendant requests that judgment in a noncapital case be pronounced against him or her in his or her absence, the court shall appoint an attorney to represent the defendant in the in absentia sentencing.

(b) If the conviction be of a misdemeanor, judgment may be pronounced against the defendant in his absence.

Penal Code Section 1191.1. Victim, parents or guardians, or next of kin; appearance and statement at sentencing proceedings; duty of court; amendment of section

The victim of any crime, or the parents or guardians of the victim if the victim is a minor, or the next of kin of the victim if the victim has died, have the right to attend all sentencing proceedings under this chapter and shall be given adequate notice by the probation officer of all sentencing proceedings concerning the person who committed the crime.

The victim, or up to two of the victim's parents or guardians if the victim is a minor, or the next of kin of the victim if the victim has died, have the right to appear, personally or by counsel, at the sentencing proceeding and to reasonably express his, her, or their views concerning the crime, the person responsible, and the need for restitution. The court in imposing sentence shall consider the statements of victims, parents or guardians, and next of kin made pursuant to this section and shall state on the record its conclusion concerning whether the person would pose a threat to public safety if granted probation.

The provisions of this section shall not be amended by the Legislature except by statute passed in each house by rollcall vote entered in the journal, two- thirds of the membership concurring, or by a statute that becomes effective only when approved by the electors.

Rules of Court Rule 4.433. Matters to be considered at time set for sentencing

(a) In every case, at the time set for sentencing pursuant to section 1191, the sentencing judge shall hold a hearing at which the judge shall:

(1) Hear and determine any matters raised by the defendant pursuant to section 1201.
(2) Determine whether a defendant who is eligible for probation should be granted or denied probation, unless consideration of probation is expressly waived by the defendant personally and by counsel.

(b) If the imposition of sentence is to be suspended during a period of probation after a conviction by trial, the trial judge shall make factual findings as to circumstances which would justify imposition of the upper or lower term if probation is later revoked, based upon evidence admitted at the trial.

(c) If a sentence of imprisonment is to be imposed, or if the execution of a sentence of imprisonment is to be suspended during a period of probation, the sentencing judge shall:

(1) Hear evidence in aggravation and mitigation, and determine, pursuant to section 1170(b), whether to impose the upper, middle or lower term; and set forth on the record the facts and reasons for imposing the upper or lower term.
(2) Determine whether any additional term of imprisonment provided for an enhancement charged and found shall be stricken.
(3) Determine whether the sentences shall be consecutive or concurrent if the defendant has been convicted of multiple crimes.
(4) Determine any issues raised by statutory prohibitions on the dual use of facts and statutory limitations on enhancements.
(5) Pronounce the court's judgment and sentence, stating the terms thereof and
giving reasons for those matters for which reasons are required by law.

(d) All these matters shall be heard and determined at a single hearing unless the sentencing judge otherwise orders in the interests of justice.

(e) When a sentence of imprisonment is imposed under subdivision (c) or under rule 4.435, the sentencing judge shall inform the defendant, pursuant to section 1170(c), of the parole period provided by section 3000 to be served after expiration of the sentence in addition to any period of incarceration for parole violation.

Prior to 1977, California had an indeterminate method of sentencing which allowed judges much discretion in handing out types of sentences and sentence length. Then the state moved to a determinate sentencing system where the primary purpose is to punish offenders, and the punishment is supposed to be in direct proportion to the seriousness of the crime. Review the statute (Penal Code section 1170) below, noting the methods in which judges are constrained in their approach to sentencing offenders.

Penal Code Section 1170. Determinate sentencing

(a)(1) The Legislature finds and declares that the purpose of imprisonment for crime is punishment. This purpose is best served by terms proportionate to the seriousness of the offense with provision for uniformity in the sentences of offenders committing the same offense under similar circumstances. The Legislature further finds and declares that the elimination of disparity and the provision of uniformity of sentences can best be achieved by determinate sentences fixed by statute in proportion to the seriousness of the offense as determined by the Legislature to be imposed by the court with specified discretion.

(2) Paragraph (1) shall not be construed to preclude programs, including educational programs, that are designed to rehabilitate nonviolent, first-time felony offenders. The Legislature encourages the development of policies and programs designed to educate and rehabilitate nonviolent, first-time felony offenders consistent with the purpose of imprisonment.

(3) In any case in which the punishment prescribed by statute for a person convicted of a public offense is a term of imprisonment in the state prison of any specification of three time periods, the court shall sentence the defendant to one of the terms of imprisonment specified unless the convicted person is given any other disposition provided by law, including a fine, jail, probation, or the suspension of imposition or execution of sentence. In sentencing the convicted person, the court shall apply the sentencing rules of the Judicial Council. The court, unless it determines that there are circumstances in mitigation of the punishment prescribed, shall also impose any other term that it is required by law to impose as an additional term. Nothing in this article shall affect any provision of law that imposes the death penalty, that authorizes or restricts the granting of probation or suspending the execution or imposition of sentence, or expressly provides for imprisonment in the state prison for life. In any case in which the amount of preimprisonment credit or any other provision of law is equal to or exceeds any sentence imposed pursuant to this chapter, the entire sentence shall be deemed to have been served and the defendant shall not be actually delivered to the custody of the Director of Corrections. The court shall advise the

defendant that he or she shall serve a period of parole and order the defendant to report to the parole office closest to the defendant's last legal residence, unless the in- custody credits equal the total sentence, including both confinement time and the period of parole. The sentence shall be deemed a separate prior prison term, and a copy of the judgment and other necessary documentation shall be forwarded to the Director of Corrections.

(b) When a judgment of imprisonment is to be imposed and the statute specifies three possible terms, the court shall order imposition of the middle term, unless there are circumstances in aggravation or mitigation of the crime. At least four days prior to the time set for imposition of judgment, either party or the victim, or the family of the victim if the victim is deceased, may submit a statement in aggravation or mitigation to dispute facts in the record or the probation officer's report, or to present additional facts. In determining whether there are circumstances that justify imposition of the upper or lower term, the court may consider the record in the case, the probation officer's report, other reports and statements in aggravation or mitigation submitted by the prosecution, the defendant, or the victim, or the family of the victim if the victim is deceased, and any further evidence introduced at the sentencing hearing. The court shall set forth on the record the facts and reasons for imposing the upper or lower term. The court may not impose an upper term by using the fact of any enhancement upon which sentence is imposed under any provision of law. A term of imprisonment shall not be specified if imposition of sentence is suspended.

(c) The court shall state the reasons for its sentence choice on the record at the time of sentencing. The court shall also inform the defendant that as part of the sentence after expiration of the term he or she may be on parole for a period as provided in Section 3000.

In addition to having determinate sentencing, California also authorizes the death penalty for first degree murder with special circumstances. The state uses a bifurcated trial, meaning that the guilt phase is followed by the penalty phase. Generally the same jury makes both decisions. This means that if death is an option at the beginning of a trial (i.e., the prosecutor has asked for the death penalty and the crime as alleged allows the prosecutor to do so), a jury must be "death-qualified," meaning that each member must be open to the possibility of sentencing someone to death. In California the sentencing procedure for the death penalty phase involves the introduction of evidence as to aggravating and mitigating circumstances. The jury hears all such evidence and weights it, ultimately deciding which outweighs which, and accordingly either sentencing the defendant to death or to life in prison without the possibility of parole. This procedure is laid out below, in Penal Code section 190.3.

Penal Code Section 190.3. Determination of death penalty or life imprisonment; evidence of aggravating and mitigating circumstances; considerations

If the defendant has been found guilty of murder in the first degree, and a special circumstance has been charged and found to be true, the trier of fact shall determine whether the penalty shall be death or confinement in state prison for a term of life without the possibility of parole. In the proceedings on the question of penalty, evidence may be presented by both the people and the defendant as to any matter relevant to aggravation, mitigation, and sentence including, but not limited to, the nature and circumstances of the present offense, any prior felony conviction or convictions whether or not such conviction or convictions involved a crime of violence, the presence or absence of other criminal activity by the defendant which involved the use or attempted use of force or violence or which involved the express or implied threat to use force or violence, and the defendant's character, background, history, mental condition and physical condition.

However, no evidence shall be admitted regarding other criminal activity by the defendant which did not involve the use or attempted use of force or violence or which did not involve the express or implied threat to use force or violence. As used in this section, criminal activity does not require a conviction.

However, in no event shall evidence of prior criminal activity be admitted for an offense for which the defendant was prosecuted and acquitted. The restriction on the use of this evidence is intended to apply only to proceedings pursuant to this section and is not intended to affect statutory or decisional law allowing such evidence to be used in any other proceedings.

Except for evidence in proof of the offense or special circumstances which subject a defendant to the death penalty, no evidence may be presented by the prosecution in aggravation unless notice of the evidence to be introduced has been given to the defendant within a reasonable period of time as determined by the court, prior to trial. Evidence may be introduced without such notice in rebuttal to evidence introduced by the defendant in mitigation.

The trier of fact shall be instructed that a sentence of confinement to state prison for a term of life without the possibility of parole may in future after sentence is imposed, be commuted or modified to a sentence that includes the possibility of parole by the Governor of the State of California.

In determining the penalty, the trier of fact shall take into account any of the following factors if relevant:

(a) The circumstances of the crime of which the defendant was convicted in the present proceeding and the existence of any special circumstances found to be true pursuant to Section 190.1.

(b) The presence or absence of criminal activity by the defendant which involved the use or attempted use of force or violence or the express or implied threat to use force or violence.

(c) The presence or absence of any prior felony conviction.

(d) Whether or not the offense was committed while the defendant was under the influence of extreme mental or emotional disturbance.

(e) Whether or not the victim was a participant in the defendant's homicidal conduct or consented to the homicidal act.

(f) Whether or not the offense was committed under circumstances which the defendant reasonably believed to be a moral justification or extenuation for his conduct.

(g) Whether or not defendant acted under extreme duress or under the substantial domination of another person.

(h) Whether or not at the time of the offense the capacity of the defendant to appreciate the criminality of his conduct or to conform his conduct to the requirements of law was impaired as a result of mental disease or defect, or the affects of intoxication.

(i) The age of the defendant at the time of the crime.

(j) Whether or not the defendant was an accomplice to the offense and his participation in the commission of the offense was relatively minor.

(k) Any other circumstance which extenuates the gravity of the crime even though it is not a legal excuse for the crime.

After having heard and received all of the evidence, and after having heard and considered the arguments of counsel, the trier of fact shall consider, take into account and be guided by the aggravating and mitigating circumstances referred to in this section, and shall impose a sentence of death if the trier of fact concludes that the aggravating circumstances outweigh the mitigating circumstances. If the trier of fact determines that the mitigating circumstances outweigh the aggravating circumstances the trier of fact shall impose a sentence of confinement in state prison for a term of life without the possibility of parole.

The list of special circumstances that qualifies for the death penalty is lengthy, and will not presented in its entirety here. It can be found in Penal Code section 190.2. Below are some examples:

- Intentional murder for financial gain.
- Murder committed by bombs or explosives
- Murder committed for purpose of preventing arrest or escaping
- Victim was a peace officer in course of duties
- Victim was a firefighter in course of duties
- Victim was a witness killed to prevent testimony
- Victim was a prosecutor, judge, or juror and killing was retaliatory

- Defendant lied in wait to kill victim
- Victim was killed because of race, color, religion, nationality
- Murder was committed during an enumerated serious felony
- Murder involved torture

Section 2: Three Strikes Law

OVERVIEW

One of California's most famous sentencing schemes, like determinate sentencing reflecting the state's "get tough on crime" approach, is its Three Strikes law. This was passed by the voters after a father (Marc Klaas) lost his daughter (Polly) to a brutal murder by someone he felt should have already been in prison indefinitely. His campaign resulted in a voter-passed proposition which sets forth severe sentences for repeat offenders. The general scheme is as follows: upon a first conviction of an enumerated violent felony, a second such conviction results in a mandatory sentence of twice the length; upon a third felony conviction which does not have to be violent, the mandatory sentence resulting is 25 years to life in prison, depending on certain criteria. The reader is referred to Penal Code sections 667 and 1170.12 for the extensive more detailed legislative approach to the Three Strikes law. Also, the Supreme Court discusses the statute in some detail in the case below.

As of late, the state's law, which has enjoyed immense popularity, has been criticized because the "third strike" need not be a violent offender. As a result, people who commit such ordinary crimes as a repeat shoplifting violation, or a repeat DUI, or passing a bad check, may become ensnared into the law's trap and sentenced to enormous sentences for what appears to be a minor offense. Accordingly, the U.S. Supreme Court agreed to hear a challenge of the law, in two related cases during the 2003 term. We'll discuss one below (the other is based on similar facts and similar analysis). The high court upheld California's law, in a narrow 5-4 decision, so as of today it still reigns. However, as this book goes to press a ballot initiative is set to be vote on by Californians in the November 2004 election, which would revise the law to require that the third strike is also for a violent felony. Early polls show large support for this initiative.

CASES

I. Ewing v. California, 123 S.Ct. 1179 (2003)

In this case the Supreme Court must decide whether California's Three Strikes law is overly punitive, thus violating the Eighth Amendment's prohibition on cruel and unusual punishment.

O'Connor, J.

BACKGROUND

California's three strikes law reflects a shift in the State's sentencing policies toward incapacitating and deterring repeat offenders who threaten the public safety. The law was designed "to ensure longer prison sentences and greater punishment for those who commit a felony and have been previously convicted of serious and/or violent felony offenses." [Cal. Penal Code Section 667(b).] On March 3, 1993, California Assemblymen Bill Jones and Jim Costa introduced Assembly Bill 971, the legislative version of what would later become the three strikes law. The Assembly Committee on Public Safety defeated the bill only weeks later. Public outrage over the defeat sparked a voter initiative to add Proposition 184, based loosely on the bill, to the ballot in the November 1994 general election.

On October 1, 1993, while Proposition 184 was circulating, 12-year-old Polly Klaas was kidnaped from her home in Petaluma, California. Her admitted killer, Richard Allen Davis, had a long criminal history that included two prior kidnaping convictions. Davis had served only half of his most recent sentence (16 years for kidnaping, assault, and burglary). Had Davis served his entire sentence, he would still have been in prison on the day that Polly Klaas was kidnaped.

Polly Klaas' murder galvanized support for the three strikes initiative. Within days, Proposition 184 was on its way to becoming the fastest qualifying initiative in California history. On January 3, 1994, the sponsors of Assembly Bill 971 resubmitted an amended version of the bill that conformed to Proposition 184. On January 31, 1994, Assembly Bill 971 passed the Assembly by a 63 to 9 margin. The Senate passed it by a 29 to 7 margin on March 3, 1994. Governor Pete Wilson signed the bill into law on March 7, 1994. California voters approved Proposition 184 by a margin of 72 to 28 percent on November 8, 1994.

California thus became the second State to enact a three strikes law. In November 1993, the voters of Washington State approved their own three strikes law, Initiative 593, by a margin of 3 to 1. U.S. Dept. of Justice, National Institute of Justice, J. Clark, J. Austin, & D. Henry, "Three Strikes and You're Out": A Review of State Legislation 1 (Sept.1997) (hereinafter Review of State Legislation). Between 1993 and 1995, 24 States and the Federal Government enacted three strikes laws. *Ibid.* Though the three strikes laws vary from State to State, they share a common goal of protecting the public safety by providing lengthy prison terms for habitual felons.

California's current three strikes law consists of two virtually identical statutory schemes "designed to increase the prison terms of repeat felons. When a defendant is convicted of a felony, and he has previously been convicted of one or more prior felonies defined as "serious" or "violent", sentencing is conducted pursuant to the three strikes law. Prior convictions must be alleged in the charging document, and the defendant has a right to a jury determination that the prosecution has proved the prior convictions beyond a reasonable doubt.

If the defendant has one prior "serious" or "violent" felony conviction, he must be sentenced to "twice the term otherwise provided as punishment for the current felony conviction." If the defendant has two or more prior "serious" or "violent" felony convictions, he must receive "an indeterminate term of life imprisonment." Defendants sentenced to life under the three strikes law become eligible for parole on a date calculated by reference to a "minimum term," which is the greater of (a) three times the term otherwise provided for the current conviction, (b) 25 years, or (c) the term determined by the court pursuant to § 1170 for the underlying conviction, including any enhancements.

Under California law, certain offenses may be classified as either felonies or misdemeanors. These crimes are known as "wobblers." Some crimes that would otherwise be misdemeanors become "wobblers" because of the defendant's prior record. For example, petty theft, a misdemeanor, becomes a "wobbler" when the defendant has previously served a prison term for committing specified theft- related crimes. § 490 (West 1999); § 666 (West Supp.2002). Other crimes, such as grand theft, are "wobblers" regardless of the defendant's prior record. Both types of "wobblers" are triggering offenses under the three strikes law only when they are treated as felonies. Under California law, a "wobbler" is presumptively a felony and "remains a felony except when the discretion is actually exercised" to make the crime a misdemeanor.

In California, prosecutors may exercise their discretion to charge a "wobbler" as either a felony or a misdemeanor. Likewise, California trial courts have discretion to reduce a "wobbler" charged as a felony to a misdemeanor either before preliminary examination or at sentencing to avoid imposing a three strikes sentence. In exercising this discretion, the court may consider "those factors that direct similar sentencing decisions," such as "the nature and circumstances of the offense, the defendant's appreciation of and attitude toward the offense, ... [and] the general objectives of sentencing."

California trial courts can also vacate allegations of prior "serious" or "violent" felony convictions, either on motion by the prosecution or *sua sponte*. In ruling whether to vacate allegations of prior felony convictions, courts consider whether, "in light of the nature and circumstances of [the defendant's] present felonies and prior serious and/or violent felony convictions, and the particulars of his background, character, and prospects, the defendant may be deemed outside the [three strikes'] scheme's spirit, in whole or in part." Thus, trial courts may avoid imposing a three strikes sentence in two ways: first, by reducing "wobblers" to misdemeanors (which do not qualify as triggering offenses), and second, by vacating allegations of prior "serious" or "violent" felony convictions.

On parole from a 9-year prison term, petitioner Gary Ewing walked into the pro shop of the El Segundo Golf Course in Los Angeles County on March 12, 2000. He walked out with three golf clubs, priced at $399 apiece, concealed in his pants leg. A shop employee, whose suspicions were aroused when he observed Ewing limp out of the pro shop, telephoned the police. The police apprehended Ewing in the parking lot.

Ewing is no stranger to the criminal justice system. In 1984, at the age of 22, he pleaded guilty to theft. The court sentenced him to six months in jail (suspended), three years' probation, and a $300 fine. In 1988, he was convicted of felony grand theft auto and sentenced to one year in jail and three years' probation. After Ewing completed probation, however, the sentencing court reduced the crime to a misdemeanor, permitted Ewing to withdraw his guilty plea, and dismissed the case. In 1990, he was convicted of petty theft with a prior and sentenced to 60 days in the county jail and three years' probation. In 1992, Ewing was convicted of battery and sentenced to 30 days in the county jail and two years' summary probation. One month later, he was convicted of theft and sentenced to 10 days in the county jail and 12 months' probation. In January 1993, Ewing was convicted of burglary and sentenced to 60 days in the county jail and one year's summary probation. In February 1993, he was convicted of possessing drug paraphernalia and sentenced to six months in the county jail and three years' probation. In July 1993, he was convicted of appropriating lost property and sentenced to 10 days in the county jail and two years' summary probation. In September 1993, he was convicted of unlawfully possessing a firearm and trespassing and sentenced to 30 days in the county jail and one year's probation.

In October and November 1993, Ewing committed three burglaries and one robbery at a Long Beach, California, apartment complex over a 5-week period. He awakened one of his victims, asleep on her living room sofa, as he tried to disconnect her video cassette recorder from the television in that room.

153

When she screamed, Ewing ran out the front door. On another occasion, Ewing accosted a victim in the mailroom of the apartment complex. Ewing claimed to have a gun and ordered the victim to hand over his wallet. When the victim resisted, Ewing produced a knife and forced the victim back to the apartment itself. While Ewing rifled through the bedroom, the victim fled the apartment screaming for help. Ewing absconded with the victim's money and credit cards.

On December 9, 1993, Ewing was arrested on the premises of the apartment complex for trespassing and lying to a police officer. The knife used in the robbery and a glass cocaine pipe were later found in the back seat of the patrol car used to transport Ewing to the police station. A jury convicted Ewing of first-degree robbery and three counts of residential burglary. Sentenced to nine years and eight months in prison, Ewing was paroled in 1999.

Only 10 months later, Ewing stole the golf clubs at issue in this case. He was charged with, and ultimately convicted of, one count of felony grand theft of personal property in excess of $400. As required by the three strikes law, the prosecutor formally alleged, and the trial court later found, that Ewing had been convicted previously of four serious or violent felonies for the three burglaries and the robbery in the Long Beach apartment complex.

At the sentencing hearing, Ewing asked the court to reduce the conviction for grand theft, a "wobbler" under California law, to a misdemeanor so as to avoid a three strikes sentence. Ewing also asked the trial court to exercise its discretion to dismiss the allegations of some or all of his prior serious or violent felony convictions, again for purposes of avoiding a three strikes sentence. Before sentencing Ewing, the trial court took note of his entire criminal history, including the fact that he was on parole when he committed his latest offense. The court also heard arguments from defense counsel and a plea from Ewing himself.

In the end, the trial judge determined that the grand theft should remain a felony. The court also ruled that the four prior strikes for the three burglaries and the robbery in Long Beach should stand. As a newly convicted felon with two or more "serious" or "violent" felony convictions in his past, Ewing was sentenced under the three strikes law to 25 years to life.

DISCUSSION

The Eighth Amendment, which forbids cruel and unusual punishments, contains a "narrow proportionality principle" that "applies to noncapital sentences." We have most recently addressed the proportionality principle as applied to terms of years in a series of cases beginning with *Rummel v. Estelle*.

In *Rummel* we held that it did not violate the Eighth Amendment for a State to sentence a three-time offender to life in prison with the possibility of parole. Like Ewing, Rummel was sentenced to a lengthy prison term under a recidivism statute. Rummel's two prior offenses were a 1964 felony for "fraudulent use of a credit card to obtain $80 worth of goods or services," and a 1969 felony conviction for "passing a forged check in the amount of $28.36." His triggering offense was a conviction for felony theft--" obtaining $120.75 by false pretenses."

This Court ruled that "[h]aving twice imprisoned him for felonies, Texas was entitled to place upon Rummel the onus of one who is simply unable to bring his conduct within the social norms prescribed by the criminal law of the State." The recidivism statute "is nothing more than a societal decision that when such a person commits yet another felony, he should be subjected to the admittedly serious penalty of incarceration for life, subject only to the State's judgment as to whether to grant him parole." We noted that this Court "has on occasion stated that the Eighth Amendment prohibits imposition of a sentence that is grossly disproportionate to the severity of the crime." But "[o]utside the context of capital punishment, successful challenges to the proportionality of particular sentences have been exceedingly rare." Although we stated that the proportionality principle "would ... come into play in the extreme example ... if a legislature made overtime parking a felony punishable by life imprisonment," we held that "the mandatory life sentence imposed upon this petitioner does not constitute cruel and unusual punishment under the Eighth and Fourteenth Amendments".

In *Hutto v. Davis* the defendant was sentenced to two consecutive terms of 20 years in prison for possession with intent to distribute nine ounces of marijuana and distribution of marijuana. We held that such a sentence was constitutional: "In short, *Rummel* stands for the proposition that federal courts should be reluctant to review legislatively mandated terms of imprisonment, and that successful challenges to the proportionality of particular sentences should be exceedingly rare."

Three years after *Rummel*, in *Solem v. Helm*, we held that the Eighth Amendment prohibited "a life sentence without possibility of parole for a seventh nonviolent felony." The triggering offense in *Solem* was "uttering a 'no account' check for $100." We specifically stated that the Eighth Amendment's ban on cruel and unusual punishments "prohibits ... sentences that are disproportionate to the crime committed," and that the "constitutional principle of proportionality has been recognized explicitly in this Court for almost a century." The *Solem* Court then explained that three factors may be relevant to a determination of whether a sentence is so disproportionate that it violates the Eighth Amendment: "(i) the gravity of the offense and the harshness of the penalty; (ii) the sentences imposed on other criminals in the same jurisdiction; and (iii) the sentences imposed for commission of the same crime in other jurisdictions.

Applying these factors in *Solem* we struck down the defendant's sentence of life without parole.

Eight years after *Solem*, we grappled with the proportionality issue again in *Harmelin*. *Harmelin* was not a recidivism case, but rather involved a first-time offender convicted of possessing 672 grams of cocaine. He was sentenced to life in prison without possibility of parole. A majority of the Court rejected Harmelin's claim that his sentence was so grossly disproportionate that it violated the Eighth Amendment. The Court, however, could not agree on why his proportionality argument failed. Justice SCALIA, joined by THE CHIEF JUSTICE, wrote that the proportionality principle was "an aspect of our death penalty jurisprudence, rather than a generalizable aspect of Eighth Amendment law." He would thus have declined to apply gross disproportionality principles except in reviewing capital sentences.

Justice KENNEDY, joined by two other Members of the Court, concurred in part and concurred in the judgment. Justice KENNEDY specifically recognized that "[t]he Eighth Amendment proportionality principle also applies to noncapital sentences." He then identified four principles of proportionality review--"the primacy of the legislature, the variety of legitimate penological schemes, the nature of our federal system, and the requirement that proportionality review be guided by objective factors"--that "inform the final one: The Eighth Amendment does not require strict proportionality between crime and sentence. Rather, it forbids only extreme sentences that are 'grossly disproportionate' to the crime.

The proportionality principles in our cases distilled in Justice KENNEDY's concurrence guide our application of the Eighth Amendment in the new context that we are called upon to consider.

For many years, most States have had laws providing for enhanced sentencing of repeat offenders. Yet between 1993 and 1995, three strikes laws effected a sea change in criminal sentencing throughout the Nation._ These laws responded to widespread public concerns about crime by targeting the class of offenders who pose the greatest threat to public safety: career criminals. As one of the chief architects of California's three strikes law has explained: "Three Strikes was intended to go beyond

155

simply making sentences tougher. It was intended to be a focused effort to create a sentencing policy that would use the judicial system to reduce serious and violent crime."

Throughout the States, legislatures enacting three strikes laws made a deliberate policy choice that individuals who have repeatedly engaged in serious or violent criminal behavior, and whose conduct has not been deterred by more conventional approaches to punishment, must be isolated from society in order to protect the public safety. Though three strikes laws may be relatively new, our tradition of deferring to state legislatures in making and implementing such important policy decisions is longstanding.

Our traditional deference to legislative policy choices finds a corollary in the principle that the Constitution "does not mandate adoption of any one penological theory." A sentence can have a variety of justifications, such as incapacitation, deterrence, retribution, or rehabilitation. Some or all of these justifications may play a role in a State's sentencing scheme. Selecting the sentencing rationales is generally a policy choice to be made by state legislatures, not federal courts.

When the California Legislature enacted the three strikes law, it made a judgment that protecting the public safety requires incapacitating criminals who have already been convicted of at least one serious or violent crime. Nothing in the Eighth Amendment prohibits California from making that choice. To the contrary, our cases establish that "States have a valid interest in deterring and segregating habitual criminals."

California's justification is no pretext. Recidivism is a serious public safety concern in California and throughout the Nation. According to a recent report, approximately 67 percent of former inmates released from state prisons were charged with at least one "serious" new crime within three years of their release. In particular, released property offenders like Ewing had higher recidivism rates than those released after committing violent, drug, or public- order offenses. Approximately 73 percent of the property offenders released in 1994 were arrested again within three years, compared to approximately 61 percent of the violent offenders, 62 percent of the public- order offenders, and 66 percent of the drug offenders.

In 1996, when the Sacramento Bee studied 233 three strikes offenders in California, it found that they had an aggregate of 1,165 prior felony convictions, an average of 5 apiece. The prior convictions included 322 robberies and 262 burglaries. About 84 percent of the 233 three strikes offenders had been convicted of at least one violent crime. In all, they were responsible for 17 homicides, 7 attempted slayings, and 91 sexual assaults and child molestations. The Sacramento Bee concluded, based on its investigation, that "[i]n the vast majority of the cases, regardless of the third strike, the [three strikes] law is snaring [the] long-term habitual offenders with multiple felony convictions ...."

The State's interest in deterring crime also lends some support to the three strikes law. We have long viewed both incapacitation and deterrence as rationales for recidivism statutes: "[A] recidivist statute['s] ... primary goals are to deter repeat offenders and, at some point in the life of one who repeatedly commits criminal offenses serious enough to be punished as felonies, to segregate that person from the rest of society for an extended period of time." Four years after the passage of California's three strikes law, the recidivism rate of parolees returned to prison for the commission of a new crime dropped by nearly 25 percent. Even more dramatically:

"An unintended but positive consequence of 'Three Strikes' has been the impact on parolees leaving the state. More California parolees are now leaving the state than parolees from other jurisdictions entering California. This striking turnaround started in 1994. It was the first time more parolees left the state than entered since 1976. This trend has continued and in 1997 more than 1,000 net parolees left California."

To be sure, California's three strikes law has sparked controversy. Critics have doubted the law's wisdom, cost-efficiency, and effectiveness in reaching its goals. This criticism is appropriately directed at the legislature, which has primary responsibility for making the difficult policy choices that underlie any criminal sentencing scheme. We do not sit as a "superlegislature" to second-guess these policy choices. It is enough that the State of California has a reasonable basis for believing that dramatically enhanced sentences for habitual felons "advance[s] the goals of [its] criminal justice system in any substantial way."

Against this backdrop, we consider Ewing's claim that his three strikes sentence of 25 years to life is unconstitutionally disproportionate to his offense of "shoplifting three golf clubs." We first address the gravity of the offense compared to the harshness of the penalty. At the threshold, we note that Ewing incorrectly frames the issue. The gravity of his offense was not merely "shoplifting three golf clubs." Rather, Ewing was convicted of felony grand theft for stealing nearly $1,200 worth of merchandise after previously having been convicted of at least two "violent" or "serious" felonies. Even standing alone, Ewing's theft should not be taken lightly. His crime was certainly not "one of the most passive felonies a person could commit." To the contrary, the Supreme Court of California has noted the "seriousness" of grand theft in the context of proportionality review. Theft of $1,200 in property is a felony under federal law and in the vast majority of States.

That grand theft is a "wobbler" under California law is of no moment. Though California courts have discretion to reduce a felony grand theft charge to a misdemeanor, it remains a felony for all purposes "unless and until the trial court imposes a misdemeanor sentence." Under California law, the reduction is not based on the notion that a "wobbler" is "conceptually a misdemeanor." Rather, it is "intended to extend misdemeanant treatment to a potential felon." In Ewing's case, however, the trial judge justifiably exercised her discretion not to extend such lenient treatment given Ewing's long criminal history.

In weighing the gravity of Ewing's offense, we must place on the scales not only his current felony, but also his long history of felony recidivism. Any other approach would fail to accord proper deference to the policy judgments that find expression in the legislature's choice of sanctions. In imposing a three strikes sentence, the State's interest is not merely punishing the offense of conviction, or the "triggering" offense: "[I]t is in addition the interest ... in dealing in a harsher manner with those who by repeated criminal acts have shown that they are simply incapable of conforming to the norms of society as established by its criminal law." To give full effect to the State's choice of this legitimate penological goal, our proportionality review of Ewing's sentence must take that goal into account.

Ewing's sentence is justified by the State's public-safety interest in incapacitating and deterring recidivist felons, and amply supported by his own long, serious criminal record. Ewing has been convicted of numerous misdemeanor and felony offenses, served nine separate terms of incarceration, and committed most of his crimes while on probation or parole. His prior "strikes" were serious felonies including robbery and three residential burglaries. To be sure, Ewing's sentence is a long one. But it reflects a rational legislative judgment, entitled to deference, that offenders who have committed serious or violent felonies and who continue to commit felonies must be incapacitated. The State of California "was entitled to place upon [Ewing] the onus of one who is simply unable to bring his conduct within the social norms prescribed by the criminal law of the State." Ewing's is not "the rare case in which a threshold comparison of the crime committed and the sentence imposed leads to an inference of gross disproportionality."

We hold that Ewing's sentence of 25 years to life in prison, imposed for the offense of felony grand theft under the three strikes law, is not grossly disproportionate and therefore does not violate the Eighth Amendment's prohibition on cruel and unusual punishments. The judgment of the California Court of Appeal is affirmed.

*****

CONCLUSION

After reviewing the history of proportionality analysis, part and parcel of the Eighth Amendment's prohibition of cruel and unusual punishment, the Supreme Court declines to rule that California's law is cruel and unusual. Instead it provides great latitude to state legislatures in determining just how punitive state sentencing statutes can be.

REVIEW

1. What was Ewing sent to prison for 25 to life for? What specific final act?

2. What is a "wobbler"? What is the significance of a "wobbler" in this case?

3. What are the three steps involved in proportionality analysis? Does this approach make sense when deciding whether a sentence is too severe?

4. Did the Court apply these three steps to Ewing's case? Did it change the approach to proportionality analysis?

5. Should one's past behavior influence one's current sentence if he or she already "did the time for the past crimes"? Give arguments on each side of the controversy.

CHAPTER FIFTEEN

Criminal Procedure in Crisis Times

OVERVIEW

Plenty of controversy has surrounded the Bush Administration's passing of the Patriot Act, which is an attempt to bolster mechanisms by which terrorist activities can be fought against in the post 9/11 era. On one side are those that argue that it is necessary to dilute individual civil rights to some extent in such a volatile and dangerous world. On the other side are those who argue that the erosion of traditional safeguards of individual liberties is a slippery slope and a dangerous venture; war on terrorists can successfully be waged without resorting to these tactics, according to this group.

Most of the portions of the Patriot Act concern federal law enforcement and not so much the states. Still, state enforcement agencies are expected to cooperate with the federal government. This has brought about an interesting dilemma in California, known for its liberal communities. Communities that believe strongly in individual civil liberties have decided not to cooperate with the federal government in enforcing provisions of the Patriot Act. As of the time this book went to press, 58 jurisdictions in California have passed such resolutions, ranging from small towns such as Arcata (population 16,300) to large cities such as Oakland (pop. 399,484), San Francisco (pop. 776,773), and Los Angeles (pop. 3,694,820).

It is too early yet to see how the drama will unfold, but the basic context is the interface between the forceful hand of federal law and the will and resolution of local communities that resist such law. One example from recent times is the distribution of medical marijuana in certain California localities legal by state law but illegal by federal law. Communities such as San Francisco and Oakland have defiantly allowed such distribution even when ordered by the federal government to prohibit "pot shops."

Below are examples of resolutions and ordinances from two California communities responding to the Patriot Act. Note the difference. Oakland's is largely symbolic, voicing the jurisdiction's opposition to the Act and its principles, and stating that "to the extent legally possible, no City employee or department shall officially assist or voluntarily cooperate with [provisions of the Patriot Act that violate rights afforded by the U.S. Constitution and its amendments]."

Arcata's resolution has actually translated into an ordinance (Ordinance 1339) which reaches beyond symbolism, making it illegal for city employees to engage in or allow any behavior that may be okay under the Patriot Act but not okay under traditional interpretations of the U.S. Constitution. City employees are prohibited from cooperating with federal investigations that adhere to the Patriot Act but violate civil liberties. Furthermore, if the federal government charges a city employee for any act based on compliance with the city ordinance, the city will provide full legal defense for the accused!

This struggle between federal and local governments demonstrates that the substantive law of criminal procedure is not always a straightforward matter of reading and interpreting court decisions. Enforcement in the real world is a crucial part of criminal procedure. The reaction of local communities who are declaring that they will refuse to cooperate with provisions of the Patriot Act is yet another testament to this.

Oakland City Council Resolution passed December 17, 2002, by a vote of 7-1

INTRODUCED BY COUNCILMEMBER Nancy J. Nadel

Resolution to Oppose the USA PATRIOT Act and Related Executive Orders

WHEREAS, the City of Oakland houses a diverse population, including citizens of other nations, whose contributions to the community are vital to its character and function; and

WHEREAS, the United States Constitution guarantees all persons living in the United States the fundamental rights including - freedom of religion, speech, assembly and privacy; protection from unreasonable searches and seizures; due process and equal protection to any person; equality before the law and the presumption of innocence; access to counsel in judicial proceedings; and a fair, speedy and public trial; and

WHEREAS, The USA PATRIOT Act signed by George W. Bush on October 26 2001, has a number of provisions that contradict the above mentioned rights and, in the words of Oakland's representative in Congress Barbara Lee, "fundamentally alters the nature of our civil liberties" and "…does little to increase public safety"; and

WHEREAS, examples of the provisions in the USA PATRIOT Act and Executive Orders that may violate the constitution and the rights and civil liberties of Oakland residents are as follows:

- Significantly expands the government's ability to access sensitive medical, mental health, financial and educational records about individuals; and lowers the burden of proof required to conduct secret searches and telephone and Internet surveillance
- Gives law enforcement expanded authority to obtain library records, and prohibits librarians from informing patrons of monitoring or information requests
- Gives the Attorney General and the Secretary of State the power to designate domestic groups, including religious and political organizations, as "terrorist organizations"
- Grants power to the Attorney General to subject citizens of other nations to indefinite detention or deportation even if they have not committed a crime · Authorizes eavesdropping on confidential communications between lawyers and their clients in federal custody

- Limits disclosure of public documents and records under the Freedom of Information Act; and

WHEREAS, Department of Justice interpretations of this Act and these Executive Orders particularly targets Muslims, people of Middle Eastern and South Asian descent and citizens of other nations, and thereby encouraging racial profiling by law enforcement and hate crimes by individuals in our community; and

WHEREAS, the Oakland Public Library Advisory Commission has already passed a resolution protecting patrons rights to privacy and confidentiality and opposing the US Patriot Act; now therefore be it

RESOLVED that the City of Oakland affirms its strong opposition to terrorism, but also affirms that any efforts to end terrorism not be waged at the expense of the fundamental civil rights and liberties of the people of Oakland, the United States and the World; and be it

FURTHER RESOLVED that the City of Oakland affirms the rights of all people, including United States citizens and citizens of other nations, living within the City in accordance with the Bill of Rights and the Fourteenth Amendment of the U.S. Constitution; and be it

FURTHER RESOLVED that, to the extent legally possible, no City employee or department shall officially assist or voluntarily cooperate with investigations, interrogations, or arrest procedures, public or clandestine, that are in violation of individuals' civil rights or civil liberties as specified in the above Amendments of the United States Constitution; and be it

FURTHER RESOLVED that the Oakland City Council calls upon all private citizens and organizations, including residents, employers, educators, and business owners, to demonstrate similar respect for civil rights and civil liberties, especially but not limited to conditions of employment and cooperation with investigations; and be it

FURTHER RESOLVED that the City of Oakland call on our United States Representative and Senators to monitor the implementation of the Act and Orders cited herein and actively work for the repeal of the Act and those Orders that violate fundamental rights and liberties as stated in the US Constitution and its Amendments.

ORDINANCE NO. 1339

AN ORDINANCE OF THE CITY COUNCIL OF THE CITY OF ARCATA AMENDING THE ARCATA MUNICIPAL CODE TO DEFEND THE BILL OF RIGHTS AND CIVIL LIBERTIES TITLE II: ADMINISTRATION; CHAPTER 2: OFFICERS AND EMPLOYEES; ARTICLE 5: DEFENDING CIVIL RIGHTS AND LIBERTIES

The City Council of the City of Arcata does ordain as follows:

Section 1: Title II: Administration, Chapter 2: Officers and Employees, Article 5: Defending Civil Rights and Liberties, Sections 2190 – 2194 are hereby added to the Municipal Code as follows:

ARTICLE 5 - DEFENDING CIVIL RIGHTS AND LIBERTIES
SEC. 2190: Purposes.
The purposes of this ordinance are as follows:

A. To protect the civil rights and civil liberties for all and to affirm the City's commitment to embody democracy, and to embrace, defend and uphold the inalienable rights and fundamental liberties granted under the United States and the California Constitutions, as set forth in Resolution 023-32, A Resolution of the City Council of the City of Arcata to Defend the Bill of Rights and Civil Liberties, adopted by the Council on January 15, 2003; and

B. To ensure that local law enforcement continues to preserve and uphold residents' freedom of speech, assembly, association, and privacy, the right to counsel and due process in judicial proceedings, and protection from unreasonable searches and seizures, even if requested or authorized to infringe upon such rights by federal or state law enforcement agencies acting under new powers created by the USA PATRIOT Act (Public Law 107-56), Homeland Security Act (Public Law 107-296), related executive orders, regulations or future enacted laws, executive orders or regulations.

SEC. 2191: No Unconstitutional Detentions or Profiling.
No management employee of the City shall officially engage in or permit unlawful detentions or profiling based on race, ethnicity, national origin, gender, sexual orientation, political or religious association that are in violation of individuals' civil rights or civil liberties as specified in the Bill of Rights and Fourteenth Amendment of the United States Constitution.

SEC. 2192: No Unconstitutional Voluntary Cooperation.

No management employee of the City shall officially assist or voluntarily cooperate with investigations, interrogations, or arrest procedures, public or clandestine, that are in violation of individuals' civil rights or civil liberties as specified in the Bill of Rights and Fourteenth Amendment of the United States Constitution.

SEC. 2193: Notification.

Management employees of the City shall promptly notify the City Manager when, in the course of City employment, the following occurs: A management employee is contacted by another law enforcement agency and asked to cooperate or assist with an investigation, interrogation, or arrest procedure under provisions of the USA PATRIOT Act (Public Law 107-56), Homeland Security Act (Public Law 107-296), related executive orders, regulation or future enacted laws, executive orders or regulations, where such procedure is in violation of an individual's civil rights or civil liberties as specified in the Bill of Rights and Fourteenth Amendment of the United States Constitution.

Upon such notification from a management employee, or upon such contact directly, the City Manager shall promptly report to the City Council specifying the law enforcement agency seeking cooperation or assistance and the actions requested of the management employee.

SEC. 2194: Defense.

The City shall provide legal defense to any management employee who is criminally charged by another entity for his or her actions in compliance with this Ordinance.

SEC. 2195: Severability.

If any section or sections of the ordinance is or are held to be invalid or unenforceable, all other sections shall nevertheless continue in full force and remain in effect.

Section 2: This ordinance will take effect thirty (30) days after the date of its adoption.

DATED: April 2, 2003.

ATTESTED: APPROVED:
s/ Dan Hauser
City Clerk, City of Arcata

APPENDIX

Selected Provisions of Article I of California Constitution

SEC. 4. Free exercise and enjoyment of religion without discrimination or preference are guaranteed. This liberty of conscience does not excuse acts that are licentious or inconsistent with the peace or safety of the State. The Legislature shall make no law respecting an establishment of religion.

A person is not incompetent to be a witness or juror because of his or her opinions on religious beliefs.

SEC. 9. A bill of attainder, ex post facto law, or law impairing the obligation of contracts may not be passed.

SEC. 10. Witnesses may not be unreasonably detained. A person may not be imprisoned in a civil action for debt or tort, or in peacetime for a militia fine.

SEC. 11. Habeas corpus may not be suspended unless required by public safety in cases of rebellion or invasion.

SEC. 12. A person shall be released on bail by sufficient sureties, except for:

(a) Capital crimes when the facts are evident or the presumption great;

(b) Felony offenses involving acts of violence on another person, or felony sexual assault offenses on another person, when the facts are evident or the presumption great and the court finds based upon clear and convincing evidence that there is a substantial likelihood the person's release would result in great bodily harm to others; or

(c) Felony offenses when the facts are evident or the presumption great and the court finds based on clear and convincing evidence that the person has threatened another with great bodily harm and that there is a substantial likelihood that the person would carry out the threat if released.

Excessive bail may not be required. In fixing the amount of bail, the court shall take into consideration the seriousness of the offense charged, the previous criminal record of the defendant, and the probability of his or her appearing at the trial or hearing of the case.

A person may be released on his or her own recognizance in the court's discretion.

SEC. 13. The right of the people to be secure in their persons, houses, papers, and effects against unreasonable seizures and searches may not be violated; and a warrant may not issue except on probable cause, supported by oath or affirmation, particularly describing the place to be searched and the persons and things to be seized.

SEC. 14. Felonies shall be prosecuted as provided by law, either by indictment or, after examination and commitment by a magistrate, by information.

A person charged with a felony by complaint subscribed under penalty of perjury and on file in a court in the county where the felony is triable shall be taken without unnecessary delay before a magistrate of that court. The magistrate shall immediately give the defendant a copy of the complaint, inform the defendant of the defendant's right to counsel, allow the defendant a reasonable time to send for counsel, and on the defendant's request read the complaint to the defendant. On the defendant's request the magistrate shall require a peace officer to transmit within the county where the court is located a message to counsel named by defendant.

A person unable to understand English who is charged with a crime has a right to an interpreter throughout the proceedings.

SEC. 14.1. If a felony is prosecuted by indictment, there shall be no postindictment preliminary hearing.

SEC. 15. The defendant in a criminal cause has the right to a speedy public trial, to compel attendance of witnesses in the defendant's behalf, to have the assistance of counsel for the defendant's defense, to be personally present with counsel, and to be confronted with the witnesses against the defendant. The Legislature may provide for the deposition of a witness in the presence of the defendant and the defendant's counsel.

Persons may not twice be put in jeopardy for the same offense, be compelled in a criminal cause to be a witness against themselves, or be deprived of life, liberty, or property without due process of law.

SEC. 16. Trial by jury is an inviolate right and shall be secured to all, but in a civil cause three-fourths of the jury may render a verdict. A jury may be waived in a criminal cause by the consent of both parties expressed in open court by the defendant and the defendant's counsel. In a civil cause a jury may be waived by the consent of the parties expressed as prescribed by statute.

In civil causes the jury shall consist of 12 persons or a lesser number agreed on by the parties in open court. In civil causes other than causes within the appellate jurisdiction of the court of appeal the Legislature may provide that the jury shall consist of eight persons or a lesser number agreed on by the parties in open court.

In criminal actions in which a felony is charged, the jury shall consist of 12 persons. In criminal actions in which a misdemeanor is charged, the jury shall consist of 12 persons or a lesser number agreed on by the parties in open court.

SEC. 17. Cruel or unusual punishment may not be inflicted or excessive fines imposed.

SEC. 23. One or more grand juries shall be drawn and summoned at least once a year in each county.

SEC. 24. Rights guaranteed by this Constitution are not dependent on those guaranteed by the United States Constitution.

In criminal cases the rights of a defendant to equal protection of the laws, to due process of law, to the assistance of counsel, to be personally present with counsel, to a speedy and public trial, to compel the attendance of witnesses, to confront the witnesses against him or her, to be free from unreasonable searches and seizures, to privacy, to not be compelled to be a witness against himself or herself, to not be placed twice in jeopardy for the same offense, and to not suffer the imposition of cruel or unusual punishment, shall be construed by the courts of this State in a manner consistent with the Constitution of the United States. This Constitution shall not be construed by the courts to afford greater rights to criminal defendants than those afforded by the Constitution of the United States, nor shall it be construed to afford greater rights to minors in juvenile proceedings on criminal causes than those afforded by the Constitution of the United States.

This declaration of rights may not be construed to impair or deny others retained by the people.

SEC. 27. All statutes of this State in effect on February 17, 1972, requiring, authorizing, imposing, or relating to the death penalty are in full force and effect, subject to legislative amendment or repeal by statute, initiative, or referendum.

The death penalty provided for under those statutes shall not be deemed to be, or to constitute, the infliction of cruel or unusual punishments within the meaning of Article 1, Section 6 nor shall such punishment for such offenses be deemed to contravene any other provision of this constitution.

SEC. 28. (a) The People of the State of California find and declare that the enactment of comprehensive provisions and laws ensuring a bill of rights for victims of crime, including safeguards in the criminal justice system to fully protect those rights, is a matter of grave statewide concern.

The rights of victims pervade the criminal justice system, encompassing not only the right to restitution from the wrongdoers for financial losses suffered as a result of criminal acts, but also the more basic expectation that persons who commit felonious acts causing injury to innocent victims will be appropriately detained in custody, tried by the courts, and sufficiently punished so that the public safety is protected and encouraged as a goal of highest importance.

Such public safety extends to public primary, elementary, junior high, and senior high school campuses, where students and staff have the right to be safe and secure in their persons.

To accomplish these goals, broad reforms in the procedural treatment of accused persons and the disposition and sentencing of convicted persons are necessary and proper as deterrents to criminal behavior and to serious disruption of people's lives.

(b) Restitution. It is the unequivocal intention of the People of the State of California that all persons who suffer losses as a result of criminal activity shall have the right to restitution from the persons convicted of the crimes for losses they suffer.

Restitution shall be ordered from the convicted persons in every case, regardless of the sentence or disposition imposed, in which a crime victim suffers a loss, unless compelling and extraordinary reasons exist to the contrary. The Legislature shall adopt provisions to implement this section during the calendar year following adoption of this section.

(c) Right to Safe Schools. All students and staff of public primary, elementary, junior high and senior high schools have the inalienable right to attend campuses which are safe, secure and peaceful.

(d) Right to Truth-in-Evidence. Except as provided by statute hereafter enacted by a two-thirds vote of the membership in each house of the Legislature, relevant evidence shall not be excluded in any criminal proceeding, including pretrial and post conviction motions and hearings, or in any trial or hearing of a juvenile for a criminal offense, whether heard in juvenile or adult court. Nothing in this section shall affect any existing statutory rule of evidence relating to privilege or hearsay, or Evidence Code, Sections 352, 782 or 1103. Nothing in this section shall affect any existing statutory or constitutional right of the press.

(e) Public Safety Bail. A person may be released on bail by sufficient sureties, except for capital crimes when the facts are evident or the presumption great. Excessive bail may not be required. In setting, reducing or denying bail, the judge or magistrate shall take into consideration the protection of the public, the seriousness of the offense charged, the previous criminal record of the defendant, and the probability of his or her appearing at the trial or hearing of the case. Public safety shall be the primary consideration.

A person may be released on his or her own recognizance in the court's discretion, subject to the same factors considered in setting bail. However, no person charged with the commission of any serious felony shall be released on his or her own recognizance.

Before any person arrested for a serious felony may be released on bail, a hearing may be held before the magistrate or judge, and the prosecuting attorney shall be given notice and reasonable opportunity to be heard on the matter.

When a judge or magistrate grants or denies bail or release on a person's own recognizance, the reasons for that decision shall be stated in the record and included in the court's minutes.

(f) Use of Prior Convictions. Any prior felony conviction of any person in any criminal proceeding, whether adult or juvenile, shall subsequently be used without limitation for purposes of impeachment or enhancement of sentence in any criminal proceeding. When a prior felony conviction is an element of any felony offense, it shall be proven to the trier of fact in open court.

(g) As used in this article, the term "serious felony" is any crime defined in Penal Code, Section 1192.7(c).

SEC. 29. In a criminal case, the people of the State of California have the right to due process of law and to a speedy and public trial.

SEC. 30. (a) This Constitution shall not be construed by the courts to prohibit the joining of criminal cases as prescribed by the Legislature or by the people through the initiative process.

(b) In order to protect victims and witnesses in criminal cases, hearsay evidence shall be admissible at preliminary hearings, as prescribed by the Legislature or by the people through the initiative process.

(c) In order to provide for fair and speedy trials, discovery in criminal cases shall be reciprocal in nature, as prescribed by the Legislature or by the people through the initiative process.

Made in the USA
Lexington, KY
15 July 2011